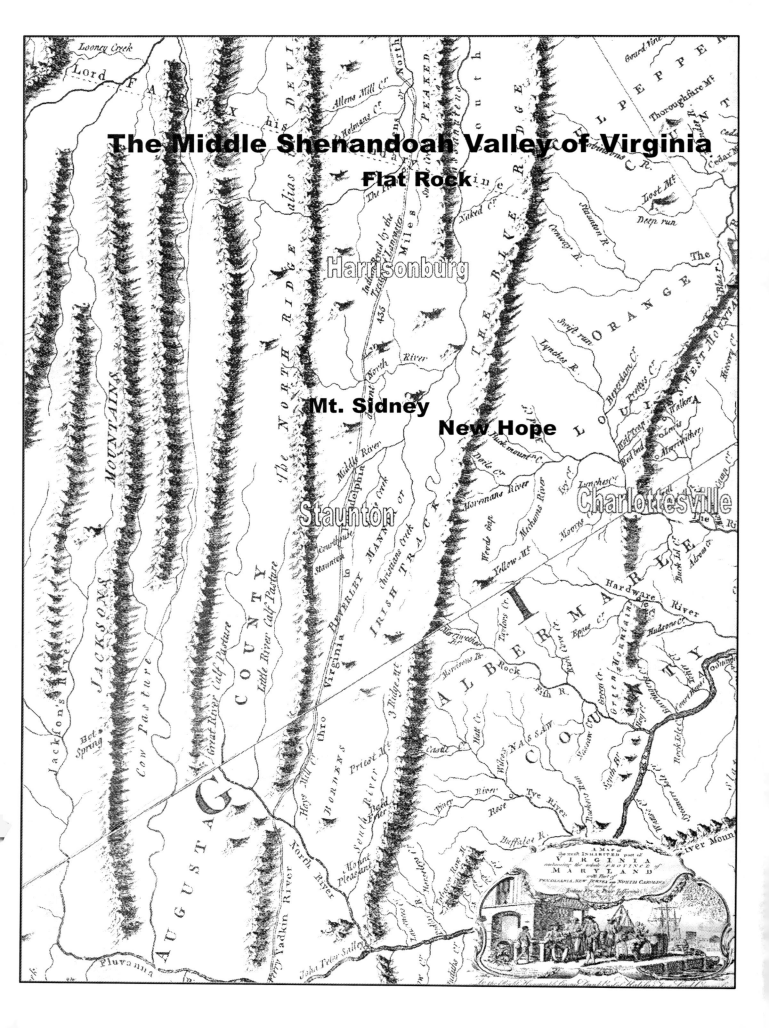

The Middle Shenandoah Valley of Virginia

Flat Rock

Harrisonburg

Mt. Sidney

New Hope

Staunton

Charlottesville

Johannes "John H." Garber

His Descendants in the Shenandoah Valley

Farmers and Ministers in Search of Religious Freedom and Peace

By

Wayne E. Garber

Wish Book Press
Studley, VA

Johannes "John H." Garber

His Descendants in the Shenandoah Valley

Wish Book Press
Post Office Box 58
Studley, VA 23162

or
WayneGarber@wishingroom.com

ISBN 0-931563-28-3
EAN 978-0-932563-28-7

This work is humbly dedicated to our Garber ancestors and the rich legacy of wonderful memories, Christian values and healthy genes that they left us.

Johannes "John H." Garber

His Descendants in the Shenandoah Valley

Farmers and Ministers in Search of Religious Freedom and Peace

Contents

Preface and Acknowledgments

The history of our Garber ancestors and the Church of the Brethren is a struggle of persecution and search for religious freedom and peace. This history is primarily intended for family descendants to assist their efforts to understand and appreciate the rich and interesting heritage of the Garber/Gerber family in America. It is impossible to study the genealogical evolution of the Garber Family without discovering its significant involvement with major historical events in America. The Garber experience in America represents in many ways a thin slice of American history. I believe it is important that we not forget who we are and what we have done.

The objectives of this book are twofold. The first objective is to compile, organize, summarize and evaluate available information (facts and traditions) about John H. Garber (Johannes Gerber) and my branch of his direct line descendants. The second objective is to provide additional documentation and historical background relating to the subject. Hopefully this micro-historical study of a few individuals may promote understanding of our heritage to future generations to help them appreciate their ancestors and their values, be of interest to those who desire to know something of our past and be an inspiration to those now living.

Several factors make the task of putting together the history of Johannes "John H." Garber and his descendants difficult:

- Very little information exists regarding John H. Garber and his ancestors. They were not people in positions of power that appeared in the history books or left personal papers.

- What we know about John's descendants, who were ministers in the German Baptist Brethren Church, is primarily based on histories and stories of what is called today the Church of the Brethren. However, they were landowners and land records have helped immensely.

- John's descendants, like many families in America, used biblical names over and over, making it easy to confuse individuals with the same name living during the same time period.

In compiling this work, I have used the sources and material that I felt would be most valuable. It is not as interesting as some people could have made it, but it is factual as far as I can determine. I have borrowed heavily from the work of Floyd Mason, who wrote *John H. Garber & Barbara Miller of Pennsylvania, Maryland and Virginia*, 1998 and Paul Coffman, who wrote *A History of Middle River Congregation, Church of the Brethren*, 1964. In compiling this document, the author has made use of Family Tree Maker software and the books, reference works and research archives held by the following institutions: The Library of Virginia, Richmond, Virginia; The Colonial Williamsburg Foundation's John D. Rockefeller, Jr. Library, Williamsburg, Virginia; Alexander Mack Memorial Library, Bridgewater College, Bridgewater, Virginia and The Augusta County Library, Fishersville, Virginia. Some materials were accessed via the Internet but most books and documents were available only in hard copy. For the most part, the author did not review the original genealogical documents cited by Mason, Coffman and others; nor did he explore all the relevant documentary collections in the United States. What is offered here is a summary of secondary sources, both old and new, supplemented by family information and personal knowledge. Some of the material comes directly from source documents and has misspelled words and grammatical mistakes which were not changed.

It has been both hard work and a pleasure to compile and write this book. My wife, Gail Garber, deserves special recognition because she supported my obsession with this project, spent many hours editing this book and endured many lonely nights while I worked at the computer. I want to acknowledge individuals who helped by providing old photographs and relevant information. I am grateful to Cleatis Garber, Dolly Garber Harner, Catherine Garber Crist, Ruby Sipe Garber, Anna Flora Smith and Mildred Renalds Wittig for their interest, help and patience with my detailed questions over many hours. I also wish to thank the many family members, all those too numerous to name, who have assisted in this endeavor by providing data and photographs.

Quotes:

"A family tree can wither if nobody tends its roots."

–Source Unknown

"They say it takes a minute to find a special person,
an hour to appreciate them,
a day to love them,
but then an entire life to forget them."

–Source Unknown

"You are not responsible for your ancestors.
We all have some who did unpleasant things."

–Source: *National Genealogical Society*

What Were They Like?

Have you ever wondered what your Garber ancestors were like? What were their habits and personalities? This generalized profile or portrait of our ancestral branch covers four generations to include:

1. Levi Garber

2. Daniel S. Garber

3. Homer F. Garber

4. Paul W. Garber.

These individuals spanning four generations of Garbers have influenced their descendants in many ways. The summary below represents generalizations that emerged from historic research and detail survey data based on interviews with those who knew them. The goal of the research and survey was to evaluate the data and then develop a general picture or character sketch of what these Garbers were like. It is hoped that the generalizations derived will help future generations understand why they are the way they are.

Garber Ancestral Portrait

Our ancestors were good, hardworking people, who lived a simple lifestyle. As a group, they exhibited some strong characteristics to include: strong faith, stubborn, serious minded, responsible, thrifty and humble. They were attractive, average-sized people with good health. Most were early-to-bed and early-to-rise, energetic and industrious, never lazy, but not overly ambitious. A few used tobacco products, none cursed, some played games and cards and many lacked a well-developed sense of humor. They rarely wrote letters, liked to visit friends and entertain, spent little time pursuing leisure activities, worrying or complaining. They were not particularly demanding of others but expected others to do their jobs. They tended to be relaxed, consistent and even-tempered, rarely grumpy or gruff, sometimes self-centered, rarely eccentric, rarely finicky or suspicious, sometimes stern disciplinarians but never cruel. Many were leaders and most were guided by their strong convictions and Christian values. They were logical, independent thinkers, often literal minded, sometimes argumentative, never absent-minded or scatterbrain. Most were not musical, particularly creative or dramatic, but some could sing. Our branch of Garbers must have had good genes because the average longevity is approximately 85 years of age. Their ailments varied, but cancer and heart disease run in the family.

Source: Wayne Garber performed the historic research and collected information on 90-plus data elements during interviews with Cleatis Garber, Dolly Garber Harner and Ruby S. Garber in December 2003. Cleatis knew all the individuals surveyed.

Garber Historical Timeline

1096 – 1099 A.D.	The Garber name dates back in history as far as the First Crusade, a Christian military expedition to recapture the Holy Land. Until this time most people in Europe had only one name. The surname Gerber (original name) appeared and is both patronymic and characteristic in origin. It is believed to be associated with the German personal name "Garibert (spear, bright)," meaning descendant of Garber.
1517	Martin Luther nails 95 Arguments citing abuses of Papal authority to Wittenberg church door.
1525	Anabaptism begins in Zurich, Switzerland, when Conrad Grebel, Felix Mantz and Georg Blaurock break with their former colleague Ulrich Zwingli and baptize themselves.
1537	Menno Simons, a Catholic priest, became an Anabaptist evangelist; his followers were known as Mennonites.
1566 – 1711	During this period the Gerbers, who were Mennonites, moved from all over Germany to Switzerland, where they resided for over 100 years. In Bern, Switzerland, Gerbers continued to be persecuted (property confiscated, homes burned, incarcerated in prisons and killed) for their religious convictions.
1605	Ulrich Gerber of Switzerland was born.
1607	Jamestown Colony, the first permanent English settlement in North America, was founded on May 13 when expeditions of James I arrived from Great Britain.
1619	Pilgrims from England arrived at Plymouth, Massachusetts, on the Mayflower.
1634	Maryland was founded as a Catholic colony with religious freedom for all granted in 1649.
1635	Christian Gerber, son of Ulrich, was born.
1661	William Penn announced his "Holy Experiment," religious and political freedom would be granted to all in Pennsylvania.
1661	Niclaus Gerber, son of Christian, was born in Steffisburg, Switzerland.
1683	Mennonite families who accepted William Penn's offer of freedom from religious persecution arrived in Philadelphia from Krefeld Germany.
1708	Alexander Mack established the first Tunker church in the village of Schwarzenau, Switzerland, when eight believers following the principles of Anabaptism and Pietism were baptized in the Eder River.
1716	Governor Alexander Spotswood led a party of 50 strong into the Shenandoah Valley for the purpose of establishing Virginia's western claims and to see if the Great Lakes were accessible from Virginia.

1723	The first Brethren congregation in America was established at Germantown, Pennsylvania (near Philadelphia).
1728	We do not know when Jo Hannes Gerber came to America, but he was found living with other German immigrants that settled in Colebrook Valley, Pennsylvania. He signed a petition that was sent to the Governor of Pennsylvania, and the signature is identical to the signature of Jo Hannes Gerber on his will in 1748.
1730	It is estimated that 15,000 Reformed church confessors (less than 100 Tunker families) had arrived in Pennsylvania from the Rhine Valley, principally Westphalia and the Palatinate. From 1727 to 1775, 324 ships of several different types brought Germans to Philadelphia.
1732	Benjamin Franklin began publishing Poor Richard's Almanack.
1732	Johannes "John H." Garber was born in Chester County, Pennsylvania. He was the son of Jo Hannes Gerber, who immigrated to America by 1728.
1744	Jo Hannes Gerber, the immigrant and father of John H. Garber, moved to some land bought by his brother Niclous Gerber/Garber and lived there from 1744 to 1748, when they both died.
1751	John H. Garber bought 200 acres on the Big Conewago in York County, Pennsylvania, and built a house. In 1752, John married Barbara Mueller (anglicized Miller) in York County, Pennsylvania, and to them were born seven sons and three daughters; his 10 children included John, Samuel, Abraham, Martin, Anna, Jacob, Daniel, Catherine, Joseph and Magadalene.
1760	Abraham Garber, son of John H. Garber, was born in York County, Pennsylvania.
1761	John H. Garber sold the 200 acres in two sections, 170 acres to John Shafer and 30 acres to Henry Neff.
1773	John and Barbara Garber moved to Beaver Dam, Frederick County, Maryland. It is believed that John and Barbara became German Baptists (Duckers) while in Frederick. John Garber and Elder Jacob Danner were ministers to the Beaver Dam congregation.
1775	Fighting begins April 19 with the British at Lexington and Concord, Massachusetts, which marked the beginning of the American Revolution.
1775	John H. Garber moved to the Shenandoah Valley in the Flat Rock/Forestville area of Shenandoah County, Virginia. Soon others followed him, and the Brethren group in the Valley grew rather rapidly.
1775	John H. Garber established the Flat Rock Church and was the first Brethren minister.
1776	The Declaration of Independence was approved July 4 by the Continental Congress.

| 1781 | British General Cornwallis surrendered to the Americans at Yorktown, Virginia, ending the fighting in the Revolutionary War. |

1781   British General Cornwallis surrendered to the Americans at Yorktown, Virginia, ending the fighting in the Revolutionary War.

1787   John H. Garber, our progenitor, died at Flat Rock, and his grave was marked by a small flat gravestone bearing the inscription – 17 J.H.G. '87, a testimony to both the sturdy life he had lived and to the modest spirit in which he had lived it.

1789   The new Constitution was approved by the states. George Washington was chosen as the first president.

1790   Abraham Garber married Elizabeth Humbert, and they soon made their home on Middle River and settled on a farm that has become known as the Garber Farm near New Hope, Virginia. Abraham and Elizabeth had seven children: John, Sarah, Daniel, Jacob, Mary, Samuel and Esther. John, farmer and minister, was the only son to become a minister and elder in his father's church.

1797   Jacob W. Garber, the fourth child of Abraham and Elizabeth Garber, was born on the family farm near New Hope, Virginia.

1803   The U.S. bought the Louisiana Purchase from France and doubled the size of the United States.

1812-1814   In the War of 1812 with Great Britain, British forces burned the U.S. Capitol and White House. Francis Scott Key wrote the words to The Star-Spangled Banner.

1823   Jacob W. Garber married Nancy Arnold of Hampshire, West Virginia. Their farm home was about two miles from Mt. Sidney and about three and a half miles from New Hope, Virginia. To them were born four sons and one daughter; their five children included Rebecca, Abraham D., Levi, Reuben and Jacob W. Garber, Jr.

1824   Abraham was instrumental in building the first Brethren church in Augusta County. He donated the land, built a brick kiln on his property, built the church building and willed it debt-free to the Middle River congregation, where he was the founder and minister of the congregation.

1828   Levi Garber was born August 21, 1828, and was the third son of Jacob Garber, a farmer.

1843   Jacob Garber purchased what was called a Louisiana (land) lottery ticket for one dollar and won the lottery. For his one dollar lottery ticket he received a 151-acre homestead offered by John and Elizabeth Miller. The German Baptist viewed the purchase of a lottery ticket as a form of gambling, which was sinful. Since Jacob was a member of the Middle River German Baptist Church, he was severely criticized by members of the congregation. Jacob kept the land; he prospered as a farmer and shared his wealth with his children. His children were fortunate because when each got married, Jacob and Nancy located them and their new spouses on nearby farmsteads. The writer believes that Jacob never held an elected church office (deacon or elder) because of this incident.

1848   Mexico was defeated and the United States gained control of the Republic of Texas and the Mexican territories in the West.

1848	Abraham Garber, 87 years old, died at his farmstead in New Hope, Virginia.
1848	The discovery of gold in California led to a rush of 80,000 people to the west in search of gold.
1850	Levi Garber married Barbara Miller on February 21, 1850. Their farm home was located one and a half miles from Mt. Sidney, Virginia, on the Buttermilk Road and about four miles from New Hope, Virginia. To them were born three sons and five daughters; their eight children included Peter, Jacob, Daniel, Lydia, Nancy, Anna, Barbara and Frances.
1851	The Annual Meeting of the Church of the Brethren was held at the Middle River Church. The proceedings were conducted and recorded in German.
1855	Daniel S. Garber, born near Mt. Sidney on August 22, 1855, was the third son of Levi Garber and Barbara Miller.
1860	Levi Garber began his ministry to the Middle River Church.
1861 -1865	The Civil War began on April 12, 1861, with the bombardment of Fort Sumter, South Carolina, and ended with the surrender of Lee at Appomattox, Virginia, on April 9, 1865. President Abraham Lincoln was assassinated.
1870	This was the beginning of public education in Virginia and Augusta County. The county built and opened 83 schools in one year.
1876	Seventy-eight-year-old Jacob Garber died at his New Hope farmstead.
1879	Daniel Garber worked on his father's farm and bought the farm from Levi about the time he and Lizzie Glick got married in 1879. Daniel and Lizzie operated the farm and reared their six children: Anthony, Ada, Homer, Martha, Minor and Cora.
1886	Homer Franklin Garber was born at the family Mt. Sidney farmstead on August 12, 1886, the third son of Daniel and Lizzie Garber.
1905	Daniel Garber bought the Knightly Mill with Joseph Norford for $6,500. He acquired the land, the water rights, the miller's house and a flour warehouse situated on land of the Valley Railroad Company near the Ft. Defiance Depot. Daniel started operating the flour mill and sawmill.
1908	Henry Ford introduced the Model T car priced at $850.
1909	Homer and Sallie Reed fell in love and eloped along with another couple. They drove a buckboard to Staunton, Virginia, and took a train to Hagerstown, Maryland, where they got married.
1910	Daniel Garber sold the family farmstead to Homer, his second son, and moved to a small, seven to eight acre homestead at Knightly, about 3 miles toward Middle River. This was the same farm that Homer's great-grandfather, Jacob Garber, had won for one dollar in the 1843 land lottery. During the next 18 years, Homer operated a typical

farming operation with livestock, crops and apple orchard and reared their five children: Cleatis, Harold, Paul, Margaret and Dolly.

1912	After operating the Knightly Mill for seven years, Daniel Garber sold a one-third interest in the mill to his son Minor Garber on July 1, 1912, for $4,000. Minor acquired the remaining interest for $8,000 in 1925, when the mill was called the Knightly Light and Power Company, Inc.
1913	Paul Garber is born at the Mt. Sidney farmstead on December 31, 1913.
1914	Levi preached and ministered to the Middle River congregation for 54 years before his death on his farm home near Mt. Sidney on November 14, 1914. Levi was elected to the office of Deacon in 1855, to the ministry in 1860 and ordained to the Eldership in 1875. Following the division of the congregation at Middle River, Elder Levi Garber carried on a great deal of missionary work in the mountain regions and in Eastern Virginia. He traveled mostly by horseback, and it is said that one riding horse carried him over 30,000 miles in his travels for the church.
1917	The United States joined World War I on the side of the Allies (Great Britain, France and Russia) against Germany.
1923	Daniel Garber died of Bright's disease (chronic inflammation of the blood vessels in the kidney) on December 30, 1923, aged 68 years, 4 months and 8 days. His estate went to his wife Lizzie and Ada and Cora, who cared for Lizzie until she died in 1948.
1925	The first Garber reunion to celebrate our Garber ancestry was held at Milton and Barbara Shaver's. B. B. Garber gave an address in which he urged the young to follow the steps of our forefathers and not betray our heritage.
1927	Charles A. Lindbergh became the first person to fly alone nonstop across the Atlantic Ocean.
1929	A stock market crash marked the beginning of the Great Depression.
1931	On December 5, 1931, Minor Garber sold the Knightly Light and Power Company, Inc., to the Virginia Public Service Company. In the early 1940s, the mill buildings were razed, but Virginia Public Service retained the land, water and dam rights. Virginia Public Service subsequently became Virginia Electric Power and then Virginia Power of Dominion Resources.
1939	Homer and Paul Garber (third son) bought the New Hope General Merchandise Store and operated it for 11 years (1940 to 1951).
1941	Japan attacked Pearl Harbor and the United States entered World War II.
1942	Paul Garber married Ruby Elizabeth Sipe at Tinkling Spring Church. Over the next 10 years, they had three children: Wayne, Don and Carolyn.
1945	Germany and Japan surrendered, ending World War II. Japan surrendered after the U.S. dropped atomic bombs on Hiroshima and Nagasaki.

1951	Homer and Paul sold the New Hope General Merchandise Store to C. William Garber for $11,000.
1954	The U.S. Supreme Court forbade racial segregation in public schools.
1959	Homer and Sallie celebrated their Golden Wedding anniversary with a large family gathering at their Waynesboro home on Wayne Avenue. It was a joyous occasion with all of their children and grandchildren present.
1963	President John Kennedy was assassinated.
1965	United States sent large numbers of soldiers to fight in the Vietnam War.
1968	Civil rights leader Martin Luther King, Jr., was assassinated in Memphis.
1969	U.S. Astronaut Neil Armstrong became the first person to walk on the moon.
1973	Homer Garber died in a nursing home on August 14, 1973; he had lived 87 years and two days and had a good quality of life until his last four months.
1974	President Richard Nixon resigned because of the Watergate scandal.
1989	After Homer's death, Sallie moved to the Bridgewater Retirement Community and began teaching handicrafts to the residents. Sallie lived to be 101 years six months and 21 days, and she died April 13, 1989.
2001	Paul W. Garber lived 87 years and six months and died on July 16, 2001.

And the Garber story is still being written...

Ancestral Backgound

The Name and Family of Garber or Gerber

Garber

Garber Coat of Arms

The surname Garber or Gerber is of Germanic origin and is an occupational name meaning, according to some authorities, a tanner or furrier, a man who prepared leather from animal hides; to others it means a grower of wheat, a harvester or farmer. As far as can be determined at this time, the Garbers date back in history as far as the First Crusade (1096-1099), a Christian military expedition to recapture the Holy Land. During this historic event, the Garbers were Knights in charge of provisions according to the interpretation of "Wade." Thus the Garbers and Gerbers have a proven historic coat of arms; however, identifying specific coats of arms is difficult. Coats of arms were granted to male individuals, not families, and inherited by sons only. Any son not first born modifies the original crest in some manner – maybe ever so slightly. Thus many different coats of arms may have been granted to individuals with the same surname and with many later modifications of each original. One Garber coat of arms especially appears appropriate for early ancestors – Knights in charge of a food supply train. The Gerber and Garver families rose to high rank and title throughout the Germanic territories. Records show that they were granted estates in Saxony, Germany, Silesia and Switzerland and in the lands under the rule of the emperors.

Until about 1100 A.D., most people in Europe had only one name. As the population increased, it became awkward to live in a village where perhaps one third of the males were named John, another sizable percentage named William. To distinguish one John from another a second name was needed. There were four primary sources for second names and they were: a man's occupation, his location, his father's name or some peculiar characteristic. The surname Garber appears to be both patronymic and characteristic in origin and is believed to be associated with the German personal name, "Garibert (spear; bright)," meaning "descendant of Garber."

In addition to needing an extra name for identification, one occupational group found it necessary to go a step further. The fighting man of the middle ages wore a metal suit of armor for protection. Since this suit of armor included a helmet that completely covered the head, a knight in full battle dress was unrecognizable. To prevent friend from attacking friend during the heat of battle, it became necessary for each knight to somehow identify himself. Many knights accomplished this by painting colorful patterns on their battle shields. These patterns were also woven into cloth surcoats, which were worn over a suit of armor. Thus was born the term "coat of arms." Some arms display characteristics of early bearer's hopes, wishes and aspirations. For example, hope is symbolized by a wheat sheaf and joy by garlands of flowers or a red rose.

There are many deviations in the spelling of our original name GERBER. Some of these deviations are listed as follows: Garber, Garbert, Garbe, Gerberd, Gerbe, Gerbor, Garibert, Garberd, Garver, Garbier and Carver. However, Gerber and Garber became the predominant and earliest way in which the family name was spelled. These names are frequently found in America and were probably borne by emigrants who came from Germany and Switzerland and even England and France.

According to Floyd R. Mason, "If you do much research on this Garber family, you will find several spellings. These include Johanns garber as signed in his will and several deeds. John H. Garber as given by Elder, David Zigler. John Carver is used in some of the tax records and John Gerber in some records. Some of the records use Hanns Garber. It may be the H. stands for Hanns and he did not use it in his signatures. Elder John Garber is found printed on a later tombstone in the graveyard. We have chosen to use John H. Garber because it is different from the other John Garbers. Since they all are the husband of Barbara Miller and parent of 10 children, we can claim them. A person who understands German said that John Garber's father's signature could be translated as John or Hannes. It looks like this … Jo Hannes. This is probably where the John H. comes from. Please note that John H.'s signature on his will (written in German) and deeds was Johannes. This suggests that John H. or J. H. is a correct rendition of his name."

A noted historian observed that the Dunkers had large families; all used the same short list of Christian names (flooding the area with Johns, Daniels, Abrahams, Samuels, Marys, Sarahs, Elizabeths, etc.) and then succeeded in making many of them their ministers. Because of their religious beliefs and misunderstanding by the general community, they necessarily became clannish, resulting in some intra-family marriages and many marriages with a few families of the same beliefs.

The widely-used term Pennsylvania Dutch refers to people who came to Pennsylvania in the 1600s and 1700s from the German Rhineland and their descendents. Actually none of them came from the Netherlands (Holland). They were called Dutch because the word Deutsch, which means German, was misinterpreted. Occasionally some of the Pennsylvania German descendents in the Shenandoah Valley were incorrectly referred to as Dutch.

Source: With minor modifications the first and fourth paragraphs come directly from Garber, Clark M., *The Garber Historical and Genealogy Record, Volume III*, 1964.

European Background of the Garbers and Gerbers

The names Garber and Gerber are synonymous, having had the same origin in Germany and Switzerland. Both history and family legend tell us that the original and correct name is Gerber. The movement of a people from place to place or from country to country often changes the names of things and people. Of course, the Garbers were at one time devout Catholics. Otherwise they would not have taken an important part in the First Crusade to the Holy Land about the year 1096.

After the crusades, Germany for hundreds of years consisted of separate states ruled by princes, often at war with each other, and not infrequently at war with foreign countries. Germany was not united until the 1800s, long after the U.S. had gained its independence from England. To compound living conditions, the princes had forced the peasants to become serfs, working for the princes without freedom to leave the estate. However, as towns grew, many serfs were granted freedom to become merchants and town workmen. Thus serfdom gradually disappeared, but it was not completely eliminated until 1807.

In 1517, Martin Luther had begun to attack the Roman Catholic Church. Princes, nobles, townspeople and peasants joined the protestant movement and reformation spread quickly. Many peasants hoped the movement would free them from serfdom. The result was a long-lasting struggle between the princes and peasants, often resulting in death. Further, each Lutheran prince and each Catholic prince had the right to force those under him to accept his religion. Protestantism survived the counter-reformation mounted by the Catholic Church but at a heavy cost.

By the late 1600s and early 1700s further unrest was developing. New ideas were being discussed and new movements founded. Many were dissatisfied with the state churches, but in most areas it was very dangerous to express any opinions at variance with such churches. However, the religious revolution for which the famed Martin Luther was responsible appealed to the minds and souls of the Gerbers. They became members of and supporters of the new faith Tunkers, a religious group which developed from the earlier Pietist or Baptist movement.

Consequently, they were the subjects of unrelenting persecution which forced them to flee from place to place and conduct their religious services under cover and secretly. Eventually their life in Germany became so difficult and dangerous that many of them fled into Switzerland where they hoped to enjoy freedom of worship. When the Gerbers fled persecution in Germany and crossed the border into Switzerland, they built houses and reared their families, only to be subjected to persecution again when the State Church of Switzerland was established and the Gerbers did not conform. Of course, they could not foresee the continued persecution which they were destined to suffer there.

In Switzerland the Garbers were divided in their religious affiliation. Some were members of the German Baptist Brethren Faith and others embraced the Mennonite Faith. However, these two faiths were so closely alike in context and rituals that the Swiss Government placed them in the same category as nonconformists.

From the Historical Sketches of Deacon Michael Gerber authored by E. P. Garber, let us examine his excerpts from the Archives of Bern, Switzerland, in which he brought to light the persecution of the German Baptist Brethren and the Mennonite peoples. "In 1566, a minister of the sect by the name of Walti Gerber was decapitated by the Government for his persistent teaching of the Taufer doctrines. The Government captured him finally through a price of two thousand dollars bounty. In 1596, the wife of one Joseph Gerber was banished for her faith and her husband was forced to furnish bail of one thousand dollars for her. In 1598, one Hans Gerber was fined for harboring Taufers or Dunkers. The following year his wife was forced to forfeit approximately twelve thousands dollars of her property. Later the husband was fined again for the same amount. In 1693, another Walti Gerber was forbidden to harbor his father because of his faith. In 1709, one Hans Gerber and wife had to hide themselves from arrest because he was a minister of a congregation of Taufers and kept on preaching contrary to Government orders. They were finally apprehended but their fate is not recorded. About this same time one Elizabeth Gerber, wife of Peter Gerber, was banished with a number of others to the West Indies. Others at this time were banished to Pennsylvania, then a new Quaker Colony. Among these was one Michael Gerber from Langnau. In 1711, a number were sent to Holland, among them one Peter Gerber. Another, Ulli Gerber, was sent to Germany. In 1711, one Hans Gerber was condemned to the galleys in Italy. This was equivalent to a death sentence, as nearly all galley slaves perished in service. He was a Deacon. Others were imprisoned and some escaped to turn up again in their homes in Emmental."

Most of the foregoing persecutions were inflicted upon the Taufers and Mennonites. Many had their property confiscated and their homes burned. Some were incarcerated in various prisons never to be heard of again. Occasionally homes were visited by the officers of the local government in an effort to force heads of families to denounce their faith. Failure to do so could bring death to the family head, burning of their property and confiscation of their goods. Eventually these religious people could no longer withstand such treatment. There was an exodus of the Taufers and Mennonites into the German Palatinate from which place they eventually migrated to America.

Regardless of such inhuman persecutions, man emerged from this period of his existence, into a new life of religious freedom, freedom of thought and expression. Eventually the Gerbers learned of a new land across the Atlantic Ocean where people were free to worship as their spirits and minds interpreted the Lord's word. Thus began the migration of our people to America, a great new Country that offered freedom of worship.

Source: Garber, Clark M., *The Garber Historical and Genealogy Record, Volume III*, 1964 with the second, third and fourth paragraphs minor modifications from "The Clifton B. Garber Family Record," 1989.

Another Account of Our European Heritage

Our Gerber ancestors (as the name was originally spelled) came from the Canton of Berne in the country of Switzerland. Their history has not always been pleasant and is often tragic, for it is the story of a people persecuted and driven from their beloved homeland because of their desire to live for conscience sake as taught by the Holy Scriptures.

Our ancestors were Anabaptists, later called "Mennonites" after Menno Simons, a leading Dutch Anabaptist. Anabaptism began as a radical expression of the Protestant Reformation begun by Luther, Calvin and Zwingli. Anabaptists broke with the teachings of Luther and Zwingli by asserting that infants, being innocent of all sin, should not be baptized; rather, baptism should occur upon the confession of faith by a believer, signifying a personal commitment to follow the teachings of Jesus Christ. Furthermore, where Luther and Calvin retained an intimate association with the secular state, Anabaptists maintained that there must be a complete separation of church and state. The Anabaptists also refused to bear arms for the state in war.

The first Anabaptists broke with the official state religion of Switzerland in 1525 and immediately persecution began. The Council of Zurich ruled that children should continue to be baptized and that any parents who refused to comply should be expelled from Zurich. This was followed by fines, imprisonment and torture. On January 27, 1527, the first martyr, Felix Manz, was drowned because of his refusal to obey the Council's order to baptize infants. Michael Sattler, author of the Schleitheim Confession, was charged with conspiring to overthrow the civil order and burned at the stake on May 20, 1527. Following this, thousands of Anabaptists were executed because of their religious convictions. On September 17, 1543, Walti Gerber was executed in Berne because of his religious beliefs. It is not known whether he was one of our ancestors.

Throughout the sixteenth and seventeenth centuries attempts were made to suppress the Anabaptists "heresy" through persecutions that included imprisonment, torture, confiscation of property and murder. Anabaptist marriages were not recognized by the State and children of such marriages were considered illegitimate.

Because of the severe persecution in Switzerland, many Mennonites fled to the Palatinate in southern Germany where they were welcomed for their agricultural skills. The Palatinate, however, offered only a temporary refuge as the country was soon ravaged by the effects of the Thirty Years' War (1616 – 1648). The country which shortly before had been so prosperous soon became a wilderness of uncultivated land marked here and there by the blackened ruins of farms and villages.

The conditions of poverty, oppression and religious intolerance in Europe provided ample reason for our ancestors to escape to a land of freedom. That opportunity came in 1661 when William Penn announced his "Holy Experiment." In Pennsylvania, religious and political freedom would be granted to all. The Mennonites found a sympathetic heart in Penn, for this Quaker, like they, refused to bear arms and understood the privations of religious persecution.

A poignant account of their departure from their homeland is given by Muller in his history of the Bernese Anabaptists: It has been frequently described how the exiled Anabaptists, laden with their scanty possessions, crossed the mountains of their native land, and with tears in their eyes, looked back to the valleys of their home. Our ancestors from Emmenthal and the Oberland found no sympathy among their fellow Swiss countrymen, as the towers of the Cathedral of Basel and the wooded heights of the Jura faded in the distance. Sitting on boxes and bundles which were piled high in the middle of the boat could be seen grey-haired men and women, old and feeble; yonder stood the young gazing in wonder at the shores as they slipped by. At times they were hopeful, at others sad, and their glances would alternate, now to the north, now to the south toward their abandoned home which had driven them out so unfeelingly, and yet whose green hills and snow-capped mountains they cannot forget. Despite the comforts of religion, their sadness could not be overcome, and from time to time someone would sing:

> Ein Herzene-Weh mir uberkam
> Im Scheiden uber d'Massen
> Als ich von euch mein Abschied nam
> Und dessmals must verlassen
> Mein Herz was bang

Beharrlich lng:
Es bleibt noch unvergessen
Ob scheild ich gleich
Bleibt's Herz bei euch,
Wie solt ich euch vergessen?
Translation:
A great heartache
Overcame me at departure
As I took leave of you
And then had to go
My Heart was anxious
Persistent, Long:
It still is not forgotten
As if I were leaving with you,
How should I forget you?

The perils of the long voyage to America were great, with much suffering, disease and death. The boats were usually very crowded, and the voyage lasted from ten to twelve weeks. Following is a translation of a 1733 journal written on the back of an old Swiss calendar. The journal was written by Jacob Beiler, a passenger on the ship "Charming Nancy."

"The 28th of June while in Rotterdam getting ready to start my _____ Zernibi died and was buried in Rotterdam. The 29th we got under sail and enjoyed only 1 ½ days of favorable wind. The 7th day of July, early in the morning, Hans Zimmerman's son-in-law died.

We landed in England the 8th day of July, remaining 9 days in port during which 5 children died. Went under sail the 17th day of July. The 21st of July my own Lisbetli died. Several days before Michael's Georgli had died.

On the 29th of July three children died. On the first of August my Hansli died and Tuesday previous five children died. On the 3rd of August contrary winds beset the vessel and from the 1st to the 7th of the month three more children died. On the 8th of August Shambien's Lizzie died and on the 9th Hans Zimmerman's Jacobli died. On the 19th Christian Burgli's child died. Passed a ship on the 21st. A favorable wind sprang up. On the 28th Hans Gasi's wife died. Passed a ship on the 13th of September.

Landed in Philadelphia on the 18th and my wife and I left the ship on the 19th. A child was born to us on the 20th – died – wife recovered. A voyage of 83 days."

The first wave of Mennonite immigration to the New World began in 1683 when a settlement was established at Germantown, Pennsylvania. The next wave of immigration began in 1709 and lasted until 1765. During this time thousands of Mennonites of Swiss origin came to Lancaster County. They settled the virgin land and through their hard work, thrift and will created one of the most prosperous farming communities in all of North America. More importantly, they were an earnest and upright people who sought to create a City of God on earth where a Christ of love and service could dwell. The passing of time has all but obliterated our knowledge of them, yet their legacy lives on. They have bequeathed to us a priceless heritage.

Source: Garber, Allan A., *The Descendants of Christian S. and Anna Garber of Lancaster County, Pennsylvania*, 1985.

Tunkers, Germany 1700s

Wittgenstein, an area in Westphalia in the central Rhine Valley, was one of the provinces where the prince permitted, to a degree, religious dissenter refuge without unbearable persecution. Alexander Mack, his wife and six other men and women were led by careful reading of the bible to reject infant baptism and a formal written creed to embrace triune (being three in one, especially of the trinity), immersion by dipping face down as the true mode of Christian baptism, and to adopt the ordinances taught by Jesus and his followers in the New Testament as the guide and rule for their lives. Briefly, they felt the example of the first century church should be followed in all its practices. In 1708, not finding these doctrines prescribed in the Christian German churches, Alexander Mack was baptized in the Eder River by one of his fellow believers, chosen by lot, and then he baptized the other seven. Thus the Tunker, or German Baptist Church, was born. The only one of the eight with a surname remotely approaching "Gerber" was George Grebi.

Tunker derives from the German verb "tunken" meaning to dip. The name was used to distinguish the new denomination from the Mennonites, some of whose dogmas are similar to those of the Tunkers, but whose mode of baptism is quite different.

Mack established the first Tunker church in the village of Schwartzenau and two additional societies in the area. Schwartzenau contained dissenters with many different and strong convictions. Although relatively free from persecution from civil authorities, the new church was not free from persecution from the state church and other dissenters. Moving was not the solution. During the first decade several groups settled at different places and met persecution from civil authorities as well as church authorities and, not surprisingly, encountered trouble within the church.

Beginning in 1719, the first Tunkers emigrated to America, with an especially large group of fifty families arriving in 1729.

Source: "The Clifton B. Garber Family Record," 1989.

Atlantic Ocean Crossings Were Dangerous

By 1730, an estimated 15,000 Reformed church confessors (less than a hundred Tunker families) from the Rhine Valley – principally Westphalia and the Palatinate – had arrived in Pennsylvania and were scattered over 300-400 miles. From 1727 to 1775, 324 ships of several different types brought Germans to Philadelphia. The ships, with an average of 300-350 passengers, were English with English captains who varied from "horrid barbarity with the passengers," to "wicked murderer of souls" to "very good captain who had much patience with us."

Journey down the Rhine River to Holland took from four to six weeks and required clearance at 26 custom houses; each clearance conducted to suit the convenience of local customs officials and was very expensive for the passengers. Passengers were detained in Rotterdam, only a few started from Amsterdam or Hamburg, another five to six weeks where necessities, food and lodging were again very expensive. By this time, many passengers had exhausted much of their resources. The second stage of the journey was from Rotterdam to an English port; 142 ships made last call at Cowes on the Isle of Wright; another delay of one to two weeks, mainly for provisions, clearing customs and waiting for favorable winds. The season for passage began in early May and ended in late October with each Atlantic crossing from England requiring at least six to seven weeks, but eight to twelve weeks were not unusual.

The ocean voyage was by far the most arduous part of the trip. The passengers were packed densely, were without proper food and quality drinking water and were subject to all sorts of diseases such as seasickness, dysentery, scurvy, typhoid and smallpox, all aggravated by frequent storms. People also suffered from constipation, headaches and infestations of lice. Children were the first to fall victim and died in great numbers. Accommodations were sparse and personal living space was limited to just barely enough room for a person to lie down to sleep. Unrelenting weather conditions such as cold, dampness, heat and storms added to the physical and emotional fatigue. Homesickness began to plague many because they remembered the comforts of home. In addition to all these factors, a few captains were reputed to have robbed passengers; some passengers resorted to hiding monies in the clothing of small children. Small wonder most Germans arrived in Philadelphia with precious little money – at most a few dollars by current values.

New arrivals in Philadelphia encountered two major obstacles. Passengers with infectious diseases were removed outside the city and received limited or no treatment. It was not until 1750 that a hospital was built on Fisher's Island in the Delaware River for the immigrants, and then only after a serious epidemic had broken out in Philadelphia. Secondly, the "Captain's List" was provided magistrates who administered "oaths of allegiance." Many Germans must have found it difficult to pledge their allegiance to England, but especially so to the Tunkers since first they had to take an oath and second agree to defend their new country (bear arms), both which were not religiously correct for them.

Without question, those starting a successful new life in the colonies were significantly fewer in number than those leaving the Rhine Valley.

Source: "The Clifton B. Garber Family Record," 1989.

The Affirmation

The following affirmation was required of the Gerbers and Garbers and the thousands of other Mennonite and German Baptist Brethren people when they arrived in the port of Philadelphia and became citizens of the Pennsylvania Colony. To many of the Garbers, the renowned Benjamin Franklin, who was at that time in charge of the Port of Philadelphia, administered this affirmation.

"We Subscribers, natives and late inhabitants of the Palatinate on the Rhine River and places adjacent, having transported ourselves and our families into the Province of Pennsylvania, a Colony subject to the Crown of Great Britain, in the hopes and expectations of finding a retreat and peaceable settlement therein, do solemnly promise and engage that we will be faithful and bear true allegiance to his Majesty, King George the Second and his successors, Kings of Great Britain, and will be faithful to the Proprietors of this Province; and that we will demean ourselves peaceably to all his Majesty's subjects and strictly observe and conform to the Laws of England and this Province to the utmost of our power and the best of our understanding."

Source: Garber, Clark M., *The Garber Historical and Genealogy Record, Volume III*, 1964.

The Garbers and Gerbers Come to America

The record of Garber and Gerber migrations to America is one of patience, courage, faith and determination. They were an industrious, frugal and, at the same time, a generous people. So begins the story of a pioneer people who played an important part in the building of our Nation. Of course, our direct ancestors were not the only Garbers or Gerbers who sought freedom and contentment in the New World. Yet they were doubtless all related in the Old Country, some distant and some closely. Over a period of approximately 75 years, beginning in the year 1700, families came from Switzerland and the German Palatinate leaving countless close relatives who did not have sufficient money for the journey or preferred not to break family ties. Across the Atlantic Ocean were the English Colonies, the land of opportunity, offering land and freedom from the privations of the Reformation.

Many different ships brought Garbers to America, including many with similar names to our ancestors.

- Hans Jacob Gerber arrived in the port of Philadelphia aboard the ship Hope, Daniel Master, Aug. 28th, 1733.
- Michael Garber, age 27, with his wife Anna and six-month-old daughter Anna. They arrived in the port of Philadelphia September 23rd, 1734, aboard the ship Hope Galley, Daniel Reidt, Master.
- Johannes Gerber, age 32, came on the ship Harle, Ralph Harle, Master. He arrived in Philadelphia September 1st, 1736.
- Hans Gerber & Hans Gerber, Jr., came on the ship Charming Nancy, Charles Steadman, Master. They landed at the port of Philadelphia October 8th, 1737.
- Hans Christian Gerber came via the ship Charming Nancy, Charles Steadman, Master. He arrived in the port of Philadelphia on November 9th, 1738.
- John Adam Gerber, age 20, arrived in the port of Philadelphia on October 7th, 1743, via the ship St. Andrew, Robert Brown, Master.
- Johannes Garber arrived in the port of Philadelphia via the ship Albany, September 2nd, 1749, Robert Brown, Master.
- Adam Gerber arrived in Philadelphia aboard the ship, Dragon, George Spencer, Master. He arrived September 26th, 1749.
- Jost Paul Kuhnroth Gerber arrived in Philadelphia aboard the ship, Leslie, J. Ballendine, Master. Arrived October 7th, 1749.
- Joseph Gerber arrived in the port of Philadelphia August 28th, 1750, aboard the ship Phoenix, John Mason, Master.
- Johannes H. Garber arrived in the port of Philadelphia aboard the ship Phoenix, John Mason, Master. He arrived August 28th, 1750, at the age of 33 years.
- Hans Gerber arrived in the port of Philadelphia on August 15th, 1751, aboard the ship Royal Union, C. Nicholson, Master.
- Johann Fredrick Garber came to America aboard the ship Phoenix, Capt. Spurrier, Master. He arrived in the port of Philadelphia September 25th, 1751.
- Johannes Garber arrived in the port of Philadelphia aboard the ship, Phoenix, on November 22nd, 1752, Reuben Honor, Master.
- Jacob Garber, age 21; Michael Garber, age 20; and Simon Garber, age 22, arrived in the port of Philadelphia aboard the ship Patience on September 8th, 1753, Hugh Steel, Master.
- Felix Gerber, age 26, arrived in the port of Philadelphia September 26, 1753, aboard the ship Windsor, John Goad, Master.
- Philip Gerber arrived in the port of Philadelphia November 10th, 1764, via the ship Boston, Matthew Carr, Master.
- Johann Christian Gerber arrived in the port of Philadelphia October 16th, 1772, aboard the ship Crawford.
- Jacob Gerber came to America via the ship Hope Galley, Daniel Reidt, Master. Arrived in the port of Philadelphia August 28th, 1773.

Source: With minor modification the material comes directly from Garber, Clark M., *The Garber Historical and Genealogy Record, Volume III*, 1964.

Church of the Brethren

Tunker was anglicized first to "Dunker" and later to "Dunkard." Another early name was German Baptist. The Tunkers preferred the name Brethren – the idea for the name comes from the eighth verse of the 23rd chapter of Matthew. Christ is addressing his disciples and the multitude and commands, "But be not ye called Rabbi: for one is your master, even Christ; and all ye are brethren." However, it was not until 1908 that officially the name of the denomination became Church of the Brethren. Since a great majority of the immigrants and their descendents for several generations spoke only German, the word "Tunker" was widely used, accepted and understood deep into the 1800s.

The Tunkers and Mennonites had beliefs and followed religious practices which were strange, not only to the original settlers of different nationalities and denominations, but also to many ethnic Germans. Their prescribed church dress, rejection of oaths, emphasis on separation from worldly matters and refusal to bear arms made them a people apart. The church prescribed the every day dress of its members; jewelry and stylish fashionable clothing prohibited the kind of entertainment they could have and forbade them to participate actively in politics and government. Without question, alcohol and tobacco production, sale and use were prohibited, as well as membership in secret societies. Consequently, they were greatly misunderstood.

Teachers that were ministers were selected by allowing every brother, so inclined, to stand up and speak (exhort). When a man appeared to be a capable and talented teacher, the members chose him their minister and ordained him by laying on hands, fasting, praying and by extending the right hand of fellowship. Ministers rose through three degrees to complete ministership. From among experienced and tested ministers, elders were chosen. In early years, an elder was usually the first or oldest teacher in the congregation. One wryly commented as to why Dunker ministers did not attend theological schools or universities was that they could not place the letters D.D. (Doctor of Divinity) after their names since their non-Dunker brethren would believe it meant "Dumb Dunker" or "Dirty Devil."

Source: "The Clifton B. Garber Family Record," 1989.

Since the Garbers of this particular lineage first came to America, hundreds of them have become Ministers, Deacons and Elders of the Old German Baptist Brethren Church. Many have also embraced the Mennonite and Amish faiths that, like the Brethren faith, were born of different interpretations of the Bible and were subjected to the terrible persecutions that all anti-Catholics suffered in the Old Country. As they spread over every State in the Union many of them found no church of their faith where they settled. Consequently, many became affiliated with other Protestant churches rather than deny their families the right to worship. Some of them have even become leaders and Ministers in other church organizations.

Source: Garber, Clark M., *The Garber Historical and Genealogy Record, Volume III*, 1964.

Migration of the Gerbers/Garbers from Europe to Virginia

11th–16th Centuries	Our Gerber ancestors lived in Germany.
1604	By the 17th century the Gerbers had moved to Switzerland. Ulrich Gerber (b 1605), Christian Gerber (b 1635), Niclaus Gerber (b 1661) and Jo Hannes Gerber (b 1701) lived in Steffisburg, Bern, Switzerland.

Abt. 1719	Jo Hannes Gerber (1701–1748) moved to the Palatinate, Germany, to a Mennonite community.
1728	Jo Hannes Gerber took a boat down the Rhine River to Rotterdam, Holland. He immigrated to America probably by way of England (Cowes on Isle of Wright). Jo Hannes arrived in Philadelphia and lived in Chester County, Pennsylvania, where his third son and our progenitor Johannes "John H." Garber (1732–1787) was born.
1744	Jo Hannes Gerber moved his family to Lancaster/York County, Pennsylvania, where they continued to live after Jo Hannes' death in 1748.
1768	Johannes "John H." Garber moved his wife, Barbara Miller and family to Frederick County, Maryland.
1775	Johannes "John H." Garber moved his family to the Shenandoah Valley at Flat Rock, Shenandoah County, Virginia.
1790	Abraham Garber (1760-1848) moved his new bride, Elizabeth Humbert, to New Hope, Augusta County, Virginia.
21st Century	Five generations of Abraham and Elizabeth Garber's descendents to include Jacob (1797-1876), Levi (1828-1914), Daniel (1855-1923), Homer (1886-1973) and Paul (1913-2001) continued to live in the areas of New Hope and Mt. Sidney, Virginia.

Migration of the Garbers within America

Two important factors were responsible for the early migration of the Garbers within America. The first and perhaps the most important cause involved the necessity for the settlement of new lands. This was inevitably brought about by large families and the need for new lands required for settlement and the homes of many, many sons. Consequently, many Garbers and their descendants came to settle along the fringe of the frontier and some even ventured into the habitat of the Indians.

Secondly, the American Revolution was fought at the time most of our early ancestors lived in York County, Pennsylvania, and the County of Frederick in Maryland. At the close of the Revolution, the soldiers returning to their homes found the "Tunkers" had taken no part in the fighting but had remained at home and had excellent farms on which they had prospered. The Garbers, as well as many other families of the German Baptist Brethren faith, adhered strongly to the tenants of their religion which prohibits them to bear arms against their fellow man. This situation so strongly disturbed the returning soldiers that again our people were persecuted for their religion. Homes and barns were burned. Cattle and other livestock were either stolen or slaughtered. Consequently the Garbers, Wines, Biglers, Millers, Swiharts, Crumrines, Ellers, Glicks, Leedys, Graybils and many others sought out new lands in which their families could be raised in comparative safety. Elder John Garber with his wagon train of family and friends went to the Shenandoah Valley of Virginia and Elder Jacob Garber with his wagon train came west to Washington County, Pennsylvania. These two movements represent the two major migrations of Garbers within America.

Source: Garber, Clark M., *The Garber Historical and Genealogy Record, Volume III*, 1964.

America's First Civil War

Garber descendants, as many other families of the German Baptist Brethren faith, were brave and patriotic people in the New World. They had moved from all over Germany to Switzerland, back to Germany and then to America to have freedom from political and religious oppression. They wanted to rear their families in as much freedom as possible. As political empires rose and fell and as State Churches changed, they wanted to remain true to their beliefs and, therefore, moved. When political and religious freedom was a problem and moving was not possible, they, like all other families, had to make compromises.

Many of our family, using the example of the "Ox in the Ditch" compromised with their religious beliefs and took combatant or non-combatant roles in the military for a few years. They returned to their civilian professions or jobs as soon as possible. A large number of them sought ways to serve the country in non-military jobs. Many of them were deferred to do work of national importance, such as farming. However, when a satisfactory job could not be obtained, many of them stood in defiance of the laws and suffered personal loss and sometimes jail. Often the best thing to do was to move to an area where the law could not find them or to an area of the opposite side.

Before the Revolution and the establishment of the new government, the land was ruled by English law. The State Church was Episcopal and all other church members were considered "Dissenters." This did not seem to be a problem to most churches as they were given a lot of freedom to worship as they pleased. The State Church had certain responsibilities assigned to them as part of the English governmental system. They were charged with the responsibility of caring for the poor and the orphans. If the other churches became too active, they found themselves in trouble with the government. After 1776, "Freedom of Religion" was getting started and has existed to this day.

During the Revolution, the colonists held their national conventions and appointed certain committees of local leaders to carry out local responsibilities. In Pennsylvania and Maryland, the main committee was the Committee of Observation. They had the responsibility of raising funds to promote the war, selecting its leaders and furnishing men, horses, rifles and food for the forces. They organized themselves with one committee member for each 100 families. These committees had full power to act as they saw fit. They were the new developing government, and there were no courts or other administrative government channels. They were responsible to no one, and there was no appeal to their decisions.

Early in the Revolution, Mennonites, Dunkers and Quakers were given freedom to remain true to their peace positions of nonviolence, but in return they would pay an additional tax of two shillings and six pence per week. This was granted at Philadelphia and Annapolis for all of Pennsylvania and Maryland, but as it was carried out in the local towns and villages, local committees were free to make their own rules and interpretations.

Those volunteering for the colonist causes were early called Associations, later called Militia Companies. The Committee of Observation made lists of those not participating, whether Loyalist or members of the Peace Churches, and they were called non-enrollers or non-associators. The war issues divided the peoples' loyalty. About one third favored the Revolution, one third the Loyalists or Tories who favored the English and one third were neutral or did not believe in this manner of settling issues. This threw the Mennonites, Dunkers and Quakers with the Tories or Loyalists and in opposition to the efforts of the Committee of Observation, at least as the Committee saw it.

The churches were bringing discipline to bear on members who did not follow the historic peace teachings of the church. Annual conferences of the churches were held each year and members were asked to remain true to the church's nonviolent principles, to refrain from participating in the war, to not voluntarily pay the war taxes and not to allow their sons to participate in the war. The Elders, to the best of their ability, tried to help members who suffered losses and collected money from church members to help those who needed help. This caused a lot of problems for the church members who wanted to be loyal to the church, loyal to the Loyalists who had brought them to the new country and loyal to the new government which was emerging.

As the war wore on and it looked as if the Patriot efforts might lose, war emotions raged. Non-associators found themselves having to pay double and triple taxes. They were having their barns burned, their livestock stolen or slaughtered, their crops destroyed and they were often beaten and/or "tarred-and-feathered." Church members would come to the aid of members suffering losses, sponsoring barn raisings and raising money for lost crops and livestock. Some members chose not to pay the war taxes or participate in the war activities and chose to wait until the authorities came and presented their papers to have taxes forced from them. This was in compliance with the Church of the Brethren Annual Conference Action. The Committee of Observation provided that non-associators could take their possessions with them and then they would seize the property and remaining possessions and sell them to fill their war chests.

Taken from several sources, these are some of the names of non-associators and others who were processed by the Committee of Observation that are descendants of Michael Miller (Sr.):

- The two step-sons and two step-sons-in-law, Samuel Garber (Sr.), Martin Garber (Sr.), Jacob Good and John Rife (Sr.)
- David Miller, the son of Phillip Jacob, Martin Garber and Samuel Garber, sons of Barbara Miller and John H. Garber
- Michael Wine, who married Susannah Miller and Jacob Miller, children of Lodowich and Abraham Miller.

Susannah Miller Wine told her children and grandchildren that Michael Wine, Jacob Miller, Martin Garber and Samuel Garber had their property confiscated by the authorities for remaining true to the nonviolent principles of their church. They lived in Frederick County, Maryland, from the 1760s to 1782 when they moved to Shenandoah County, Virginia. It is stated that Maryland Dunkers fared better than Pennsylvania Dunkers and that is perhaps why many of them moved from York County, Pennsylvania, to Maryland in the 1760s.

From a list of Dunkers taken into court and fined in 1776 are listed those who are a part of the Miller family. It seems that the Committee of Observation, not knowing how to deal with the following Dunker leaders, called them into court and fined them. When they did not pay their fines, officials confiscated their land and sold it and paid their fines for them. Some say that the court gave them permission to destroy these records and therefore the records of some of these confiscations are not available. Perhaps this action was done in order to silence them and force their compliance with the activities of the Committee.

- Elder Jacob Danner 10 pounds
- Eld. Samuel Danner, son of Jacob Danner 6 ½ pounds
- Eld. Martin Garver, son of John H., 7 ½ pounds – then remitted
- Eld. Samuel Garver, son of John H., 6 ½ pounds – remitted
- John Garver (may be Eld. John H.), 6 ½ pounds, then remitted the same day
- Elder Daniel Miller, son of Lodowich Miller, 4 ½ pounds
- Elder Michael Wine, son-in-law Lodowich Miller, 6 ½ pounds reduced to 5 ½ pounds (1782 farm and land confiscated)
- Christopher Steel, brother-in-law of Michael Wine, 5 ½ pounds reduced
- April 12, 1776, John Garver, Michael Garver, Samuel Garver fines remitted.

Suspected Loyalist sympathizers were watched very closely by local committee members and their advisers. Mennonites and Dunkards were closely watched as some thought they were Loyalists. Mennonites Henry Newcomer and Yost Plecker were jailed in 1781.

In 1781, there was a case taken into the courts in Fredericktown, charging seven persons of treason. This is referred to as the Traitor-Loyalist Trials. They were tried and found guilty. Three of them were hanged and put on display according to English Law. The other four were later pardoned and released. Some believe that Yost Plecker, a Mennonite, and Peter Suman, a Dunker, were chosen not because they were part of the plot charged but because they were Dunkards and Mennonites and by using this means it would cause more non-associators to join the Patriot causes. Peter Suman was the Dunkard layman chosen, and he was one of the three hanged according to English Law. His Dunkard Elder, Peter Arnold, and some church members took him down and gave him a church burial. The others in the case were pardoned.

Government leaders, local, state and national, either misunderstood or chose to take advantage of the church leaders and members who stayed loyal to their beliefs when they were opposite to the laws and practice of the land. The following issues created a lot of difficulty:

- Early German Baptist Elders interpreted their German Bibles very literally. They accepted the Scriptures to mean that we are subject to earthly Kings and we are under principalities and princes....etc. and thus they were dubbed "Tories."
- Several of the Anabaptist denominations opposed the "taking of an oath" for any reason. One source says sometimes was acceptable but for many the word "yes" or "no" was all that could be given. Early Americans often found themselves faced with having to give an "oath of allegiance" to first one government and then another. Refusal to do so was considered as having "aided the enemy." Laws were passed in Pennsylvania and Maryland to permit their land to be seized and sold.
- Some of the Anabaptist denominations believed that nonviolent means of settling disputes were the only acceptable means.
- They also opposed killing, even in the time of war, and many of them refused to participate or to carry a gun. For these reasons, many of them were persecuted by the State during the time of the Revolutionary and Civil Wars.

These are reasons that some of our families moved to new land areas where they had freedom to worship and raise their families. During times of national crises, members of many families were divided into different positions. Some went with the position of the State in which they lived. This resulted in families being divided and family members were often on opposing sides. Many families moved to Virginia, West Virginia, Kentucky, Ohio, Indiana, Illinois and farther west because of the issues surrounding the Revolutionary and Civil Wars.

Owning slaves was also a burning issue at this time. During the Civil War, much of the same conditions existed. The Church of the Brethren opposed owning slaves. Elders were purchasing the slaves and freeing them. They did not want to participate in the war for aforesaid reasons.

The writer has read many accounts where the Dunker families in the Shenandoah Valley fed and housed leaders and soldiers first of one and then another. They saw the soldiers as human beings and were willing to care for their needs as brothers.

Source: With minor modifications the material comes directly from *Mason, Floyd, John H. Garber & Barbara Miller of Pennsylvania, Maryland and Virginia*, 1998.

The Shenandoah Valley of Virginia

The hills and valleys were beautiful and fertile. The streams were crowded with fish and on land wild animals were plentiful – primarily bears, beavers, buffaloes, deer, elk, black and grey foxes, coons, hares, muskrats, opossums, otters, skunks, wild turkeys and wolves. There were no rats, crows, blackbirds or honey bees until the white man arrived. To encourage the growth of grasses and similar vegetation for pasturage for buffalo, elk and deer the Indians annually burned, at the end of the hunting season, the rivers and large creek bottoms providing a prairie-like condition. The mountain sides, high hills and marshy lowlands were thick forests, and some large trees were along the streams. But river bottoms and creek meadows were pasture lands.

Before 1730 – 1732, the date usually accepted for the arrival of the first permanent white settlers, a long power struggle existed between several Indian tribes for possession of the central valley. Even after peace was more or less established between the white man and the Indians, many migratory tribes and groups used the Shenandoah Valley as a highway for their trading, military efforts against one another, hunting and fishing grounds and even as a change in climate. Some upstate New York and Canadian Indians would visit regularly to escape the severe northern winters. One conflict never resolved was that of private ownership. The Indians firmly believed that anything the land, air or water provided belonged to them, if needed, even the white man's stock and crops. Predictably, on occasion, this led to bloodshed and death.

The Blue Ridge Mountains were a natural barrier to the English who had settled in the Tidewater and Piedmont areas east of the mountains. A few explorers led expeditions into the valley in the late 1600s. And a very few adventurous people stayed without land rights. In fact, Middle River was first known as Cathey's River after a family by that name had "squatted" near the river. Around 1700, English interest increased in the Shenandoah Valley as trade with the Indians was becoming very profitable and with the need to find a direct route to the Great Lakes. In addition, the continued threats of raids and open war against English settlers east of the Blue Ridge by the Indians caused those east of the Blue Ridge to want a permanent settlement in the valley to serve as a buffer between them and the Indians.

The valley had been under the jurisdiction of Orange County east of the Blue Ridge. But by 1738, the valley had sufficient growth that the Colonial legislature created Augusta County reaching westward to lands on the Ohio and Mississippi Rivers. By 1745, the new region had sufficient qualified inhabitants for county officers and courts and became independent of Orange County. Staunton (originally known as Beverley's Mill Place) became the county seat. As early as 1742, monies were raised in Augusta to provide for the poor and orphans, maintain the militia for protection from the Indians, the killing of wolves preying on livestock and for other purposes. Because Augusta County was far too large to serve efficiently its rapidly growing populace from Staunton, it was quickly and often reduced in size. Rockingham County was carved out of Augusta County in 1778 with Harrisonburg the county seat.

Slaves were introduced into the area after the first permanent white settlers arrived – even some ministers owned them. However, slavery was always opposed by the Dunkers. Slaves never exceeded 12% of the total population in the Augusta-Rockingham area.

Into this region first came the English, French, Irish, Scotch-Irish and Welsh pioneers. Then around 1750 the Germans, including a few Dunker families, began migrating from York County and surrounding Pennsylvania countryside, through Maryland into the Shenandoah Valley.

Source: "The Clifton B. Garber Family Record," 1989.

U.S. Generation No. 1

Johannes "John H." Garber & Barbara Miller

Home of John H. Garber and Barbara Miller

York County, Pennsylvania
Picture Was Probably Taken about 1900. Log Cabin Was Removed before 1919.

Ancestors of Johannes "John H." Garber

There is conflicting opinion as to where the Garber family originated, but the preponderance of evidence established it first in Switzerland. Doubtless Garbers migrated from Switzerland to Westphalia, the Palatinate, Alsace and elsewhere and this gave rise to the theory that their original residence was somewhere other than in the province of Berne, Switzerland. Floyd Mason and others believe that our ancestors went from Germany to Switzerland to Germany and then to America. We know that they were in Switzerland during the seventeenth century, were Mennonites and were martyrs when necessary to their faith. The ancestor tree starts with Ulrich Gerber of Switzerland and traces the ancestry to John H. Garber of Flat Rock, Virginia.

Generation One
Ulrich Gerber of Switzerland was born around 1605 and married Barbara Farni. They lived in Steffisburg, Bern, Switzerland, and had three children: Hans Gerber born Jan 13, 1631, in Steffisburg; Anni Gerber born January 22, 1632, in Steffisburg; and Christian Gerber born March 20, 1635.

Generation Two
Christian Gerber born March 20, 1635, in Steffisburg, Bern. He and his wife moved to Markirch, Alsace, before February 1674. They were both called Anabaptists at the baptism of their sons in 1671 and 1684. He was probably expelled in 1671.

Generation Three
Niclaus Gerber born November 21, 1661 and married Anna Bachman in Steffisburg. He was called the son of Christian Gerber the Anabaptist at the baptism of his daughters Barbara in 1689 and Anna in 1691. There are no more children found for him in Steffisburg after 1691. He may be the Mennonite Claus Gerber who was living at Immelhausenhof, Germany, in 1731. Niclaus and Anna had four children as follows:

1. Barbara Gerber born July 7, 1689, in Steffisburg, Switzerland

2. Anna Gerber born October 4, 1691, in Steffisburg, Switzerland

3. Niclous Gerber born about 1700 [added by Davis]

4. Jo Hannes Gerber born about 1701 [added by Mason and others].

Note: Mason believes that Jo Hannes Gerber and his brother, Niclous Gerber, had immigrated to America by 1729.

Generation Four
Mason believes that Niclous and Jo Hannes Gerber families were as outlined below.

Niclous Gerber born about 1700 and died in 1748. He married Elizabeth (unknown) and their children are as follows:

1. Elizabeth Garber born about 1722 (?) and married Jacob Good who was born in 1722.

2. Samuel Garber born 1732, died in 1793, and married Mary Long.

3. Martin Garber born about 1737, died before 1804, and married Anna Preston born in 1749 and died in 1802.

4. Anna Garber born (?) and married John Rife (Reiffe) who was born in 1724 and died about 1787.

Jo Hannes Gerber/Garver was born about 1701 and died in 1748. He left a will and, while he did not name his children, he gave instructions for the administrators of the estate to take care of the wife and children. We believe he immigrated about 1728, and Mason and others have determined that the following are likely the children.

1. John Gerber born (?), died 1804, and married Catherine __?__.

2. Michael Garber buried beside Johannes Garber in Garber Cemetery and father of Elder Samuel Garber of Augusta County, Virginia.

3. Johannes "John" Garber born about 1732, died in 1787, and married Barbara Miller born in 1733 and died in 1808.

4. Daniel Garver born about 1738 and bought land in Frederick County, Maryland. (No more information.)

5. Nicholas Carver born in 1742 and moved to Virginia in 1783. (No more information.)

Mason believes that Niclous Gerber emigrated from Switzerland to Pennsylvania on August 19, 1729, on the ship Morton House with other Mennonites. We do not know when Jo Hannes Gerber migrated to America, but he arrived by 1729. The brothers Niclous and Jo Hannes Gerber are believed to have lived together on one tract of land in Chester County, Pennsylvania, from time of immigration to about 1744. Niclous Gerber and his wife Elizabeth owned the land, and Jo Hannes Gerber and his wife built on the land that his brother owned.

Generation Five
Johannes "John H." Garber was born in America about 1732, died in 1787 in Flat Rock, Virginia, and married Barbara Miller who was born in 1733 and died in 1808. The life of John Garber is the starting point for this family history.

Source: With minor modifications the material comes directly from *Mason, Floyd, John H. Garber & Barbara Miller of Pennsylvania, Maryland and Virginia*, 1998.

Author's Note: Johannes "John H." Garber is the starting focus of this family history because he was the first of our ancestors born in America.

Who Was Jo Hannes Gerber (Father of John H. Garber)?

We do not know when Jo Hannes Gerber came to America. Floyd Mason gives the date of entry of Niclous and Elizabeth Gerber as 1729. Niclous was a brother to Jo Hannes, who was found living with other German immigrants that settled in Colebrook Valley, Pennsylvania. Dr. Henry gives us some help as he writes, "Few Germans were in Pennsylvania before 1700. Peter Becker, the first Brethren minister in 1719, came to Germantown, Pennsylvania. This became the Mecca for the newcomers. Here they found their kinsmen and fellowshipped with the sons of their mother tongue."

The early Germans came in great numbers and soon made their way across the Susquehanna. They began to clear the forest, build log cabins, construct roads and communications and establish homes on the frontier. It wasn't long until they were molested and, in some cases, murdered by the Indians. In 1728, a petition was sent to the Governor of Pennsylvania signed by 76 German settlers asking for protection against the Indian outrages. Tolzman gives the petition and the names of the 76 signers along with their signatures. They were settlers in Colebrook Valley, Pennsylvania. Jo Hannes Gerber and Christian Stoner signed together, and the signature is identical to the signature of Jo Hannes Gerber on his will in 1748. This gives us some proof that Jo Hannes Gerber was in Pennsylvania as early as 1728. He later moved to some land bought by his brother Niclous Garber and lived there until they both died and left the land in their wills in 1748.

Mason writes, "In order to understand this, one has to understand that German Lutheran, Mennonite and Dunker/Tunker immigrant families that came to America lived together, worshipped together and intermarried the first two generations in the New World. It was rough going, the elements, Indians, wars, English rule and American efforts to colonize and form a new republic."

Michael Danner, Sr., got some land from William Penn and helped the settlers move to the lands near Hanover, Pennsylvania, in what is today York County, Pennsylvania. He was a German Baptist Brethren and/or Mennonite. These two sons of Niclaus Gerber of Germany came to America and are believed to have lived together on one tract of land, first in Chester County, Pennsylvania, and then in Lancaster County, Pennsylvania. They built homes there and reared their families. They were Mennonites by faith and farmers and shoemakers. Many families did this as they began their existence in the new country as they moved from one area to another; they often lived together until they could get enough money to buy land of their own.

This was true of brothers and sisters as well of parents and their children in those times. Often the father would see his children build homes on his land, and later he would have the land resurveyed and sold to his children. Sometimes this would be listed in the deeds as "for a few dollars and love."

Niclous Garber and his wife Elizabeth owned the land. John Gerber and his wife built on the land that his brother owned. They are believed to have lived in Chester County and/or Lancaster County, Pennsylvania, from the time of immigration to about 1744 when they moved to the area that later became York County, Pennsylvania. They lived here only a few years from 1744 to 1748, when both died. They wrote their wills and instructed their executors to distribute their estates to the wives and children on an equal basis. Niclous named two of his four children. Samuel was to have first chance at the land, and the second unnamed son was to have second chance. If neither took the property, it would be sold and the money divided on an equal basis. Hanns/John Gerber owned no land, and his estate was composed of buildings and personal property.

This information helps support the idea that the son of Jo Hannes Gerber became the German Baptist Minister, working with Elder Jacob Danner and Daniel Leatherman in the Maryland and Pennsylvania mission churches. It was this Johannes "John H." Garber who moved to Flat Rock, Virginia, and helped establish the first church at that place.

Source: With minor modifications the material comes directly from *Mason, Floyd, John H. Garber & Barbara Miller of Pennsylvania, Maryland and Virginia*, 1998.

Jo Hannes "John" Gerber Will – The Father of John H. Garber

In the name of God, amen, I John Gerber of the County of Lancaster being very sick and weake in Body but of perfect Mind and Memory, thanks be given unto god thee fore, calling unto mind the mortality of the body and knowing that it is appointed, for a man once to dye, do make and order that this my last will and testimony, that is to say principally and first of all I give and recommend my Soul into the hands of god that gave it, and for my body, I recommend it to the earth to be buried in a Christian like & decent manner and as touching such worldly estate, I give devise and dispose of the same in the following manner and form:

1) - It is my will and I do order that in the first place all my just debts and funeral charges be paid and satisfied.

2) - It is my will, that my wife, shall live along with my children together as long and as good as they can but in case they cannot stay no more together there my said children shall give her a liven and all necessities as long as she lives.

3) - It is my will that my eldest son shall have three pounds current money and then the children all will shear and shear alike.

4) - It is my will that Samuel Bechtly and Andrew Hershey shall be my soul executors of this my last will and testament, and to take gear of my plantation as long till my youngest son is of age and I do hereby utterly disallow revoke and disannul all and every form of testaments will legacies and executors by me in any ways be for this time named, willed and bequeathed ratifying and confirming this and no other to be my last will and testament. In witness there of I have hereunto set my hand and seal the 5th day of March 1748.

Signed Jo Hannes Gerber (German)

Note: Mason has determined in his book on the Niclous Garber Family Record the names of the four children and how the will was settled. About 1752, Michael Miller, a neighbor, lost his wife and soon thereafter married Elizabeth Garber and became the executor of the Niclous Garber estate. In 1754, he went into court with the executors and reported that he now had enough money from the estate to settle the estate according to directions from the will.

Mason believes that John Gerber/Carver, the oldest son of the second family (Jo Hannes Gerber/Garver), was wealthy enough to pay Michael Miller the sum that was needed for this distribution. John Gerber/Carver also made settlement with his brothers and sisters and became the owner of the 100 acres of land that Niclous owned and an additional 44 acres of land adjoining to the north, which he purchased before he died in 1804.

Source: *Mason, Floyd, John H. Garber & Barbara Miller of Pennsylvania, Maryland and Virginia,* 1998. The will was written in German and Mason typed this English translation from a certified hand-written translation on March 25, 1998, making the best guess of some words that are hard to read, Lancaster County, Pennsylvania, Will Book Y – Vol. 1 – Page 192.

When Was John H. Garber (the son) Born and Who Were His Ancestors?

John H. Garber's parents are still not certain. We have researched all the records that we can find. Many have written that he was born in 1717. This is to agree with the immigrant who signed his papers Johannes H. Gerber in 1750 at an age of 33. S. R. Garver on his Internet home page states that this was in error and he gives another family for this immigrant. We have rejected a birth of 1717 as being too old. The Elder David Zigler who gave us the name John H. Garber also said that "he was a little past the meridian of his life when he died." He writes that Barbara was 54 years old at the time of his death, which closely corresponds to his age at his demise. Also Elder Zigler wrote, "Martin Garber, like his father, died comparatively a young man." His death occurred in 1814, at age 53. Coffman says he was about 54 years of age when he died.

I have hand-written copies of records of John H. Garber by J. Carson Miller and writings of others that agree with the age suggested by Elder Zigler. It is from these records that I have established for my records the date of birth about 1732.

Finding the parents of John H. Garber is a recently-solved mystery. The fact that he wrote John Garber, Sr., in his will was likely to distinguish himself from his first son, John Garber, and not to mean that his father was not also a John Garber or Gerber. We believe that John H. Garber was born in Chester County, Pennsylvania, and, like the Michael Miller and Niclous Carver/Garber families, moved to the area of Lancaster County, Pennsylvania, later called York County about 1740s.

We give you the following as a result of our ten years of research with the Garbers. A John Gerber Will is located on the same pages as Niclous Gerber. Both of these men died in 1748 and recorded their Wills in Lancaster County, Court House. They are there for all to see. See Book Y, Vol VII, p 192 and Book A VI p 165. We agree with S. R. Garver in his home page that Niclous Gerber and John Gerber were brothers. While Niclous named his wife and two of his four children, John did not give the names of either wife or children. John and Niclous Gerber used one of the same Executors, Samuel Bechtel, a Mennonite minister.

He also used Andrew Hershey. The executers were instructed to pass his farm on to his heirs. While the Will doesn't give the names of the wife and children, S. R. Garver on his home page gives the children as John Garber d 1787, Martin Garber b c1733, Daniel Garber b 1738 and possibly Nichlous Carver b 1742. We believe that Martin Garber was a son of Niclous and Elizabeth Gerber.

We have never found where this administrative record was ever recorded. If John H. Garber, the son, was 16 years of age and there were no other heirs, it may be that the executors allowed him to retain ownership of his father's land and never officially recorded it. As stated before he owned land in York County, Pennsylvania, and Frederick County, Maryland, while living in Virginia.

There is some evidence that John Gerber (Jo Hannes Gerber), the father, was an immigrant from Switzerland and moved to Chester County, Pennsylvania. Michael Danner, Sr., was a big land developer in the area near Hanover, Pennsylvania, in the 1740s. We believe that about the time that Niclous Gerber, Michael Miller and Samuel Bechtol moved to the same area, in 1744, John Garber moved in with his family. They must have been neighbors and likely brothers from the old country. It is known that Michael Danner, Sr., sold land to immigrant Mennonite, Dunker and Lutheran families and that they lived, worshipped and celebrated life together in the land which was then Lancaster County, soon to be York County, Pennsylvania. It was Michael Danner's son, Elder Jacob Danner that became a Dunker minister and took John H. Garber to new lands on Beaver Dam Creek in Maryland. Here they farmed and ministered to new Dunker churches as they formed. John H. Garber was a new minister under the leadership of the older Elder Jacob Danner.

We believe that John H. Garber was a neighbor of Barbara Miller who he married and became the parents of the big Garber Family.

Source: *Mason, Floyd, John H. Garber & Barbara Miller of Pennsylvania, Maryland and Virginia, 1998.*

Glimpses of John H. Garber and Barbara Miller

Johannes Garber, Sr., better known as John H. Garber, was born in 1732 and died November 1787. On January 2, 1751, he bought 200 acres on the Big Conewago in York County and built the log house pictured at the beginning of this chapter. In 1752, he married Barbara Mueller, anglicized Miller, who was born in 1733 and died in 1808. They lived in the log house in York County, Pennsylvania, for about 15 years, where they started their large family. John farmed and cobbled boots and shoes. On December 14, 1761, he sold the 200 acres in two sections, 170 acres to John Shafer and 30 acres to Henry Neff. According to Mason "We have not found the other land that he is reported to be paying land taxes on while living in Virginia."

On June 3, 1767, John bought from Jacob Danner 21.5 acres called "Garbers Good Luck" along Israel Creek in Frederick County, Maryland. In the spring of 1768, John sold his home and moved his family to Frederick County, where he made his home for the next seven years. He was now known as John H. Garber and became very active in the ministry. He joined Jacob Danner in preaching the gospel to scattered churches and helped build the Beaver Dam congregation, where he was ordained to the eldership of the church. While in Maryland, two of his sons married daughters of Elder Jacob Stoner. In 1775, John moved to the Shenandoah Valley of Virginia, near Flat Rock, where he was a farmer and shoemaker. John was a leader and the first Brethren minister in the Valley. Six of these sons and two sons-in-law were distinguished ministers of the Church of the Brethren. According to Mason, they were, like their father, pioneer ministers, "who ministered to many early families as they moved into undeveloped territories in Virginia, West Virginia, North Carolina, Tennessee, Kentucky and Ohio. They preached to these families in their barns and homes, often under the tree, and helped them form new congregations, often called Societies and eventually helped them build their first house of worship." One son was a deacon.

To John H. and Barbara Garber were born seven sons and three daughters to include:

1. Samuel b 1756 d 1814 m Mollie Stoner. Moved to Tennessee in 1811. Eleven children.

2. John b 1758 d 1819 m Barbara Zook. Nine children.

3. Abraham b 1760 d 1848 m Elizabeth Humbert. Settled near New Hope, Virginia. Seven children.

4. Martin b 1761 d 1824 m Rebecca Stoner. Lived in Maryland and Flat Rock area.

5. Anna b 1762 d 1837 m Daniel Miller b1752 d 1820. Lived in Shenandoah and Rockingham Counties. Eleven children.

6. Jacob G. b 1766 d 1836 m Susanna Humbert c 1771 d 1854. Remained in the Flat Rock area. Three children. Jacob inherited the home place.

7. Daniel b 1769 d 1849 m Susanna Miller b 1780 and later Elizabeth Shank. Donated land for the Garber's Church of the Brethren near Harrisonburg. One known son.

8. Catherine c 1771 d 1835 m Elder John Flory b 1776 d 1845. Lived near Cooks Creek – Garber Meeting House, Harrisonburg. Ten children.

9. Joseph c 1773 d 1854 m Catherine Leedy b 1777 d 1845. Moved to Tennessee and later to Montgomery County, Ohio.

10. Magdalene b 1774 d 1832 m Elder George Wine b1774 d 1845. Lived near Ottobine, Rockingham County, Virginia. Eight children.

The members of the Anabaptist denominations in early America, Mennonites, Dunkers (Brethren) and Quakers, because of their beliefs and practices, were subjected to much abuse and mistreatment. This became a serious problem from about 1750 to the beginning of the American Revolutionary War. The struggle for religious liberty or freedom had been their objective – the right to practice these beliefs and to worship and live in accordance with one's faith without external constraint was, on a day-to-day basis, now quite a problem.

Mason "believes from tradition that has come down through the years, that the land sold to Shaffer and Neff, was sold by officers of York County, to pay off War Taxes levied against John Garber. Because of his Dunker religious beliefs, he would not pay these taxes but would participate in the County's plan for Dunker and Mennonite non-associators. The County would notify the owner of the land of anticipated action of Confiscation. They would then give the family a designated time to move all personal property and animals from the property. The officers would then sell the land, keep the amount of taxes levied, and return the balance to the previous owner."

An important reason the Garbers, at that particular time, welcomed the opportunity to move into a more isolated area lay in their church doctrine which stood strictly opposed to bearing arms against their fellow man. Here again our ancestors suffered persecution and unpleasantries because of their religious convictions. Homes were burned, livestock stolen and some of the people suffered personal injuries. All of this came at the hands of irate soldiers returning from the battlefields of the American Revolution. This situation also accounts for the wagon train of Garbers and their Brethren friends who settled in the Shenandoah Valley.

John Garber arrived in the Shenandoah Valley during its frontier period and witnessed its transitions to a more developed world. These frontier Valley settlers saw a patchwork of wooded land and significant but small areas of open grassland. The Garber farm home was established a mile or so west of a large flat rock on a fertile tract of land. John cleared forest land, erected a log cabin, planted diverse crops and cobbled shoes for his neighbors and his own family. The paramount concern was to secure food for themselves, so they cultivated a broad range of field crops, corn, grasses and cereal grains and husbanded various types of livestock, horses, cows, swine, sheep and barnyard fowl. Whenever the opportunity arose, they produced cash crops. Livestock raising allowed them to drive to market along the most miserable frontier roads cattle, swine and turkeys.

Johannes Garber's Spring on His Farm at Flat Rock, Virginia. Picture 2005

With seven grown sons to help subdue nature, the family prospered and founded a good estate. John had not only the means but also the leisure and inclination to make himself useful to his neighbors. He expanded his ministerial work and traveled extensively on horseback to bring the gospel message to scattered settlers. He established the Flat Rock Church and was the first Brethren minister to settle permanently in Virginia. He cultivated friendly relations with the Indians and demonstrated what intelligent industry and good management could do in building a home in the American wilderness. He was loved and admired not only by those who knew him but also by the scattered settlers and roving Indians. In fact, some of his Indian friends were present at his death, attesting to his peaceful life and treatment of his fellow brethren.

Johannes Garber's Spring House, Picture 2005

The principal mode of travel for early settlers was walking. Barbara was widely known for having walked twice to Maryland and Pennsylvania and back to visit relatives and friends. John and Barbara are buried in a small Garber family graveyard near the site of their log house, not far from the present Flat Rock Brethren Church.

An Account of John H. Garber's Move to the Shenandoah Valley

In his *History of the Brethren in Virginia*, Zigler says that about the year 1775 or 1776 John Garber (John H. Garber) of York County, Pennsylvania, made a trip into the northern part of the Shenandoah Valley. The purpose of his visit is not known. On May 22, 1775, John returned the 21.5 acres to Jacob Danner from whom he had purchased the land and moved to the Shenandoah Valley in the Flat Rock/Forestville area of Shenandoah County several miles west of New Market. The Garber home was established a mile or so west of a large flat rock on a fertile tract of land. Soon others followed him and the Brethren group in the Valley grew rather rapidly.

From an article by the Rev. Freeman Ankrum published in the *Brethren Evangelist*, "What was it that motivated them? What caused them to leave the safe known for the dangerous unknown? There was safety in eastern Pennsylvania and in Carroll and Frederick County sections of Maryland. In the Shenandoah Valley of Virginia, west of the Blue Ridge Mountains, the Indian still roamed at will by the side of the beautiful Shenandoah River, 'The Daughter of the Stars.' Any settler who braved the forest-covered valley did so at his own risk, for the long arm of 'Uncle Sam' could offer him little, if any, protection. Was there some force that drew them, or was there some unsettling circumstances and conditions that caused them to leave the scenes of their first homes, literally driving them out? Our early church fathers, fresh from the land of oppression and wars of no end, were looking for peace and freedom with the right to worship God without let or hindrance."

During the period of the Revolutionary War from 1775 to 1781, we find that there was a migration from the fertile fields in the vicinity of York County, Pennsylvania, and from the rolling hills in and around Pipe Creek Valley, Maryland. While news traveled slowly in the wilderness, nevertheless it traveled. The hunter, the explorer and the passerby all carried messages to civilization.

In the year 1768, there was a family by the name of Henry Kagey living on Smith Creek, not far from the present city of New Market, Virginia. To this section of the "forest," as it was called, John Garber and the members of his family came in 1775. Their location was in the Valley not far from the present village of Forestville. In fact, the hills and valleys were covered with such growth of trees that when a group settled on the banks of Holman's Creek in Shenandoah County in 1800, there was no difficulty in naming their settlement, "Forestville."

To this section came the Wines, Moyers (Myers), Bowmans, Garbers, Millers and others. Some of the Bowmans went farther south to Franklin County, Virginia, where we find them, down to the seventh generation, faithful to the cause. Some tarried not long in Franklin County, but journeyed on farther south, and we find them in Tennessee, still faithful to the established work of their ancestors. Other names that are easily recognized include:

- In 1776, John Glick, an elder from Lancaster County, moved to Brothers Valley. He too settled in the Flat Rock area.

- The following ministers and elders moved from Stony Creek and Brothers Valley to the Shenandoah Valley of Virginia:

  - Daniel Good in 1786, Jacob Good in 1785, John Kagey, Jr., about 1800, Christian Meyers about 1795.

  - About 1800, John Kline, the father of the famous Elder John Kline, moved from Brothers Valley to Virginia.

- In 1769, Daniel S. Arnold married Elizabeth, daughter of Michael Wine and Susannah Miller, and moved into the Stony Creek congregation where he was elected to the eldership that year. In 1785, he moved to the Beaver Run Church in Hampshire County, Virginia. Many relationships exist between this Arnold family and the Brethren families of the Shenandoah Valley.

When John Garber came to the Valley, he brought five of his seven sons with him and left two older sons, Martin and Samuel, in the Beaver Dam section of Maryland. Their wives were sisters, daughters of Elder Jacob Stoner of Frederick County, Maryland. The brothers had tarried in Maryland before joining their father, mother, sisters and brothers. Martin and Samuel and their families and Michael Wine and his family were part of a wagon train of six families who settled in the immediate neighborhood of Flat Rock, Virginia. In a little more than two weeks they pulled up alongside the great flat rock and made their camp in the vicinity of John H. Garber's home. Martin purchased a tract of 400 acres near his father. Of the six families who came with this wagon train, at least five settled in the immediate neighborhood.

When John Garber came to this section of the Valley, it was a matter of getting settled and proceeding to hew from the rugged and rocky wilderness a home for themselves. John was a minister; in fact, he was the first Brethren minister to come to this section of the state. However, the first seven or so years were more or less a family enterprise. It was quite a number of years before a church building was erected.

This is probably the chimney of Johannes Garber's house
located one mile west of Flat Rock, Virginia, and several miles southwest of Forestville, Virginia.
The building attached to the chimney was built in the 20th century.

The settlers in the lonely wilderness were gladdened in 1785 when six more families came to Flat Rock, doubling the membership. One told another back in Pennsylvania and Maryland, and so yearly arrivals were the rule. By the year 1787, 32 families in all had come, and a larger part had settled in the Flat Rock section, though some went on farther south to Linville Creek and probably Cook's Creek. The village of Timberville, some six miles south of Forestville, received its name from the same basic fact, that of forests of timber.

The year 1787 records the first known death among the settlers. It had been 12 years since John Garber, his wife Barbara and their younger children had come to Flat Rock. The first seven years they had pioneered the forest. The last five, his form had taken on Patriarchal stature, leaving him loved and admired by all who knew him. In the autumn of 1787, he became ill; on September third, he made a will. The will was probated on December 27th of the same year denoting that between these dates he closed his eyes in death. His birth was thought to be in the year 1732; therefore, he was, at the time of his death 55 years of age. It has been recorded that all his family except one was present at his passing. Tradition also persists that there were some of his Indian friends present to witness the event.

John Garber was very likely the first of the Virginia Brethren to pass to his reward and the first to be interred at Flat Rock. Here in the family plot beyond the spring where the ground slopes toward the sun, his weary body found its last resting place. It is marked by a small flat gravestone bearing the inscription – 17 J.H.G. 87' a testimony to both the sturdy life he had lived and to the modest spirit in which he had lived it.

Johannes "John H." Garber's Headstone, 1732 – 1787, Picture 2005

Author's Note: The small flat gravestone disappeared in the mid part of the 20th century and was replaced by a mass-produced carved stone.

Some months following the death of John Garber, another migration brought to the Valley a larger group of settlers. Among these were the Bowman brothers, Peter, Benjamin and Joseph, two of whom were ministers. They settled south of Flat Rock in the Linville Creek section. They left a brother, Jacob, in Somerset County. Joseph became an outstanding churchman and civic leader. He lived on a farm purchased June 15, 1787.

About this time, there was a migration away from Flat Rock. As the families grew, there was need for more land. On the 26th of April 1790, John Flory, who had lived at Flat Rock for several years, married Catherine Garber, Elder John's second daughter, and they moved to their new home near the main road, later the Valley Pike, three miles southwest of Harrisonburg, in Cook's Creek congregation. Almost at the same time, her brother Daniel Garber married Susan Miller, daughter of Jacob Miller of Flat Rock, and moved to the settlement on Cook's Creek. In the year 1790, Abraham Garber, older brother of Daniel and Catherine, married Elizabeth Humbert, daughter of one of the early settlers at Flat Rock and went to make their home on Middle River in Augusta County.

Source: Zigler, *History of the Brethren in Virginia*, 1914.

The Flat Rock Church

Elder John H. Garber was the founder of the Flat Rock Congregation, near Forestville, which is the mother church of all the Dunkers in the Shenandoah Valley of Virginia. Jacob David Wine, in his book, *A History of Flat Rock, Church of the Brethren*, 1962, gives the following account of early church members. "Among the early settlers in the Flat Rock vicinity were the Branners, Zirkles, Bowmans, Pences, and Harpines, of the Lutheran Church; the Garbers, Wines, Glicks, Myers, Kageys, Goods, Clines, and Neffs, of the Tunkers. In 1775, John Garber came from York County, Pa., and settled on the farm owned in 1907 by his great-granddaughter, Lydia Garber. He was the father of seven sons and three daughters. Six of the sons became preachers of the Gospel and served the church in Virginia, Ohio, West Virginia, and Tennessee. The first church at Flat Rock was built in 1841, on a lot deeded to the church by Michael Wine; the new church was dedicated October 6, 1907. Prior to 1841, the meetings of the church were held in homes of the members. The dwelling houses were often so constructed that all the space on the main floor, except the kitchen, could be thrown together for religious meetings."

Source: Wine, Jacob David, *A History of Flat Rock, Church of the Brethren,* 1962

Flat Rock Church of the Brethren (Mother Church), Built 1907

Johannes "John H." Garber Will

In the name of god amen, I John garber Senior of the State of Virginia & County of Shenandoah being sick and in a low state of health in body but of perfect mind and memory do make and ordain this my last will & testament in manner and form following, Viz: that my well beloved wife Barbara and the five youngest of my children as now are living with us shall continue living on said place & plantation where on I now live until February the first day in the year 1790 and so continue the same in farming as now as if I were alive with all furniture belonging to the same till said time and that all my just debts be paid in the same manner as if I were alive and at the end of the said time it is my will that my beloved wife shall remain living on this my place and in the same house during her natural life and that she is to have her bed and a good spinning wheel and the choice of one of the milk cows to be kept and found in feeding and stabling during her life and her cubbert, and the choice of two sheep to be kept in manner as aforesaid with the cow so that she may have no just cause or reason to complain, and if so that there is fruits of planted trees she shall have liberty to have of them as she may want for her use and then at the end of said time as aforesaid all my remainder of my moveables whatever shall be appraised and then that my beloved wife shall have a full third part of all said moveables and not any of said moveables to be sold but of the remainder after her third taken out, it shall then be equally divided among all my said children the names are as following John, Samuel, Martin, Anna, Abraham, Jacob, Daniel, Catherine, Joseph & Magdalene. The two cows as Anna had she shall be charged five pounds to be in part of her share in said moveables and further the land and plantation I now live on which is two hundred and seventy eight acres be the same more or less (excepting near about 8 acres of the same tract belonging to my son-in-law Daniel Miller so as the line now between us made) and as aforesaid that my son Jacob shall have said place and plantation for him his heirs and assign for ever and that the said my son Jacob shall pay for said place four hundred pounds, Virginia currency in gold or silver or the value thereof and if there remains yet any debts unpaid they shall be paid out of said four hundred pounds and the remainder of said four hundred pounds then each of my children as aforesaid and the said my son Jacob to go equal in share again with the others and further that the said Jacob shall pay to my beloved wife his mother during her natural life yearly and every year five pounds in cash or any produce as may be agreeable to her, and to find her a riding creature that is sufficient at any such time as she may sees need of one and to keep her a garden for her use, further it is my will that my two sons Jacob and Daniel are to have cash twenty five pounds out of said remaining sum of four hundred pounds as it were forgot first above and then are both to go equal shares with the rest of the remaining sum, and further that if my son Jacob should die without an heir then my son Daniel shall stand in his place in every particular as above said and if so that Daniel should die without an heir my wife shall be on said place in every thing in particular as aforesaid during her life and widowhood but if she marries again then has no privilege to live on said place and further if my son Joseph shall live at the end of said time of the year 1790 he shall be put out to learn a trade such as may be suitable for him and Magdalene to stay with her mother till she comes of age if so that any of the said children should die with out heir then each child shall fall equal sharer of the remaining estate as afore said and further that my son Jacob or any of the others as shall or may survive living on said place shall not be hurried or bought in pay out to the others of my children as long as their mother is living and remains on said place and then not to be made to pay in such short time as may become hurtful to him. Lastly I likewise constitute & ordain my son Samuel & Martin to be the sole executors of this my last will & testament and do hereby utterly disallow & revoke all former testaments, wills, legacies & executors ratifying & confirming this and no other to be my last will & testament of witness whereof I have here unto set my hand and seal this fourth day of September in the year of our lord one thousand seven hundred & eighty seven - - - 1787.

Signed Sealed and published & Pronounced and declared by the said John garber Senior as his last will & testament in the presence of - Michael Wine, Johannes Glick and Jacob Neff.

Johanns garber (seal)

At a Court held for the County of Shenandoah on Thursday the 27th day of December 1787. The Last Will and Testament of John Garver dec. was proved by the affirmation of Michael Wine & John Glick Jun'r Witnesses thereto to be Recorded on the motion of Samuel & Martin Garver, Exors., therein mentioned a probate thereof is granted them in due form having affirmed to the same & given bond & security according to the Law.

Test
John Williams CBL

Source: *Mason, Floyd, John H. Garber & Barbara Miller of Pennsylvania, Maryland and Virginia*, 1998. Mason typed this will from a handwritten copy of the original in April 1995. Will Book B Page 409, Shenandoah County, Virginia.

The Germans of the Valley

The Germans came into the Shenandoah Valley mostly from Pennsylvania looking for good land, and a great many of them stopped in Shenandoah, Rockingham and Augusta Counties. They evidently had money and seem to have paid cash for their lands as much then as the same lands were worth in 1900.

The Germans of the Valley, like most of their race, were simple, sturdy, modest, frugal and honest folk. Their style of living and their industry were the chief causes of their prosperity. The majority of them, especially the Mennonites, Tunkers and Quakers, owned no slaves, since they believed the institution of slavery to be evil, unjust to the slave and displeasing to God. There was doubtless also some antipathy toward the Negro race. As a result, the proportion of Negroes has always been smaller in the Valley than other parts of the State. Most of the Germans did not care to possess very large estates; their farms were usually of a comparatively small size, containing generally about as much land as the owner, with the assistance of his family, could keep in a good state of cultivation. On a few acres, carefully tilled and well fertilized from the stable yards, surprisingly large crops were produced.

The dress of the early settlers was of the plainest and most primitive sort, generally being of their own manufacture. Prior to the Revolutionary War, the married men usually shaved their heads and either wore wigs or white linen caps; but when the war began, this fashion was abandoned, partly, perhaps, from patriotic considerations, but chiefly from necessity. Owing to the interruption of trade with England, wigs and white linen for caps were hard to obtain. The men's coats were generally made with broad backs and straight, short skirts, having pockets on the outside with large flaps. The waistcoat skirts were long, extending nearly halfway down to the knees. The breeches were short, barely reaching to the knee, and had a band surrounding the knee and fastening the band, brass or silver buckles. The hats worn were made of either wool or fur, having broad brims and low crowns.

The female dress was generally the short gown and petticoat made of the plainest materials. The German women mostly wore tight calico caps on their heads, and in the summer season they were generally seen with no other clothing than a linen shift and petticoat – feet, hands and arms bare. In hay and harvest time, they joined the men in the labor of the meadow and grain fields. Their custom, of the females laboring in the time of harvest, was not exclusively a German practice, but was common to the northern people. Many females were expert mowers and reapers.

The German's barn was usually the best building on his farm. He was sure to erect a fine large barn before he built any dwelling house other than his rude log cabin. There were none of our primitive immigrants more uniform in the form of their buildings than the Germans. Their dwelling houses were seldom raised more than a single story in height, with a large cellar beneath; the chimneys in the middle with a very wide fireplace in one end for the kitchen, in the other end, a stove room. Their furniture was of the simplest and plainest kind, and there was always a long pine table fixed in one corner of the stove, with permanent benches on one side. On the upper floor, garners for holding grain were very common. Their beds were generally filled with straw or chaff, with a fine feather bed for covering in the winter.

A common practice at weddings was to determine who the next bride would be. German settlers in Augusta County, in lieu of the now popular "throwing the bridal bouquet," used it. After the bride and groom had retired, all of the young men and women went to the bedchamber. One by one they stood at the foot of the bed with their backs to the occupants. Taking a rolled-up stocking in their hand, they threw it over their shoulder. The men aimed for the groom's head and the women for the bride's. The first one of each sex to hit his target would be the next of that sex to wed.

Source: With some modifications from Wayland, John W., *The Virginia Magazine of History and Biography*, *"The Germans of the Valley,"* October 1902.

U.S. Generation No. 2

Abraham Garber & Elizabeth Humbert

Middle River Meetinghouse, 1824

Photograph of a painting by the artist, Mrs. Janet Tanner,
who painted it from information provided by Mrs. Nelia Ray
(New Hope, Virginia) and gave it to the Middle River Church of the Brethren in 1966.

Church Founded by Abraham Garber

Glimpses of Abraham and Elizabeth Garber

It is known that Dunkers were settled on Christians Creek by 1750, with even larger settlements farther north on the lower bottom land of Middle River and in the Crimora area, approximately six miles from New Hope, before 1790. These people were brave pioneers who came into this area and settled on the fertile soil along Middle River. They had to brave the dangers of the wilderness. They worked hard to clear the land, build their homes and produce their food and other things they needed.

In *History of Augusta County, Virginia* by I. Lewis Peyton, he makes reference to Middle River: "In the generations between 1770 and 1850, they (the Brethren) put their roots down deeply and many felt "at home" in the Great Valley of Virginia. They emigrated from Pennsylvania and Maryland about the year 1752, and settled on the waters of SHANADORE (Shenandoah), and have increased to about thirty-six families; whereof thirty-six persons are baptized. Some of them keep the seventh day Sabbath by means of their connection with the Tunkers of Ephrata. These have also been much harassed by reason of their militia law and their scrupling to take an oath."

In 1790, Abraham Garber, who was born 1760 in York County, Pennsylvania, married Elizabeth Humbert. Elizabeth was also born in 1760 and was the daughter of Jacob Humbert, one of the early settlers at Flat Rock. They made their home on Middle River and settled on a farm that has become known as the Abraham Garber Farm near New Hope, Augusta County, Virginia. The farm is located about 1/2 mile west of the Middle River Church of the Brethren on the north side of the Knightly Mill road and is owned by the William Garber family, who are descendants of Abraham and Elizabeth Garber. An old farm lane leads over a bluff toward Middle River to the site of Abraham and Elizabeth's house, which was dismantled about 1990. The wooden frame house was situated on the side of the bluff and built on large slabs of flat limestone. A concrete retaining wall surrounds the lower side of the front yard and contains two very large black walnut trees to provide shade. Nearby is a former chicken house where many pieces of the house are stored to include solid four panel doors, floor joists, step treads, window shutters, wooden flooring and baseboard molding. Some parts of the house were sold, and Dolly Garber Harner has a fireplace mantle with carved acorns. At the base of the bluff is a brick spring house that provided water for drinking and household purposes. Fifteen feet from the spring are the remains of a standing brick chimney that probably belonged to the wash house. Beyond the spring and chimney is a vast expanse of rich river bottom land running to Middle River. The farm also has a large pasture field on the south side of the Knightly Mill road that runs up and around Middle River Church cemetery.

A. Garber Chicken House with dismantled house stored inside, 2007

Abraham Garber Homestead Site, 1995

A. Garber Front Yard with Walnut Trees, 2007

A. Garber Part of Front Foundation, 2007
Notice chicken house in the background.

A. Garber Foundation Stones, 2007

A. Garber Back of Wash House Chimney, 2007

A. Garber Corner of Retaining Wall, 2007

A. Garber Ruins of Bank Barn, 2007

A. Garber Spring House, 2007

Bishop Miller first organized the Tunker, or German Baptist Church, in Augusta County about the year 1790. Abraham may have been one of the first members of the Church to move to Augusta County. The Brethren had very little communication with the outside world. Church services and activities were held in homes, lofts, barns and, quite possibly, schools. In fact, some ministers' homes had hinges attached to the top of walls so the walls could be swung conveniently from the bottom to hooks in the ceiling, thus quickly expanding the meeting space. In Peyton's *History of Augusta County* we find this reference to Middle River: "Elder George Boone, a brother of Daniel Boone, also ministered to the Augusta Brethren. He had been ordained to the ministry in the old Stony Creek Church in Brothers Valley, Pennsylvania, in 1770, and was known to be among the Muhlenberg County, Kentucky, Brethren by 1785. About 1800, he preached in the Elder Abraham Garber home meeting-house, which had been built along Middle River, Virginia, in 1790." According to Mason, Abraham and Elizabeth moved to Madison County, Ohio, about 1809, and then returned about 1815, to the Garber farm near New Hope, Virginia. He is believed to have owned farmland in Ohio, Rockingham County and Augusta County, Virginia.

Abraham was instrumental in building the first Brethren Church in Augusta County in 1824. Merle Hamilton, "Garber Family Record," stated, "He donated and built the first house of worship of the Church of the Brethren in Augusta County. This was a commodious brick building erected in the year 1824, on a beautiful and convenient location on his farm. This has been the scene of many sacred events and other scenes." In addition to donating the land to Middle River congregation, Abraham built a brick kiln on his property to make bricks for the new church, willed it debt-free to the church and, in general, provided overall leadership and resources.

Abraham was the minister at Middle River and the founder and father of the congregation. At his death, the membership had increased to more than 500 members and was one of the largest congregations in the Valley. However, the members were widely scattered, and the church could no longer meet their needs. Thus, Middle River became the mother church to two new churches, Pleasant Valley in 1854 in Weyers Cave and Barren Ridge in 1856 and provided support and staff for both churches. The Annual Conference was held at the Middle River Church in 1851, and the proceedings were conducted and recorded in German. Attendees came from as far away as Ohio, Pennsylvania, Maryland and Kentucky. The nearby church cemetery is well kept and has many interesting epitaphs. The earliest date is 1829 and some of the dates are written differently from any found elsewhere. One Civil War veteran killed at the Battle of Piedmont is buried here.

Abraham and Elizabeth Garber had four sons and three daughters to include:

1   John b 1792 d 1854 m Catherine "Kitty" Miller da of Samuel Miller, Apr 9, 1816, married by Abraham Garber. Five children. John, farmer and minister, was the only son to become a minister and elder in his father's church.

2   Sarah "Sallie" b 1793 d ? m Christian Whitmore.

3   Daniel b 1793 d 1883 farmer m Elizabeth Dunston April 19, 1824.

4   Jacob W. b 1797 d 1876, farmer m Nancy Arnold da of Samuel Arnold March 10, 1823. Five children

5   Mary b 1805 d 1864 m John Arion. Three children.

6   Samuel b 1806 d 1892 farmer, m Anna Peters da of George Peters and Rebecca Rhodes. Seven children.

7   Esther b 1813 d 1879 m Abraham Stoner May 15, 1833, married by Abraham Garber. Three children.

Father and four sons are buried at Middle River Church.

John Garber and Peter Miller were co-ministers and elders at Middle River Church from 1824-1854. Strangely they died within a month of each other and at a time that their work was culminating in the opening of new churches at Pleasant Valley and Barren Ridge and just six years after the death of Abraham. John (died of the flux-discharge of larger quantities of fluid material) and Catherine are buried at the Middle River Church.

Abraham's 1843 will, lengthy and detailed, in part provided "his well-loved son Samuel shall have the lands on which I live except one acre of meetinghouse and shall have $1,500." Such land, contiguous to the present church, has remained continuously with Samuel Garber's heirs. After Samuel, it was occupied by Samuel's son, William "Bill" F. Garber, and also by William's son, Charles Garber. The farm continues to be occupied by Abraham's descendants. Abraham's tombstone at Middle River Church of the Brethren reads as follows:

Headstone of Abraham Garber

Abraham Garber
Nov. 10, 1760 - Feb. 16, 1848
Elizabeth Humbert - His Wife
Died 1838
Founder and Elder of the Middle
River Cong(regation). Donated and
built the first Church of the
Brethren in Augusta Co.
in 1824
In remembrance of
their lives and service.

Abraham Garber Will

Will of Abraham Garber, son of John H. Garber and Barbara Miller. Wife Elizabeth Humbert. Written November 29, 1843. Probate January 24, 1849, Augusta County, Virginia (Courthouse Record at Staunton, Will Book 27, Page 287) Abraham's 1843 will, lengthy and detailed, in part provided:

"…my daughters Mary and Esther. My son Samuel shall have the land I live on with the exception of 1 acre on which the meetinghouse of our society stands, except also the house in which I dwell goes to Samuel. He shall also have 34 acres of the northern part of the ROUND HILL LAND for $5,900.00 against the $1,500.00 bequest. Daughter Sarah gets lands lying on Meadow Run adjoining lands of Casper Coiner and John Miller.

My 7 children: John Garber, Daniel Garber, Jacob Garber, Samuel Garber, Sarah Garber, Mary Garber and Esther Garber."

Witnesses were Jacob Miller, Solomon Peters and Samuel Garber.

The Second Middle River Church – c1884

The Building of the Middle River Congregation - Church of the Brethren

Up to 1824, there had been very few church houses built by the Brethren in Virginia. The time had come, however, when buildings were needed, and this was especially true for the holding of love feast services. In an unpublished history, Dr. John S. Flory wrote about the church house built at Middle River. "In 1824 they built a church. The story of this enterprise reads almost like a story out of legendary lore. It runs like this. In the summer of 1824, Abraham Garber led a group of workmen to the backside of his farm and set them to building a brick kiln. This finished, he set them to digging up the clay and preparing it for a large kiln. In a seemingly short time there was a stack of bricks sufficient for a large building. The next step was to set the men to work, under the direction of an experienced bricklayer, to erecting the walls of the church.

So efficiently was everything managed, it is said that before the snow began to fly the walls were up, the building roofed and furnished with hastily constructed benches, and the big fireplaces, one at each end, were ablaze with hickory wood from the forest. If this story, as it has come down to us, is not literally true in every detail, it is certainly true in its general purport, and is highly representative of the time and the spirit in which our Brethren went about establishing themselves and the church they loved."

Before the end of 1824, the congregation was organized with Abraham Garber as the first Elder. Dr. Flory wrote: "At the same time he presented to the congregation a will, which conveyed to them the church building along with the plot of ground on which it stood, all free of debt, as a freewill gift to the newly organized Brick Church Congregation of Augusta County, Virginia."

The building of a new church was a signal to expand. An organization meeting elected two young men to the ministry, John Garber and David Miller. John Garber was the oldest son of Abraham, and Peter Miller was the son of David Miller. It is not known who David Miller was or where he came from. He was born in 1750 and died in 1828. Peter Miller was married to Barbara Lear. They had three sons and one daughter. John Miller, one of Peter's sons, was born in 1814 and later married Fannie Brower and settled near Mt. Sidney. He was the ancestor of Elder S. D. Miller, a longtime leader in the Pleasant Valley Congregation. His wife's name was Mary. These young men were installed ministers, and prospects for the church were bright. The new church house and the addition of new ministers helped attract other settlers to Middle River. As sections of the counties farther north were more fully occupied, more of the newcomers went on southward into Augusta County. They found fertile soil along Middle River well suited to the building of their homes.

The period from 1824 to 1850 was a period of growth and development for the Brick congregation on Middle River. The building of the house of worship was the second in the Valley and the first in Augusta County. The congregation had an able staff of officers headed by Abraham Garber, who led the work until his death in 1848 at the age of 87. During this period, John Garber and Peter Miller were the other elders, and the ministers were Daniel Brower, Jacob Brower and Martin Garber. The membership had increased to more than 500 members, and the Shenandoah Valley had become a leading center of Brethren influence. Middle River was the only congregation of the Brethren in Augusta County, but seven other congregations were in Shenandoah and Rockingham Counties.

During these years, the Annual Meeting of the then-German Baptist Brethren had been held from time to time in Pennsylvania, Maryland, Virginia and Ohio. In 1851, it was held at the Brick Church on Middle River. This was an important meeting with quite a number of Brethren present from several states. It opened on Friday evening and continued through the following Tuesday. Elder George Hoke from Ohio was Moderator. The Annual Meeting was held at Pentecost, as was the custom at that time, and a copy of the proceedings was found written in the German language. Attendees came from as far away as Ohio, Pennsylvania, Maryland and Kentucky.

With membership over 500, Middle River was one of the largest congregations in the Valley and its members were widely scattered. Meetings had been held in various homes and schoolhouses in different parts of the territory served by Middle River. After careful consideration, the congregation reached a general agreement to build two new church houses. One was to be several miles north of the Brick Church and the other several miles south. After these two new churches were properly staffed, the territory would be divided into three congregations. The church to the north was Pleasant Valley; the one to the south was Barren Ridge. In 1854, when John Garber and Peter Miller died, the Pleasant Valley Church was under construction and was built and dedicated two years later. John Miller was ordained elder and placed in charge of the Pleasant Valley Church, and John Brower was ordained and placed in charge at Barren Ridge.

When the congregation was divided, there were nine ministers at Middle River. Their allotment with that of the membership was determined by the congregation lines, which on the whole proved satisfactory. In these allotments the parent church, Middle River, had slightly more than 200 members with Martin Garber and Daniel Brower elders and John Brower, Levi Garber and Daniel Yount as ministers. Pleasant Valley had around 150 members with John Miller as elder and Abram D. Garber as minister. Barren Ridge started with about 100 members, and John Brower was elder with Enoch Brower minister. It seems that these new congregations were officially started in 1865.

Source: With some modifications this material comes directly from Coffman, W. Paul, *A History of Middle River Congregation, Church of the Brethren*, 1964.

Author's Note:
The Middle River Church of the Brethren stems from the Flat Rock Congregation situated in the Shenandoah Valley north of Timberville, Virginia. Abraham and Elizabeth Garber were both of the Flat Rock congregation. The Brethren at that time were known as German Baptist Brethren and were a pietistic denomination. They were distinguished from other Christian denominations by their emphasis on pacifism, separation from all worldly matters, a prescribed dress code for its members, triune baptism, an annual love feast and an annual meeting at which doctrinal questions and religious and moral practices were debated and ruled on.

The prescribed dress code for men in 1790 was a broad-brimmed, black hat, a black coat with no collar which was worn buttoned up to the throat and black broadcloth felt trousers. The prescribed dress code for women was a plain street-length gown and a prayer covering resembling a pilgrim's bonnet. The wearing of jewelry was verboten to both sexes. Triune baptism as practiced by them was immersing the recipient in a kneeling position in water three times, first in the name of the Father, second in name of the Son, and third in the name of the Holy Ghost. This form of baptism led to non-Brethren referring to them as Tunkers, then as Dunkers and lastly as Dunkards. Their communion service included a self-examination period, the washing of feet as practiced at the Last Supper of Christ and partaking of unleavened bread and wine. From the organization of Augusta County in 1745 until 1824, there were no Brethren churches in the county. The few Brethren people living there held services in their homes and barns. The first love feast held in the county was in the loft of a building on Abraham Garber's farm.

If the Brethren way of life was to survive in the New Hope community, the Brethren living there needed to have a church. The church building was a simple rectangular brick structure with a chimney and fireplace at each end to keep the congregation warm in the winter. After completing erection of the building, Abraham Garber held a congregational meeting; he was named elder, and Peter Miller and John Garber were elected to the ministry.

Jacob W. Garber & Nancy Arnold

Portrait Etching of Jacob Garber Using Charcoal and Chalk, c1840

Jacob W. Garber, Sr.

Glimpses of Jacob and Nancy Garber

Jacob W. Garber, Sr., better known as Jacob Garber, was born in 1797 and died 1876. Jacob was the fourth son of Abraham and Elizabeth Garber. On March 10, 1823, he married Nancy Arnold of Hampshire, West Virginia, who was born April 12, 1805. Their farmstead was located about two miles from Mt. Sidney and about three and a half miles from New Hope, Virginia (west of Knightly Store and east of Mt. Sidney).

Jacob was a very successful farmer but not an important leader in the Middle River German Baptist Church. The reason probably lies in my research from the Augusta County, Virginia, *Heritage Book*, 1732–1998, which revealed that in 1843 Jacob purchased what was called a Louisiana (land) lottery ticket for one dollar. Jacob's ticket won the lottery; he presented his receipt and received a 151-acre homestead offered by John and Elizabeth Miller. It is the author's conjecture that the Millers disposed of their land by lottery because the ailing economy of the United States had been mired in a deep depression since 1839. Few people had money to buy a farm, and many were moving westward for cheap land.

The German Baptist viewed the purchase of a lottery ticket as a form of gambling and, therefore, a sin. Since Jacob was a member of the Middle River German Baptist Church, he was severely criticized by members of the congregation. However, Jacob kept the land; he prospered as a farmer and shared his wealth with his children. His children were fortunate because when each got married, Jacob and Nancy located them and their new spouses on nearby farms with homes, where they reared their families and spent their lives. The writer believes that Jacob never held an elected church office (deacon, minister or elder) because of this incident, a fact which had been kept quiet and unknown to all descendants.

To Jacob and Nancy were born four sons and one daughter to include:

1. Rebekah b 1823 d 1886 m 1846 Daniel Miller b 1816 d 1901 farmer and son of Elder Peter and Barbara Miller. Two children.

2. Abraham D. b 1824 d 1911 minister of Pleasant Valley Congregation m 1848 Magdalene Wine b 1827 d 1868, da of Michael and Catherine (Arnold) Wine. Second marriage 1869 to Sophia Byrd Hayes, widow of James Hayes and da of William and Hannah Showalter of Rockingham County, Virginia. Ten children.

3. Levi b 1828 d 1914 farmer and minister for 55 years of Middle River Congregation m 1850 Barbara Miller b 1825 d 1868 da of Elder Peter Miller and Barbara Laird. Eight children.

4. Reuben Arnold b 1836 d 1884 m 1857 Mary Flory b 1836 d 1898 da of Daniel and Christine Flory. Seven children.

5. Jacob W. b 1842 d 1908 farmer, m Susan A. Ham b 1848 d 1934 da of Robert Ham and Mary Douglas of Green County, Virginia. Ten children.

Nancy died February 29, 1868, about age 68.

Jacob's tombstone at Middle River Church of the Brethren in Augusta County reads as follows:

In Memory of
Jacob Garber m Nancy Garber
Born
Oct. 28, 1797
Died
Sept. 25, 1876
Aged
Yrs. 78 Mos. 11

Jacob and Nancy are buried at the Middle River Cemetery, New Hope, Virginia.

Jacob and Nancy Garber Headstone

Inter-Virginia Romance and Marriage
Garber-Arnold, 1822-23

One hundred and forty years ago a fruitful marriage of abiding interest in Garber history was affected amid fascinating circumstances. In the spring of 1822, April love was tapped in youthful hearts. It was destined to ripen into marital commitment. Until then, however, the young lovers had not met, and they lived in widely distant places. One attained his manhood in the fertile Shenandoah Valley of Virginia. The other cultivated her womanhood before the majestic mountains of West Virginia.

Abraham Garber, prosperous farmer and patron of Middle River Brethren Church near New Hope, Virginia, commissioned his third son, Jacob, to go to Romney, West Virginia, to purchase some horses. The vigorous man of mid-twenties was hospitably entertained in the home of Samuel Arnold where there was a bevy of marriageable daughters. Nancy of seventeen summers captured the affections of Jacob and he secured her promise to correspond with him.

A year later, March 1823, Jacob returned to Romney on a similar mission but with the avowed intention of securing a companion for the return journey and the remainder of his life. Nancy's wholehearted love for Jacob enabled her to say; "Where thou dwells I shall dwell; thy people shall be my people; and thy God shall be my God." This irrevocable dedication sustained her in the arduous honeymoon on horseback and the uncertain future among strangers.

Jacob's parents and his sisters and brothers warmly welcomed the young bride. Ere long the newly wedded couple was established in their own home three miles east of Mt. Sidney, Virginia. The property was bought from a Mr. Moses who had built in 1819 a substantial two-story brick house, which is still in use. Through industry and economy the original hundred and sixty acres were extended with the purchase of adjoining farms. These were sufficient in number to provide a farm home for each of the children, namely: Rebekah (Mrs. Daniel Miller), Abraham D., Levi, Reuben Arnold, and Jacob William.

The last named, being the youngest, inherited the parental homestead and continued the filial care of the aging parents. In May 1865, this Jacob married Miss Susan A. Ham of nearby Greene County. She exemplified the loving and faithful devotion of a dutiful daughter-in-law. They shared together the beloved companionship of pioneering parents whose trust was in the Lord, and witnessed their earthly departure in the triumph of Christian faith. Blessed indeed is the family whose God is the Lord.

Source: Garber, Dr. John A., "Inter-Virginia Romance and Marriage, Garber-Arnold," 1822-23 Dr. Garber is a retired minister in Decatur, Georgia, and son of Jacob W. and Susan A. Garber.

The Jacob Garber House

This two-story brick and frame L-shaped house had a gabled metal roof and three chimneys. Its 16 windows (two to sash) measured 12x28 inches, and the green shutters were full length with a half pivot. The transom entrance had square columns and the porch was one story. The interior contained 10 rooms (6 large and 4 small) with a ceiling height of 8 feet; an open string stairway (one flight) with small round newel, round handrail and square spindles; and a small vegetable cellar. The doors were six-panel, heavy, handmade, and painted, and the hardware was common hinges of flat outside iron. The walls were plastered and papered; the floors were made of pine boards of different widths supported by oak logs; and the mantels were plain, handmade and painted.

Source: Mc Cleary, Ann, *Eighteen Century to the Present, Historic Landmarks of Virginia,* 1982.

The farm acreage totaled 160 acres. The hilltops were used for crop farming and the sides of the hills were used for grazing cattle. The farm has three sources of water, two ever-flowing streams and a pond. The house faced to the west onto Garber Road, which has been closed since about 1900. Originally, the house had a one-story ell, which was replaced by a two-story ell in the early twentieth century. A large carved stone was imbedded near the top of one of the chimneys with the date 1818. The stone was given to Dr. Adam Garber, a university professor in the Atlanta area, by Anna Smith. Charles W. and Anna Smith lived in the house from 1946 until 1974 and reared eight children. The house and well became unsafe for cattle and were burned and bulldozed in 1998 by the owner of the farm, Lowell Garber. To locate the house site, take Route #608 one mile north of New Hope, Virginia, and turn west on Knightly Mill Road (Route #776); go about two miles to foot of hill past Knightly Store (burned), turn in gate by a small house and follow road through woods about a half mile.

Drawing of Jacob Garber House, c1960

U.S. Generation No. 3

Home of Jacob and Nancy Arnold Garber, Built 1819

The Jacob Garber House, Picture c1900
(L-R) Ida, unknown, unknown, Susan, Arthur, Adam, Aunt Becca, Jacob, Cora, Ada Byrd, Abraham D., Sophie and George Garber

Painting of Jacob Garber House, c1960 (Notice Stucco on Bricks)

Christmas Dinner at the Jacob Garber House, 1966
(L-R) Alice Smith, Sylvester Smith, William Smith, Charles W. Smith Jr., Harriett Caroline Noon Smith and
Olga Whitmer, Picture Taker - Anna Smith (Notice Walnut China Closet)

The Jacob Garber House, Just before It was Burned and Bulldozed, 1998

Source: Information and photographs provided to the writer in 2005 by Anna Flora Smith of Mt. Sidney, Virginia. Anna lived in this house for about 30 years and reared eight children.

Jacob Garber Farm Deed from the Lottery

This Indenture made this 11th day of January in the year of our Lord one thousand eight hundred forty three between John Miller and Elizabeth, his wife, of the County of Augusta, State of Virginia of the one part and Jacob Garber of the County & State aforesaid of the other part of their hand witnesseth that the said John Miller and Elizabeth, his wife, for and in consideration of sum of one dollar well and truly paid unto them by the said Jacob Garber at and before the signing and delivering of these presents, the receipt whereof is hereby acknowledged have granted bargained and sold and by these presents do grant, bargain, sell and convey unto the said Jacob Garber his heirs, executors to a certain tract or parcel of land lying, in the said County, adjoining the lands of George Shreckhise, William Bull & others. It being (the) south eastern part of the tract formerly owned by the said John and Samuel Miller containing by recent survey one hundred and fifty one acres. Roods & nine poles and bounded as follows by beginning at a stone by the road on Shreckhise's line thence N 60 E 10 poles to a pine thence S 79 E 152 poles to a pine SW 85.5 poles to a locust stump between 3 hickories thence S 62 E 5 poles to a blown down pine thence S 41/2 W 94 poles to one white oak and two gums thence N 87 1/2 W 64 poles to two white oaks thence N 62 W 28 poles to the road thence N 1 & E 37 1/4 poles to a rock in the lane thence N 69 W 45 poles to white oak thence N 8 3/4 E 15 poles and links to a stone thence N19 W 17 poles to a stone in draft thence N 8 E 36 poles crossing the meadow to a stake thence running along the meadow N 78 ½ E 20 poles to a stone thence N 27 ¾ W 77 poles to the beginning. To have and to hold the above named tract or parcel of land with all and singular the appurtenances there unto belonging or in any wise appertaining free from all manner of encumbrance or encumbrances. To the only proper use and behoof of the said Jacob Garber his heirs assigns administrators & c forever. And the said John Miller and Elizabeth his wife for themselves their heirs assigns executors to do hereby grant bargain sell & convey the above named tract of land to Jacob Garber his heirs and assigns forever the rights & title whereof the said John Miller and Elizabeth his wife do hereby warrant and by these presents forever defend against the claim or claims of all and every person or persons whatsoever. In testimony whereof they have hereunto set their hands and afixed (affixed) their seals the day and year first above written.

Signed John Miller (Seal)

Elizabeth Miller (Seal)

AUGUSTA COUNTY TO WIT

We Samuel Harnsberger and Thomas P. Wilson Justices of the Peace in the County aforesaid do hereby certify that John Miller a party to the within deed personally appeared before us in our County and acknowledged the same to be his act and deed and desired us to certify said acknowledgment to the Clerk of the County Court of Augusta in order that the said deed may be admitted to record. And we further certify that Elizabeth Miller wife of the above named John Miller and a party to the within deed personally appeared before us in our county and being examined by us privately and apart from her husband and having the aforesaid deed fully explained to her, she said Elizabeth acknowledged the same to be her act and deed and declared that she had willingly signed sealed and delivered the same and that she did not wish to retract it given under our hands and seals this 11th of January 1843.

Signed Samuel Harnsberger (Seal)

Thomas P. Wilson (Seal)

Augusta County Court Clerk's Office June 15th 1843

This deed from John Miller and wife to Jacob Garber was this day presented in the office aforesaid and being acknowledged by the said Miller and wife she being also privily (privately) examined and having relinquished her dower before two justices of the peace for this County with the certificates of said justices hereon endorsed and admitted to record.

Teste: Jefferson Kinney Clerk

Source: Wayne Garber typed in January 2005 this hand written deed record from the Augusta County Land Courthouse, Staunton, Virginia, (Deed Book 64 - page 63).

Sketches of Two Shenandoah Valley Communities

Since 1790, many Garber descendants have lived in the general vicinity of New Hope and Mt. Sidney, Virginia. William Patterson, a long time New Hope area resident, stated in 2006 that in the early 20th-century, "there were so many Garbers in New Hope that you could not throw a rock without hitting one." Certainly many Garber generations have contributed to the development and prosperity of the New Hope and Mt. Sidney communities. What is presented is a short historical sketch of each community.

The Town of New Hope

New Hope is located in the heart of the beautiful Shenandoah Valley about twelve miles east of Staunton and nine miles northeast of Waynesboro, Virginia. The village of New Hope is situated in the historic area of Augusta County near the confluence of Meadow Run (formerly Long Meadow Run and, before that, Beaver Run), Christian's Creek and Middle River (formerly Cathey's River). William Beverley received an 118,491-acre land grant in 1736, in consideration for inducing a large number of settlers to the community. The Beverley Land Grant embraces the site of the present city of Staunton. The Kerr family, which settled in the New Hope area around 1730 to 1732, was one of the first settlers.

It seems that little is known about the origin and early history of New Hope. Although the village has an inspirational name, no one knows the origin of the name. Three stories are given for the name. The first story explains that, in 1772, settler John Kerr made a land entry for 400 acres and named the land for his dream of finding new hope in this new land. Another story suggests that the area's first settlers were stricken with a disease or extreme hardship of some kind and the residents became disheartened. One of the residents offered an encouraging word by stating, "Let's not be discouraged. Let's look for the best. Let's watch for new hope." Waddell's *Annals of Augusta County* states, "It would be interesting to know the origin of the names of the many small towns and villages in Augusta County, but with the exception of five or six, no one living can tell by whom and why the names are applied." What we know is that its name appeared many years before the Battle of Piedmont during the Civil War.

The evolution of New Hope sprang from the building of the Stout-Fretwell-Garber General Merchandise Store (built 1804), the Dickerson-Fretwell Tavern (built 1818) and postal operations (started 1829), which then resulted in community and commercial developments such as churches, family farmsteads, grist mills and early houses.

Looking down the New Hope Road, photograph taken c1850

Note: Photographs of both the store and tavern may be found in *The History of New Hope, Virginia* by Owen Early Horner and Wayne Edward Garber, ISBN 0-9752745-9-7.

The Stout-Fretwell-Garber General Merchandise Store was a two-story brick building with a basement, main floor and second floor. Around 1818, the Dickerson-Fretwell Tavern, which sits at the northeast corner of Routes 608 and 616, was built and served as a tavern and stagecoach stop. The New Hope Post Office was established on March 3, 1829. During the 1830s and 1840s, the village slowly grew with the building of more houses on New Hope Road near the general merchandise store and tavern.

In 1824, the first Tunker or German Baptist Church (Middle River Church of the Brethren) was built near New Hope. The old New Hope Church, first called Providence Church (New Hope United Methodist Church), was built in the spring of 1850. Both churches served as hospitals for Confederate soldiers during the Civil War. In the late 19th-century, New Hope was the largest village in the present Middle River District and in 1882 was the fifth largest community in Augusta County. The village could not boast of any innovative town planning since New Hope was laid out as a string of lots on each side of the road. By 1884, the village of New Hope could boast of having forty houses, a graded schoolhouse, a post office, a saddler shop, a Methodist church with parsonage, a Dunker church, three stores, two resident physicians, a Masonic Hall, two blacksmith shops and the usual workshops. Since 1884, the general lay-out of the village has changed very little.

The Town of Mt. Sidney

Mt. Sidney, developed in 1826 by Hugh Glenn and Henry B. Roland, is located north of Staunton on U.S. 11 and west of Interstate 81 in North River District. Until the new highway was built, it was included in Middle River District. There are several stories regarding the origin of the name. Joseph A. Waddell, in *Annals of Augusta County, Virginia*, relates the tale of the three sons who were told to mount their horses: Mt. Sidney, Mt. Jackson and Mt. Crawford. Mr. Hanson, in his book on origin of place names in Virginia, states that Charles Curry named it for Sir Philip Sidney. Waddell also states that it is probable that the term "Mount" is one brought over from Ireland, since you find place names there preceded by the word "Mount." No matter how it was named, Mt. Sidney has been a village in Augusta County since April 8, 1826. It was on that date that the first deed was written for a lot (lot #17 one-half acre) in the new town and was sold to Joseph Rankin, Jr. By 1829, the land tax book of Augusta County, District 2, shows the names of William Campbell, Josiah Cathron, Joseph Coiner, John Deary, Hugh Glenn (still owning 17 lots), Gilbert James, Nathaniel Hurst, James Gilbert, Christian Landis, Sr., Christian Landis, Jr., Henry B. Roland (11 lots), Jacob M. Parsons, David Ross, Samuel Rankin and Jonathan Sheetz.

On March 19, 1878, the *Staunton Spectator* gives the following account of the origin of Mt. Sidney, located north of Staunton on U.S. 11: "In 1812, when traveling from Harrisonburg to Staunton, one would follow the old road over which old Charley Bockett carried the first mail from Winchester to Staunton. Where Mt. Sidney is, or rather just below, Capt. Samuel Frame lived where the late Addison Hyde lived. Adjoining him below was one Roland who owned the old Plow and Harrow Tavern. No one remembers where he came from or when. He had four sons: John, a cavalry officer on the north frontier; David, George and Henry B. Henry B. Roland succeeded Capt. Frame as commandant of the Cavalry Company of the old 32nd Regiment, which held its musters in October at old Peter Hangar's, the Willow Spout. Capt. Roland married Patsy Glenn, daughter of Hugh Glenn, who then lived at the west side of what is now the village of Mt. Sidney. About 1828, he laid-off and gave name to the village of Mt. Sidney. He operated a store for several years in the heart of the village. Capt. Roland studied medicine and moved to Indiana. Another store was operated by Michael Mauzy a few hundred yards west of the Plow and Harrow near the intersection of the Keezletown Road with the Valley Pike."

The original plat shows 41 lots, with the main street being Washington Street, running north and south. Two cross streets named Bolivar and La Fayette, and another side street named Marion. All names were for champions of freedom. In 1826, Hugh Glenn sold 13 of the 24 lots on the east side of the main street (Washington). He retained lots 1 and 2 for himself. In 1830, Hugh Glenn went bankrupt. Born in 1775 in Augusta County, Virginia, he was married three times: Elizabeth McCausland, Rebecca Turk Anderson and Susan Taylor of Albemarle Co., Virginia. It is from tax records that the year of his death, 1833, is determined. He left no will. Susan Taylor Glenn died after 1870 but before 1884.

In December 1829, the inhabitants asked for permission to hold a lottery to raise $5,000 to build a market, town hall and other public buildings. The deed records show that Mt. Sidney had an Academy and proof that a school was there as early as 1826. From 1813 to 1829, the post office was located in the Plow and Harrow Tavern near the intersection of the Valley Pike and the Keezletown Road; then the post office moved into a separate building.

Mt. Sidney Train Station, c1870s, Torn Down in 1940s

In the manuscript of Mt. Sidney by Nelson F. Fogle in 1967, he lists the following businesses as being there in the 1800s and early 1900s: blacksmith shop, planing mill, post office, Ritchie's store, town hall, Methodist Church (white), Methodist Church (colored), hotel, tavern and barroom, Harper's store, Shumake-Johnson store, copper shop, the watering trough, Bell's undertaking establishment, Flavin-Watson tin shop, Lutheran parsonage, Lutheran Church (St. James), bar room and tavern, Mt. Sidney school, Potter shop, Mt. Sidney Academy and Dr. William Crawford's office. In 1966, he lists a grocery store and filling station, antique shop, Cleaning and Dye works, Shenandoah Tailoring Company, post office, bank, town hall (now apartments), another grocery store, the two Methodists churches, grade school, trailer court, Huffman Transfer and a barber shop and beauty salon.

Source: The Mt. Sidney material with minor modifications is taken directly from the "Katherine Gentry Bushman Papers" at the Library of Virginia, Richmond, Virginia. Bushman was past president of the Augusta County Historical Society.

U.S. Generation No. 4
Levi Garber & Barbara Miller

Levi Garber, c1910

Elder Levi Garber

Glimpses of Levi and Barbara Garber

Levi Garber, better known as Elder Levi Garber, was born August 21, 1828, and was the third son of Jacob Garber, a farmer. It has been written that "Levi and Barbara Miller saw much of each other at family gatherings at Pleasant Valley." They fell in love and married on February 21, 1850. Barbara was born February 25, 1825, in Augusta County and died August 1, 1878, at age 53 years. Their farm home was located 1.5 miles from Mt. Sidney, Virginia, on the Buttermilk Road and about four miles from New Hope, Virginia. The Levi Garber farm was first owned by Jacob Garber, his father, who won the farm in a lottery with the purchase of a one dollar ticket, which he presented to the owners John and Elizabeth Miller. It has been reported that Jacob gave each of his children a farm, and Levi was given the lottery homestead on Buttermilk Road. Levi farmed to support his family but spent a considerable amount of his time helping others and preparing for the ministry.

Levi was about 5' 8" tall, thin and probably weighed about 160 pounds. He lived a frugal life style, was religious and very strong in faith, a well-respected church leader, even-tempered, very honest and modest. When Levi had a moment for relaxation, he liked to go to the Knightly Mill to fish for perch and suckerfish.

To Levi and Barbara Garber were born three sons and five daughters to include:

1. Peter b 1850 d 1932 m 1876 Emma Catherine Cline b 1852 d 1915. Four children.

2. Jacob A. b 1853 d 1915 m 1873 Mary Elizabeth "Lizzie" Myers b 1853 d 1928. Five children.

3. Daniel S. b 1855 d 1923 m 1879 Elizabeth "Lizzie" Glick b 1860 d 1949. Seven children.

4. Lydia Catherine b 1857 d 1936 m 1880 Jacob H. Flory b 1853 d 1927. Six children.

5. Nancy Jane b 1859 d 1890 not married.

6. Anna Rebecca "Becky" b 1861 d 1940 m 1920 Enos F. Garber (2nd cousin) b 1860 d 1934.

7. Barbara Elizabeth b 1863 d 1949 m 1889 Joseph S. Norford b 1870 d 1940. Three children.

8. Frances "Fannie" V. b 1866 d 1925 m 1900 Jacob L. Huffman b 1862 d 1950. Four children.

Flax was grown on the Levi Garber farm, and linen was spun from the flax. In the 1880s, a five-gallon lard can filled with flax was found in a secret attic of the house, where it had been hidden during the Civil War. From the flax, Ada Garber Reed and Cora Garber made linen doilies in the 1920s. When Cora died an old maid, Katherine Garber Crist found these doilies in Cora's hope chest and gave one to Wayne Garber in December 1991.

Levi was elected to the office of deacon in 1855, to the ministry in 1860 and ordained to the eldership in 1875. Following the division of the congregation at Middle River, Elder Levi Garber carried on a great deal of missionary work in the mountain regions and in Eastern Virginia. He traveled mostly by horseback, and it is said that one horse carried him over 30,000 miles in his travels for the church. His work required Levi to visit places located in the Blue Ridge Mountains, e.g., Wayside, Bluffdale and Sugar Hollow. When the government established the Shenandoah National Park in the 1930s, all the people living in this territory had to move out, so Levi's work came to a stop. Middle River also had an interest in the Mountain View Chapel on the Rockfish Road until it was discontinued and the church building torn down. Levi's entire ministerial life was devoted to serving the Middle River Congregation.

Levi Garber Farm House, Built c1840

In 1868, the Court of Augusta County authorized Levi to perform marriage ceremonies.

Rev. Levi Garber, Certificate and Order Authorizing Celebration of Rites of Marriage

In Augusta County Court January the 27th 1868 Rev. Levi Garber having produced credentials of his ordination and also of his being in regular communion in the German Baptist Church in this county. This day appeared in court and together with Isaac Flory his security entered into a bond in the sum of fifteen hundred dollars payable with condition as prescribed by law, which bond was acknowledged in court by the obligor's thereto and ordered to be recorded and thereupon the said Levi Garber is by the court duly authorized and empowered to celebrate the rites of matrimony according to law, the said bond having been duly stamped as required by law.

> Copy Teste
> Signed by: William A. Burnett, Clerk
> Virginia Augusta County to Wit

We Martin Garber a regular ordained Bishop in the German Baptist Church of said county and Christian Kline and Abraham D. Garber and Isaac Flory regular appointed and set apart as deacons or overseers of the said Church do hereby certify that our Brother Levi Garber is a regular ordained preacher in our said church and he is in regular communion in the said church. Given under our hand and seal this 22nd day of December 1860.

Signed   Martin Garber (seal)   Abraham D. Garber (seal)
                Christian Kline (seal)   Isaac Flory (seal)

Source: The original document of authorization was provided to Wayne Garber by Catherine Garber Crist of Harrisonburg, Virginia. The writer typed it on February 22, 2004.

Levi preached and ministered to the Middle River Congregation for almost 55 years before his death on November 10, 1914, at his farm home at Mt. Sidney. Before his death, he called several of his grandchildren to his bedside for a talk. The following information was copied from the original handwritten statement in the possession of Cora Garber.

Last Words of Levi Garber, November 7, 1914

These are the last words of our father Elder Levi Garber to his great grand children Cleatis, Harold and Paul Garber. He called their Papa and Mama (Homer F. and Sallie Bell Garber) to bring them to him. Taking them by the hand he said: "Now my little boys I am soon going to die, and then a man will come, put me in a big wooden box, they will take me to the church, put me in a deep hole, cover me up with dirt and pile it over me. After a while the good man will come, take the dirt off of me, and take me to the good place to live with him. Be good boys, love Papa and Mama, and some day you will die too, and then we will live together again a long time."

Witnessed by: Jacob A., Anna R., Homer F. and Sallie B. Garber and Jacob H. and Lydia C. Flory

Source: The original handwritten statement was in the possession of Cora Garber, granddaughter of Levi Garber. The document was provided to Wayne Garber by Cleatis Garber of Waynesboro, Virginia.

Obituary *Staunton News-Leader*

Garber, Elder Levi, born near the Middle River Church, Augusta County, Virginia, Aug. 21, 1828, died Nov. 10, 1914, aged 86 years, 2 months and 19 days. Bro. Garber had been a great sufferer for about six or eight years with cancer in the mouth, but bore his affliction very patiently. In his younger years he was a great missionary. His field was mostly in mountain territory, and his mode of travel was nearly all done on horseback, as was the custom in those days. He was married to Barbara Miller Feb. 21, 1850. She was a daughter of Elder Peter Miller. She preceded him to her eternal home thirty-six years. He remained unmarried the remainder of his days. He was elected to the ministry in 1860, and was ordained to the eldership in 1875. He was senior elder of the Middle River Congregation until he got too feeble, which compelled him to resign. The Lord blessed him with eight children. One daughter preceded him many years ago. Four daughters and three sons survive him. The eldest son is a senior elder of the Valley congregation; the second son is elder of the Greenmount congregation, Rockingham County, Virginia; and the third son is deacon in the home church. All the children are members of the Church of the Brethren. Services by Brethren Ministers H. C. Early and B. B. Garber. Text Rev. 14:13 – J. F. Miller, Grottoes, Virginia.

Obituary *Harrisonburg Daily News Record*

Elder Levi Garber, Nov. 10, 1914, Dies at Mt. Sidney
Father of Rev. Jacob A. Garber of Greenmount Had Been Suffering from Cancer for Years
Elder Levi Garber, a prominent minister of the Church of the Brethren, died yesterday morning at 11 o'clock at his home at Mt. Sidney. He had been suffering with cancer for years. Elder Garber was a son of the late Jacob W. Garber, Sr., and Nancy Arnold of Hampshire County, West Virginia. He was eighty-six years old last August and was born in the Mt. Sidney neighborhood, where he spent practically his entire life. His wife, who was Miss Barbara Miller, died thirty-six years ago.

Surviving Mr. Garber are seven children – Elder Peter Garber of Weyers Cave, Elder Jacob A. Garber of Greenmount, Daniel S. Garber of Ft. Defiance, Mrs. Lydia B. Flory of Dayton, Miss Anna R. Garber at home, Mrs. Barbara E. Norford of Ft. Defiance, Mrs. Fannie V. Huffman of MacDoel, California, and Mrs. Susan A. Garber of Dayton, a sister-in-law. The funeral service will be held from Middle River Church of the Brethren tomorrow morning at 11:00 o'clock.

Levi Garber Headstone

Eld. Levi Garber
Born
Aug. 21, 1828
Died
Nov. 10, 1914

"Served as minister to the Church of the
Brethren for 54 years."

On August 1, 1928, the Middle River Church held a commemoration of Abraham Garber and his grandson Levi Garber. The program stated, "In loving remembrance of Abraham Garber, Founder and Elder of the Middle River Congregation who donated the land and built the first house of worship for the Church of the Brethren in Augusta County, Virginia, and also his Grandson, Elder Levi Garber whose 100th birthday we celebrate today and who has served as minister of the congregation for 54 years and as Elder for 39 years.

The Ministry of Levi Garber to the Middle River Church

During the last quarter of the nineteenth century, the church at Middle River continued to expand and develop. Sunday school was conducted in connection with the preaching service. When this work began we are not sure. Mrs. Nelia Ray remembers that when she was a little girl and while the old Brick Church was still in use, that there was a Sunday school. She says there were several classes but no separate rooms except for the children who met in the kitchen. They had very little literature. The Bible was used as a textbook. She tells us that Walter B. Yount, as a young man, taught the children in the old kitchen. He was Mrs. Ray's teacher. She says that he would tell them Bible stories and then ask questions about the stories.

About this time there was an interest in higher education. For many years two German sects, Dunkers and Mennonites, had made the mistake of not educating their children. That changed when the Church began to see the need of educated leadership. More members were attending institutions of higher learning. It was becoming evident that people would need to be trained for positions in society. Elder D. C. Flory, a member of the Middle River Congregation, established a school at Spring Creek, Rockingham County, in 1880. This school was later moved to Bridgewater and became Bridgewater College. This school and many others were connected with the Church of the Brethren.

It became evident that the old Brick Church was becoming inadequate. On March 28, 1884, the church council "almost unanimously agreed to build a church on the grounds of the old Brick Church." Construction of the new church must have started soon thereafter and continued through the summer. By October it was far enough completed that a date was set for the dedication of the new building. The Minutes state: "It was unanimously agreed to have the new church dedicated on the 23rd day of November and have communion meeting on the 27th."

Second Middle River Church of the Brethren, Built 1884

The new church was larger than the Brick Church and was of frame construction. The Church had three doors on the north side and was heated by stoves instead of fireplaces. It was plenty large for the accommodation of the Congregation. The middle door was a double door, while the one on either side was a single door. There was a table for the ministers at the south side of the building. At each end there were raised benches. In August of 1885, the Church authorized the digging of a cistern for the Church use and in February of the following year authorized that a pump be placed in the cistern. In the early part of 1886, the cistern was put into use. In 1902, the church lot was enlarged by the purchase of additional land for $200. In 1905, the council decided to have the cemetery lots staked off and numbered. In 1906, the council decided that a levy be made on the Church (Congregation) high enough to cover the present indebtedness and give ample funds for next year's expenses. The money was to be raised by solicitation. Brethren Homer Garber and Samuel Garber were named to do the work. In 1907, a committee was appointed to solicit funds and carpet the church floor. Additional Sunday school rooms were provided in 1910. Electric lights were installed in the church in 1916. In 1921, more Sunday school rooms were added and a furnace was installed. On November 13th of that year, the remodeled building was dedicated with I. N. H. Beahm delivering the sermon. A piano was purchased in 1925. The organ was installed in 1949. A Sunday school class provided individual communion cups in 1932. The basement was excavated in 1943 providing a fellowship hall and additional facilities.

The ministerial work of the church was cared for across the years by the home ministers on the free-ministry basis with the exception that for a time prior to the securing of a pastor, the home ministers were paid a small amount for their services. In 1937, Brother Samuel A. Harley became the first employed pastor of the Middle River Church. The parsonage was built in 1939 on a lot donated by Wade G. Flory. The pastors having served the Middle Church are as follows:

Samuel A. Harley (1937-42);
D. Howard Keiper (1942-47);
Floyd H. Mitchell (1947-52);
John W. Gosnell (1952-57);
Frank Y. Garber (interim 1957-58);
Marvin E. Clingenpeel (1958-65);
Fred A. Driver (1965-71);
Warren D. Bowman (interim 1971-72);
R. Thomas Fralin, Jr. (1972-78);

Auburn A. Boyers (interim 1978-79);
Brian S. Hildebrand (interim 1979-80);
Dennis L. Brown (1980-1990);
Brian S. Hildebrand (part time 1990-94);
Fred Bowman (interim 1994);
Harold Sonafrank (1994-1998);
Wendell Flory (interim 1998-1999);
Charles Smith (interim 1999-2000);
Chester Fisher (2000-2005);
Nathan Myers (2005-present).

A plan of reorganization was drafted and adopted in 1949. In 1961, this plan was revised and enlarged and served as a basis and guide for the organization and administration of the church program. Plans for a new building got underway in 1956. A large and representative Planning Committee was appointed with Joe Humbert as Chairman and Mrs. Kelly Chapman, Jr., as Secretary. A financial campaign was conducted and a building fund was started. Preliminary plans were drawn by Forrest Groff, the denominational Building Counselor. J. E. Harper of Staunton was secured as architect to do the construction drawings and supervise the construction. A few years later Arthur Dean, who had succeeded Forrest Groff as Building Counselor, made new preliminary drawings which determined the plan of the new building.

Fourth Middle River Church of the Brethren, Picture Taken 2004

The contract for construction was let in February 1964 to J. S. Mathers, Inc., of Waynesboro. A ground-breaking service was held on Sunday, March 8, 1964, and construction began immediately. A cornerstone laying service was held on Sunday, July 19, 1964. The fellowship hall, kitchen and restrooms were added in 1975.

Note: The sanctuary of the Middle River Church burned in 2006 due to an electrical fire and was rebuilt in 2007 at the cost of one million dollars.

Source: Coffman, W. Paul *A History of Middle River Congregation, Church of the Brethren*, 1964.

Author's Note:
The Church of the Brethren held its Annual Meeting in Rockingham County in 1861. Interestingly, the Rockingham Register reported on May 24, "The men and women were segregated, the men on one side of the church, the women on the other. Not a woman had on a hoop skirt, a jockey cap, a chignon resembling a waterfall, crinoline figured woolen petticoat showing below a hooped skirt or a piece of jewelry. They wore no bonnets, but a prayer covering made of cotton netting woven in hexagonal meshes." As recently as 1884, a member had to resign from a bicycle club and the Young Men's Christian Association (YMCA), another was expelled for worldliness in his amusements and in 1886 another was charged with having been entertained in his home with a brass band. In 1911, a young lady was disfellowshiped for persisting in wearing a hat rather than a bonnet.

The Tunker (Church of the Brethren) Society changed between 1905 and 1920 from a nonconforming one to a more or less conforming one. After a long and bitter struggle, the church abandoned many of its restrictions and accepted more modern-day practices by abandoning its dress code, its ban on the use of musical instruments in church services, its ban on members holding public office and the practice of using free ministers.

The Civil War

By recognizing slavery as an institution in some states and by failing to deny expressly the right of a state to withdraw from the union of states created by the Federal constitution, the framers of that document planted the seeds of the American Civil War. These seeds of conflict were nurtured by a sectionalism resulting from different economic systems in the Northeastern and Southern regions of the country. The economy of the North was based on commerce, manufacturing and small family-worked farms; whereas that of the South was based on specialized-farming on large plantations worked by slave labor. With two such different economies, national governmental policies which were beneficial to one region were not necessarily beneficial to the other.

Source: May, C. E., *Life Under Four Flags In North River Basin of Virginia*, 1976.

The Civil War and the Middle River Congregation

During the third quarter of the nineteenth century there was much trouble in this country. It was the time when the slavery question and the problem of States Rights were before the people. It was the period of the Civil War and reconstruction. It presented many problems to the Brethren as well as others. The Brethren did not believe slavery to be right and they did not believe it was right to engage in warfare. The stand of the Brethren brought much persecution and they were often misunderstood. While the war raged, many lost most or all of their material possessions but maintained their faith in their God and way of life. In the midst of suffering and war, they tried to live in peace and give service to their fellowmen. The church house was used as a hospital during and after the Battle of Piedmont that was fought in sight of the church. Some of the soldiers who died were buried in the church cemetery. Wooden markers were placed to mark the graves, but they have long since disappeared.

After the war started, laws were passed requiring men to serve in the Confederate Army. Many of the members of the Church of the Brethren refused to engage in warfare. Many were arrested and persecuted. Some of the leaders of the Church, along with others, influenced the Virginia General Assembly to pass an exemption act that exempted those who opposed war on religious grounds. This law was passed after a number of Brethren were already imprisoned, some in Richmond and some in Harrisonburg.

In the spring of 1862, while these men were in prison, a general council meeting was held at the Middle River Church. At this council Benjamin F. Byerly and Christian Kline were appointed to go to Richmond to secure the release of the men imprisoned there. Under the exemption law a man had to pay $500 and two percent of the assessed value of his property in order to be released. The members of the Church quickly responded and a large sum of money was raised to get the men released. It was some time before they were released, as there seemed to be some confusion about the matter and officials hesitated to accept the money.

Among those imprisoned were: Elder John Kline, Joseph Beery, Gabriel Heatwole, Sr., John A. Kline, Joseph M. Kline, Christopher Miller, George Holler, Daniel Hert, Samuel Wine, John Swartz, Jacob Knupp, Martin Click, Hue Brunk, Henry Brunk, Henry Nisewander, Jacob Snell, Philip Hollar, George Wine and Jackson Showalter. This list of names is from Zigler's *History of the Brethren in Virginia*.

When these men were permitted to return to their homes, there was great rejoicing even though large fines had bought their liberty. The rejoicing was short-lived because almost before they were out of the shadow of the prison walls, the Confederate Congress passed a conscription act requiring all men between 18 and 45 to serve in the Confederate Army. This law was passed April 16, 1862. This caused more trouble for the Brethren. On April 21, 1862, an exemption was made for ministers in the regular discharge of their duties.

After much work by the Brethren and others, with the help of Col. John B. Baldwin in the Confederate Congress, a law was passed on October 17, 1862, which exempted members in good standing of the Mennonites, Friends (Quakers), Nazarenes and Dunkards if they either secured a substitute or paid into the public treasury the $500. Again the Brethren responded nobly and many fines were paid for exemptions.

As the Confederacy became weaker, the substitute law was repealed and there was fear that the exemption law for religious objectors would also be repealed. The Brethren and others kept pressure on the Confederate Congress that this law is kept and they were successful in their efforts.

In 1864, Sheridan was sent to the Shenandoah Valley with orders from General Grant to destroy and lay waste to this fertile valley from which the Confederate Army still received many supplies. Sheridan laid waste to the Valley; burning, pillaging and destroying whatever was of any value or would be of any value to the Confederate Army. The loss was in millions of dollars and the Brethren, along with their neighbors, shared in this great loss. The army destroyed fences, burned houses, barns, mills and other buildings, drove off the horses and cattle, killing sheep and hogs. It was a time of great suffering and loss of material possessions. The Brethren were glad that their lives were spared and that they did not have to engage in the taking of human life, even though much of their property was destroyed and they were persecuted for their beliefs.

Source: Coffman, W. Paul, *A History of Middle River Congregation, Church of the Brethren*, 1964.

Levi Garber Picture Story

House at Rockland Mills on Route 276 North of Weyers Cave Along North River, 1904
L-R Aunt Becky, Jacob L. Huffman, Frances Garber Huffman,
Levi Garber with long beard, Joe Norford, wife Barbara Garber Norford, son Earl

Sleigh Ride, c1899
Back Row, Far Left, Levi Garber, son Daniel S. Garber beside Levi

Family gathering at Uncle Abe Garber's
when Aunt Frances "Fannie" V. Garber was married in February 1900.

Levi Garber with Family (German) Bible, 1902
L-R, Levi Garber with beard, Becky Garber (Levi's daughter, standing left), Frances Garber Huffman (Levi's daughter standing right), Jacob L. Huffman (Husband)

Four Generations, c1912
(BR, L-R) Levi Garber and Daniel S. Garber
(FR, L-R) Homer F. Garber with Harold L. Garber

Levi Garber Casket Receipt from William Henry Willberger
Founder of Willberger Funeral Service

Bottle of Oats, 1864

This bottle of oats has the following label attached,

"Oats my father (Levi) raised during the (Civil) war, 1864."
Signed: Rebecca (his daughter).

The year 1864 has significance because General Sheridan's Union Forces burned the crops in the surrounding fields, hundreds of barns and mills including the original Knightly Mill building during his Shenandoah Valley scorched earth campaign. The bottle of oats was given to Harold Garber by Ada Reed and Cora Garber in the 1960s and is in the possession of Frederic Garber.

U.S. Generation No. 5

Daniel Samuel Garber & Elizabeth "Lizzie" M. Glick

Daniel and Lizzie Garber with Sons and Daughters, 1910

Standing - Anthony, Ada, Homer, Martha, Minor and Cora Garber (center)
Seated - Daniel and Elizabeth (Lizzie) Garber

Glimpses of Daniel and Lizzie Garber

Daniel S. Garber, the third son of Levi Garber and Barbara Miller, was born in 1855, near Mt. Sidney. While growing up, Daniel worked on his father's farm and then bought the family farm from Levi about the time he and Lizzie got married in 1879. Elizabeth Margaret "Lizzie" Glick, born 1860 and died in 1949, was the daughter of Samuel T. Glick and Rebecca Wine. Daniel operated his father Levi's farm for about 11 years before it was officially conveyed on March 24, 1890. Daniel and Lizzie bought the 146 acres of farm land, barn and house for $8,000. Daniel was an active, lifelong member of the Middle River Church of the Brethren and served as a deacon. He and Lizzie reared six children on the farm.

Daniel was industrious, frugal and saved his money. On May 31, 1905, he bought the Knightly Mill with Joseph Norford for $6,500. He acquired the land with water rights, the miller's house and a flour warehouse situated on land of the Valley Railroad Company near the Ft. Defiance Depot. Daniel began operating the flour mill and sawmill. In 1910, he sold his farm of 141 acres to his son, Homer. Daniel and Lizzie moved to a small (seven to eight acres) homestead at Knightly, about three miles toward Middle River. The farm was officially conveyed to Homer and Sallie on April 1, 1915, for $10,162 with a down payment of $963. After operating the Knightly Mill for seven years, Daniel and Joe Norford sold a one-third interest in the mill to Minor Garber on July 1, 1912, for $4,000. Minor acquired the remaining interests in the Knightly Mill on March 12, 1925, for $8,000, when the mill was called the Knightly Light and Power Company, Inc.

In retirement, Daniel was one of the first school bus drivers in Augusta County. He received a contract from Augusta County to provide school transportation for kids in the Knightly area. He purchased a truck and built a wooden frame school bus with bench seats that ran the length of the truck bed. He drove children to New Hope School for several years. When he was not busy, he liked to sit in a wooden chair by the wood stove to keep warm. On December 30, 1923, Daniel died of Bright's disease. His estate went to his wife Lizzie and daughters Ada and Cora, who cared for Lizzie until she died in 1949. Daniel invested the money he received from Homer for the farm and Minor for the mill, and his estate supported Ada and Cora all their lives.

Daniel was 5'8" tall, well-built and weighed about 175 pounds. He had brown hair, a beard and brown eyes, never smoked, chewed or cursed, rarely read, never played cards or games, never told jokes and never corresponded with others. He was a willing and hard worker, a very good manager and businessman, was early to bed and early to rise, liked to fish, had no special abilities, rarely visited friends or told stories and was sometimes a stern disciplinarian who expected one to do the job. Daniel was an honest, reserved, even-tempered and responsible individual, never grumpy, rarely argumentative but sometimes stubborn, literal minded, always logical and energetic but not a strong leader. He liked to sing, was not artistic and was strong in faith, generally relaxed, carefree, honest, humble and modest.

Lizzie was a small woman, standing only 4' 9" tall, thin and weighing less than 95 pounds. She had black hair, brown eyes, small features and was very supple. She wore bonnets, tight-waist dresses down to her ankles (old Brethren style) and capes. Lizzie was a housewife who loved to talk to anyone, was very easy going, not a disciplinarian and did not worry. Lizzie enjoyed life, fed her chickens and a cat, milked the cow, liked to sing, was sometimes industrious and possessed no special skills or abilities. She was even-tempered, never grumpy, frequently stubborn, serious but happy and lighthearted, carefree, strong in faith, thrifty, humble, honest, sensitive and modest.

Some German families were slow to change their ways and integrate into the culture of America. Elizabeth (Lizzie) Glick Garber started school speaking German but was teased badly by the other children for not speaking English. This childhood experience so impacted Lizzie that she would not allow German to be

Daniel and Lizzie, Before 1910

spoken in her house. So her children, Anthony, Minor, Ada, Martha and Homer, were not allowed to learn or speak German; however, Cora was taught some German by Lizzie after the older kids left home.

To Daniel S. and Elizabeth "Lizzie" Garber were born three sons and four girls to include:

1. Anthony A. b 1880 d 1951 m 1904 Ada Early b 1885. Five children.

2. Ada b 1881 d 1962 m 1902 David Reed b 1877 d 1903. No children.

3. Regina b 1884 d 1884 during birth.

4. Homer Franklin b 1886 d 1973 m 1909 Sallie Belle Reed b 1887 d 1989. Five children.

5. Martha D. b 1888 d 1914 m 1913 Roy W. Slonaker b 1888. Mother and child died during birth.

6. Minor William b 1891 d 1966 m 1912 Rena Barbara Western b 1892 d 1982. One child.

7. Cora V. b 1899 d 1985. Never married.

In 1919, Daniel and Lizzie celebrated their 40th wedding anniversary at their home.

CELEBRATED THEIR
FORTIETH WEDDING
ANNIVERSARY
——— *1919*

On Sunday, March 9. Mr. and Mrs.
D. S. Garber celebrated their fortieth
wedding anniversary at their home
near Fort Defiance. A sumptous dinner was served at 2 o'clock.

All their children and grand-child-
ren were present as follows: Mr. and
Mrs. A. A. Garber and four children,
Noah, Clarence, Ruth and Pauline:
Mr. and Mrs. H. F. Garber and four
children, Cletis. Harold. Paul and
Marguaret; Mr. and Mrs. M. W. Gar-
ber and daughter. Catherine: Mrs
Ada Reed and Miss Cora Garber
Others present were Mr. and Mrs.
John R. Garber, Ada, Mary, Ruby and
Lawrence Garber.

Daniel and Lizzie's 40th Wedding Anniversary
Celebration, March 9, 1919

Daniel Garber's Ledger of Family Transactions

It was important to Daniel that he and Lizzie treat all of their children in an equitable manner, so he kept a ledger of all transactions. The ledger has been copied as follows:

Property of Anthony A. Garber — Received his legacy from home

1	Horse	$75.00
1	Buggy and Harness	$63.00
1	Saddle & Bridle	$9.00
1	Watch	$4.00
	To Cash	$50.00
10-15-1909	To Cash on Lot	$300.00
1911	To Bonds	$500.00
2-22-1911	To Sale Bill	$35.75
	Total	$1,016.75*
11-16-1915	To Credit on Personal Account	983.25
	Total	$2,000.00

* Daniel miscalculated and the real total was $1,036.75.

Property of Homer F. Garber — Received

1	To Buggy	$85.00
	To Harness	$12.00
1	To Horse	$125.00
2-22-1911	To Sale Bill	$825.00
	Total	$1,047.00
	By Down Payment on Farm	$953.00
	Total	$2,000.00

Property of Minor W. Garber

		Received
9-11-1909	To Cash for School	$40.00
10-25-1909	To Cash for School	$10.00
11-26-1909	To Cash for School	$65.00
3-12-1910	To Cash for School	$30.00
4-15-1910	To Cash for School	$75.00
6-1-1910	Cash	$10.00
	Total	$230.00
1911	For Buggy and Harness	$115.00
7-12-1912	To Interest on Mill	$700.00
	Total	$1045.00
4-1-1915	To Settle Bonds	$932.00
1-17-1917	To Cash	$23.00
	Total	$2,000.00

Property of Martha D. Garber

		Received
Feb. 1910	To Cash	$25.00
July 1910	To Cash	$15.00
Aug.	To Cash	$15.00
Sept.	To Cash	$60.00
Sept.	To Cash	$2.00
Sept.	To Cash	$5.00
Sept.	To Cash	$20.00
Oct.	To Cash	$5.00
Nov. 19	To Cash	$5.00
Dec.	To Cash	$75.00
Feb.	To Cash	$5.00
March	To Cash	$35.00
April 3	To Cash	$35.00
April 24	To Cash	$5.00
June 17	To Cash	$25.00
	Total	$332.00
July	To Cash	$16.00
April 1912	To Cash	$15.00
May	To Cash	$25.00
Nov.	To Cash	$40.00
	Total	$428.00

Daniel made no ledger entries for daughters Ada and Cora, who lived at home with Lizzie and him.

Source: The original ledger of family transactions was provided to Wayne Garber by Dolly Garber Harner of New Hope, Virginia.

Humbert-Knightly Mill

One of the two most significant mills on Middle River was the Humbert-Knightly Mill, located on Route 778 where the road crosses Middle River. According to C. E. May, the Humbert-Knightly was known first as Allison Mill, next as Humbert's Mill, then as Hope Mill and finally as Knightly Mill. This mill was established on a small grant of land to Robert Wiley and a tract of land Jacob Fisher acquired through several purchases.

The Knightly Mill Log Dam over Middle River, c1905
Notice the Swinging Bridge Above the Dam.

Jacob and David Humbert purchased, on May 10, 1819, a mill seat on Middle River with the right to raise the mill dam to such a height as might be necessary. The mill dam was built before July 27, 1833, per an agreement between Daniel and Jacob Humbert and William Allison. The Humbert Merchant Mill and sawmill situated on a seven-acre tract of land on Middle River was conveyed to Samuel Garber on January 22, 1853. Four years later, it became known as the Hope Mill when a half interest was conveyed by William Beard to David Beard. Over the next fifty years, either a full or partial interest in the mill was conveyed many times to the following people: Mansfield Marshall, Harrison Ross, David Myers, Christian Cline, Joseph Cline, John Wampler, D.A. Garber, John M. Cline, D. Baxter Lucas, Joseph Norford, Daniel S. Garber and Minor Garber.

Daniel Garber and Joseph "Joe" Norford formed a company to buy and operate the Humbert-Knightly and Ft. Defiance Mills. In 1905, the mills were conveyed and Daniel Garber operated the Knightly Mill from 1905 to 1912 and Joe operated the Ft. Defiance Mill. The Knightly Mill facility consisted of a log dam on Middle River, a millrace, a five-story frame mill house with two waterwheels, a wheat elevator, a sawmill, water rights, miller's house and a flour warehouse situated on land of Valley Railroad Company near the Ft. Defiance Depot.

The mill ground wheat for local farmers and bought wheat from farmers to grind and resell. Daniel employed his son, Minor Garber, who worked in the flour mill and sawmill in the wintertime. Daniel kept black snakes in the mill for mouse control, which proved to be very effective. The products sold were white flour and whole flour that were labeled "White Lilly," and the tag line on the flour sacks was "None Better." A black woman who lived nearby at Knightly made underpants out of one of the flour sacks and showed off her bottom, which said "None Better."

Daniel was instrumental in getting a bridge over Middle River at the Knightly Mill. He viewed a bridge as essential for growing the business of the mill. Below, local politicians visit the bridge site to monitor construction. Daniel is standing in the center of the Knightly Steel Truss Bridge (STB) built by the Champion Bridge Co. of Wilmington, Ohio. It is a single-span, pin-connected camelback Pratt truss bridge, which carries Route 778 across Middle River just south of Knightly. The bridge is 182 feet long and was one of five STB bridges across Middle River.

Knightly Bridge (Structure No. 6149) under Construction, 1915
Daniel S. Garber stands in the center. The Knightly Mill is in the background.

Rebuilt Humbert-Knightly Mill, photograph taken in 1870s
Note the wagons full of wheat waiting to be unloaded.

In 1912, Daniel sold a one-third interest in the mill company for $4,000 to his son Minor because he did not like the dust associated with the milling business. Minor Garber's interest included the land, the water rights, the dam rights, the miller's house and the flour warehouse on the land of the Valley Railroad near Ft. Defiance Depot. About 1916, Minor Garber installed two dynamos in the mill to generate electricity and built an electrical distribution system in the Mt. Sidney, Ft. Defiance and New Hope areas. He employed Ralph Gordon to work in the mill and Ralph's son, George Gordon, to help run the electric business. He acquired the remaining interest for $8,000 on March 12, 1925, when the mill was called the Knightly Light and Power Company, Inc. The mill produced electricity while continuing to grind flour. It is believed that the residents of Mt. Sidney and Ft. Defiance were provided electrical service within a few years. Parts of the New Hope area were not provided electrical service until 1927 because not enough residents would subscribe a sufficient amount of money to help build the line.

The period 1910 to 1940 was a time of rural electrification efforts in America and consolidation in the electric power industry. On December 5, 1931, Minor Garber sold all the property, real, personal, mixed, franchises, contracts, rights of way, easements, privileges, buildings, machinery and equipment to the Virginia Public Service Company. About 1940, Virginia Power discontinued flour milling operations and power generating and razed the buildings, but it retained the land and water and dam rights. Virginia Public Service bought the mill for its distribution system and used it mainly for reserve power until World War II. Virginia Public Service subsequently became Virginia Electric Power and then Virginia Power of Dominion Resources.

SOURCES: The material for this section was partly based on the book *My Augusta* by C. E. May, 1987, and on an interview conducted with Catherine Garber Crist, daughter of Minor Garber, at her house in Harrisonburg, Virginia, on January 15, 2004.

Minor Garber working at the Knightly Mill, c1912
(L to R: Ralph Gordon, Minor Garber)

The Deaths of Daniel and Lizzie

Obituary *Staunton News-Leader*
Garber, Daniel S., of Ft. Defiance, Virginia, was born near Mt. Sidney, Virginia, Aug. 22, 1855, departed this life, Dec. 30, 1923, aged 68 years, 4 months and 8 days. He was the third son of Elder Levi and Barbara Miller Garber. On March 9, 1879, he was married to Lizzie M. Glick, of Weyers Cave, Virginia. To this union were born three sons and four daughters. He united with the Church of the Brethren at the age of fifteen, and was called to the deacon's office ten years later; which office he filled in a most creditable manner. His counsel and good judgment were frequently sought. His exemplary life in the home, in the community and in the church is worthy of the highest esteem. For several years his health had not been good. Dec. 30 he succumbed to a severe attack of Bright's disease, passing without pain, peacefully into the realm of the departed. He is survived by his widow, two daughters, three sons, nine grandchildren, one brother Elder Peter Garber of Weyers Cave and four sisters.

Garber
Daniel S.
Aug. 22, 1855 - Dec. 30, 1923

Elizabeth M., His Wife
Aug. 26, 1860 - Mar. 8, 1949

"Let our fathers will be done."

Note: Buried at Middle River Cemetery, New Hope, Virginia.

After Daniel's death, his personal property was offered for sale at a public auction as evidenced below.

C. H. HILBERT, Auctioneer

PUBLIC SALE

=== OF SOME VALUABLE ===

PERSONAL PROPERTY

Having decided to make sale, we will sell at public auction, on the premises of the late Daniel S. Garber, 3 miles east of Fort Defiance, Va., on the Knightly Mill road, on

Wednesday, March 26, 1924

AT TEN O'CLOCK, A. M.

The following personal property: Two Republic one-ton trucks, in good running condition; one 125-gallon gas tank and pump, two ice hooks, some quarry tools, drills and hammers, shovels and picks, one good gas drum, four good oil drums, several oil barrels, one road wagon and bed, in good condition; one sleigh, two Oliver plows, pair of double trees, one neck yoke, one mower, one pair of scales, one ascetyline drum, two sets of small pulley blocks, one corn scoop, one riding saddle, one buggy pole, one cultivator, one double shovel plow, one single shovel plow, one stretcher, two iron wheels for low wagon, two pair work harness, one pair check lines, two work bridles, one pair buggy harness, one work collar, some other harness and collars, one 4-prong fork, one cutting box, two good Jersey cows, two pair breast chains, one grind

H. F. GARBER
M. W. GARBER | Executors

THE McCLURE COMPANY, INC., PRINTERS, STAUNTON, VA.

Public Sale Notice

Daniel's wife, Elizabeth "Lizzie" Margaret Glick Garber, passed away March 8, 1949. She died at her house at Knightly and had received good care from Ada and Cora, her daughters. Her memorial service was held at Middle River Church of the Brethren where she was a member for many years. The inspirational memorial message was written and delivered by Floyd Mitchell.

A Message from a Flower

We have gathered here this afternoon in a memorial service for our departed Sister. Our purpose is not to exalt her life, for nothing that we say or do can change any part of the life which has so recently departed. Her life has been its own witness, and you know that better than I. Our purpose here is to bring a message to the living that we who have not yet reached this stage might be prepared to receive the rewards which it offers. Our presence here and all these flowers symbolize our love and appreciation for the life of Sister Garber. These beautiful flowers are certainly a high tribute to her, for she was a great lover of flowers. Each Sunday that she was able to attend Church, she brought along a beautiful flower. Visit her home and there were always beautiful flowers all around. She loved flowers very much.

Thus in this memorial service there is nothing more appropriate for us to think about than flowers – for flowers symbolize the life which has gone on, and present to us in a parable form a great message of inspiration for our own lives.

> We muse on miracles who look
> But lightly on a rose!
> Who gives it fragrance or the flint
> Of glory that it shows?
>
> Who holds it here between the sky
> And earth's rain-softened sod?
> The miracle of one pale rose
> Is proof enough of God.
> –Edith Daley

Each flower speaks to us a message if we but take time off "from the maddening maze of things" and see its parable of life.

A flower in the springtime shoots forth new life from the quiet dead earth. The sun-warmed and rain-moistened earth sends forth new life. That life grows and in its season buds forth, swells and blossoms. It then is an object of beauty and admiration; its fragrance is wonderful and sweet, and we mortals gaze with satisfaction upon its splendor. But the bloom however beautiful is also fragile and frail. And no matter how much we admire its splendor soon it will begin to fade and finally wither away. We are sorry to see its beauty go; we miss it dearly, but go we know it must. But then we notice again, and there where once was a lovely bloom is now a seed. Thus we are made to realize that the flower is not dead, but has only entered into another life, from whence it will continue to live in beauty and loveliness.

Life is as a flower. We are born into a world, not by any wish of our own, but because of a divine plan of God. We grow into life and develop into a personality of beauty. Life blossoms forth with beauty, enjoyment and happiness. But like the flower of nature, God has ordained that the flower will wither and fade away. We mourn the passing of the flower, which was so dear to us for we "recall the glorious companionship we've had." But as we lower the past physical bloom into the earth, we know that this is not the end, but only a change in the form of life; from that of physical to that of spiritual; from that which was temporary to that which is permanent; from that which has faded to that of new and eternal beauty.

Christ gave comfort to those who mourn the passing of their loved ones in these words: "Let not your heart be troubled, ye believe in God, believe also in me. In my Father's house are many mansions: if it were not so, I would have told you. I go to prepare a place for you. And if I go and prepare a place for you, I will come again, and receive you unto myself; that where I am, there ye may be also." John 14:1-4. Flowers that have followed the plan of nature have a life that lives on after the passing of the bloom, and so with life. If life is lived according to the divine plan of God there will be a life which lives on after the passing of this physical bloom.

Mrs. Garber would always bring her flower along to Church with her. During the service she would often look at that flower, as if it spoke to her a message – and that it did, and thus it does to each of us if we but observe. When she arrived at Church the flower was always fresh cut, pert, beautiful and fragrant. But during the service frequently the bloom would begin to wither and fade, until before very long its beauty would be gone, and it was then discarded. And like the flower which she loved, she, though once in the beauty of the blossom of life, now has withered and faded away. The body she has now discarded for it has served its purpose, but life goes on. She has now returned unto God from whence she came. "The spirit shall return unto God who gave it."

We go from God to God – then though
The way be long,
We shall return to Heaven our home
At evensong.

We go from God to God – so let
The space between
Be filled with beauty, conquering
Things base and mean.

We go from God to God – Lo! What
Transcendent bliss
To know the journey's end will hold
Such joy as this!
–Evelyn Healey

So may we live that when our summons comes to join those who have gone on before, we will be ready to go, and prepared to receive the rewards which God has in store for us. May the bloom of our lives have prepared a soul that will live on eternally with our Father in Heaven.

Message by Floyd H. Mitchell
Pastor at Middle River Church of the Brethren

Daniel and Lizzie Garber's Picture Story

Sitting on the Back Porch, c1902
Daniel and Lizzie, Ada and Cora Garber

Elizabeth "Lizzie" Glick Garber, c1900

Ada R. Garber, c1899

Ada and New Husband, David Reed, 1902

Young Couples
(Standing) Ralph and Lena Gordon, Anthony Garber and Ada Early
(Sitting) David and Ada Garber Reed, 1903

Anthony Garber with His New Bride
Ada Early Garber, c1904

Minor Garber Plowing, c1905

Five Garber Maidens, All First Cousins, c1906
(Standing) Lena, Rebecca, Anna Rebecca, (Sitting) Sarah Catherine and Ida

Farmer Daniel Garber with Virginia Fruit, c1907

Garber Ladies, 1910
(BR) Ada Garber Reed, Cora Garber and Martha Garber
(FR) Sallie Reed Garber, Rena Western (Garber) and Ada Early Garber

Martha Garber Slonaker, c1913

Wedding Picture, 1913
Martha Garber & Roy Slonaker

Daniel Garber Farmstead at Knightly, 1912

Four Generations of Garbers in the Fields Making Hay, 1913

Lizzie Garber Feeding the Chickens, 1916

Lizzie Garber Feeding the Cow and Chickens, 1916

Daniel and Lizzie Eating Watermelon, c1917

Daniel and Lizzie Garber in the Buggy, 1920

The Garber Family, c1920
(L-R) Anthony, Ada, Daniel, Homer, Lizzie, Minor and Cora Garber

Daniel and Lizzie Garber's Grandchildren, c1920
(Standing) Harold, Noah, Ruth, Pauline, Clarence and Cleatis Garber
(Sitting) Paul, Daniel, Margaret, Lizzie and Catherine Garber

Grandchildren Margaret and Catherine Garber, 1923

Brothers and Sisters, August 21, 1923
(BR) Joe and Barbara Garber Norford, Nancy Garber Moomaw, Enos and Becky Garber
(FR) Jacob and Lydia Garber Flory, Peter Garber, Daniel and Lizzie Garber

Daniel S. Garber's School Bus (One of the First in Augusta County), 1920

Grandchildren Playing
(L-R) Catherine, Margaret, Cleatis and Harold Garber, c1925

Daniel and Lizzie Garber House at Knightly, c1940

Lizzie Garber and Children, October 28, 1942
(BR) Minor, Anthony and Homer Garber
(FR) Ada Garber Reed, Lizzie and Cora Garber

Homer Franklin Garber & Sallie Belle Reed

Wedding Clothes, 1909
(L) Charles and Mary Early Wampler, (R) Homer and Sallie Garber

Glimpses of Homer and Sallie Garber

Homer Franklin Garber, the fourth child of Daniel and Lizzie Garber, was born August 12, 1886, and died 1973. He attended Centennial Public School through the sixth grade. The public school operated only about five months of the year to allow students to help plant and harvest crops on the farm. As a teenager, he worked both on the family farm and in his father's Knightly Flour Mill but did not like millwork because of the dust. After finishing school, he worked for Daniel on the farm. In 1909, Homer and Sallie Belle Reed fell in love and eloped with another couple, Charles and Mary Early Wampler to Hagerstown, Maryland. On October 25, 1909, he married Sallie Belle Reed, who was born 1887 and died 1989 and was the daughter of John and Amanda Shiflet Reed. The picture on the previous page presents the two couples in their wedding clothes.

Black Rock Spring, August 1909
(L) Homer and Sallie Garber (C) Ben and Lena Reed (R) Minor and Rena Garber

After the honeymoon, Homer continued to operate the family farm and bought it in 1910 for $10,162 from his parents, Daniel and Lizzie Garber. However, the title was not conveyed until April 1, 1915. This was the same farm that Homer's great-grandfather, Jacob Garber, had won for one dollar in the 1843 land lottery.

To Homer and Sallie Garber were born three sons and two daughters to include:

1. Cleatis Franklin b 1911 m 1942 Doris Elizabeth Miller b 1921. Two children.
   Second marriage to Nancy Moore 1986.
2. Harold Lavern b 1912 d 2002 m 1937 Norma Isabelle Fisher b 1918 d 1998. Three children.
3. Paul Wilson b 1913 d 2001 m 1942 Ruby Elizabeth Sipe b 1919. Three children.
4. Margaret Elizabeth b 1915 d 1981 m 1940 Walter Wesley Woodside, Sr. b 1916 d 1983. Three children.
5. Anna Lee "Dolly" Virginia b 1928 m 1948 Owen Early Harner b 1929. Five children.

After selling the farm in 1928, Homer lived on a nine-acre farmstead near New Hope. He worked for the Knightly and Ft. Defiance Mills as a truck driver delivering flour to Richmond and North Carolina, ran a grocery store with his son Paul and worked as a finish carpenter for a small Waynesboro house contractor. Sallie was a homemaker and worked in the New Hope Grocery store with Homer and Paul. In 1950, they bought a house in Waynesboro, Virginia, and Sallie pursued arts and crafts.

Homer was not a strong leader or particularly ambitious, but he worked hard and provided for his family. He was about 5'8" tall, a muscular 185 lb. man with black hair and brown eyes. Homer smoked a pipe and cigarettes, chewed apple tobacco, never cursed, read the newspaper and Bible, played checkers, never wrote letters, sometimes told jokes and enjoyed repairing and building things since he was a "jack-of-all-trades." Homer loved Sallie; he was henpecked and did what Sallie wanted. He was an even-tempered, relaxed individual, easy to get along with, a neat dresser, literal minded, never argumentative, frequently stubborn, thrifty and rarely stern or angry. Homer had no creative or artistic talents, was strong in faith, was both serious and lighthearted, rarely got in a hurry, and was humble, honest and modest.

Sallie was 5'4" tall, weighed 135 lbs. and was a pretty woman with black hair and brown eyes. She was bossy with Homer and the kids, never read, did not particularly like housework, cooked until her later years, liked to stay up late and watch wrestling on TV and sleep late, was materialistic, wanted new things and liked stylish clothes with colorful hats and costume jewelry. Sallie played canasta and Chinese checkers, sang and played the piano and enjoyed gardening. Her special ability was arts and crafts, which she did not develop until she and Homer moved to Waynesboro, Virginia. At age 65, Sallie became a "Grandma Moses" by painting flower/bird pictures, painting collectibles and metal trays, making handbags and refinishing furniture. Homer supported her artistic pursuits by making or repairing furniture and picture frames. Sallie was a willing worker, sometimes a perfectionist and a spendthrift, frequently a stern disciplinarian, demanding of self, hard to please, frequently argumentative, sometimes moody and frequently stubborn. Sallie was strong in faith, rarely worried but serious, never lazy, sometimes lighthearted, frequently nervous, rarely thrifty, rarely egotistical, honest, not modest or humble and a neat dresser.

In 1959, Homer and Sallie celebrated their golden wedding anniversary with a large family gathering at their Waynesboro home on Wayne Avenue. It was a joyous occasion with all of their children and grandchildren present. Around 1972, Homer and Sallie sold their Wayne Avenue home and had an auction to sell their household belongings. Antique dealers were present in force to buy Sallie's handicrafts and collectibles. Homer was getting weaker and entered a nursing home, where he died October 14, 1973. He lived 87 years and two days and had a good quality of life until his last four months. Sallie rented an apartment several blocks away from their Wayne Avenue house for several years, then moved to the Bridgewater Retirement Community and began teaching handicrafts to the residents. She was in good health until she lost her eyesight due to an operation on her retinas. Then her health began to decline, and she lost the will to live. Sallie lived to be 101 years six months and 21 days but the quality of her life the last seven to eight years was not good. She died April 13, 1989.

Homer and Sallie Garber's 50th Wedding Anniversary, 1959

Obituary for Homer F. Garber, *Waynesboro News-Leader* (Tuesday, October 16, 1973)
Homer Franklin Garber, 87, a well-known resident of Waynesboro, who made his home at 615 14th Street, died at 10:30 PM Sunday evening at the Staunton Manor Nursing Home in Staunton. He had been in ill health for the past five years and had been a resident of the Staunton Manor Nursing Home since March 9, 1972.

A son of the late Daniel S. and Elizabeth Glick Garber, he was born on Aug. 12, 1886, at Mt. Sidney where he lived his early life. He later lived near the New Hope community for 20 years and had been making his home in Waynesboro for the past 24 years. Mr. Garber farmed in his early life and operated a mercantile business at New Hope for 11 years. He had been associated with the Ft. Defiance Mill and in later years was a carpenter and cabinetmaker.

Mr. Garber was a life long member of the Middle River Church of the Brethren, where he was a former Sunday school teacher and former Deacon. He was also a member of the Reserve Police Force of Waynesboro and the Waynesboro chapter of the A.A.R.P.

On Oct. 25, 1909, he married the former Miss Sallie Reed, who survives him. Besides his wife, he is survived by five children, Cleatis F. Garber of Saigon; Harold L. Garber of Waynesboro; Paul W. Garber of Route 1, Waynesboro; Mrs. W. W. (Margaret) Woodside of Arlington; and Mrs. Owen (Dolly) Harner of Route 1, Ft. Defiance. Also surviving are 16 grandchildren; 13 great-grandchildren; and one sister, Miss Cora Garber of Harrisonburg.

Funeral services will be held at eleven o'clock Wednesday morning from the Middle River Church of the Brethren with the Rev. Tom Fralin in charge of the services. Burial will be in the adjacent cemetery. His body now rests at the Lindsey and Koontz Funeral home at Weyers Cave where the members of the family will receive friends from 7:30 until 8:30 this (Tuesday) evening. His body will be taken to the Church to remain for an hour prior to the services, and relatives, friends, and active and honorary pallbearers are asked to meet at the Church at 10:45 Wednesday morning. Active pallbearers will be Harold L. Garber, Jr.; Frederic C. Garber; David Garber; Wayne E. Garber; Walter W. Woodside, Jr.; James O. Harner; and Michael G. Harner.

Obituary for Sallie Belle Garber, 101, *Waynesboro News-Leader* (Died April 13, 1989)
Sallie Belle Garber, 101, widow of Homer F. Garber, and a resident of the Waynesboro and New Hope communities for a number of years, died at 4:35 Thursday morning at the Bridgewater Home where she had made her home for the last 13 years.

She was born Sept. 23, 1887, in the Laurel Hill area of Augusta County, the daughter of the late John R. and Amanda Elizabeth Shiflet Reed. She had formerly resided at Mount Sidney and New Hope prior to moving to Waynesboro. She was a member of the Middle River Church of the Brethren, the New Hope and Waynesboro Home Extension Clubs for over fifty years, and the Waynesboro Women's Club. She was also a member of the Council of Organizations for the Woodrow Wilson Rehabilitation Center. On Oct. 25, 1909, she married Homer F. Garber, who preceded her in death on Oct. 14, 1973.

Mrs. Garber is survived by sons, Cleatis F. Garber of Falls Church; and Harold L. and Paul W. Garber, both of Waynesboro. She also leaves one daughter, Dolly Harner of New Hope; 16 grandchildren; and 35 great-grandchildren. A daughter, Mrs. Margaret Woodside, preceded her mother, Mrs. Garber, in death in April 1981.

Funeral services will be held at two o'clock Saturday afternoon in the Middle River Church of the Brethren. Her pastor, the Rev. Dennis L. Brown, will conduct the services and burial will be in the adjacent cemetery. Her body now rests at the Lindsey Weyers Cave Funeral Home where friends may call, but the family will receive friends in the parlor of the Middle River Church of the Brethren one o'clock until one-forty-five Saturday afternoon.

Homer and Sallie Garber are buried at Middle River Cemetery, New Hope, Virginia.

Homer and Sallie Garber's Headstone

Jacob Garber Lottery Farm Deed History
Buttermilk Road, Augusta County, Virginia

Grantees	Deed Book	Page	Date Conveyed	Acreage	Price & Grantors
Jacob Garber	64	63	6-15-1843	151	Presented a $1 receipt (lottery ticket) for homestead of John & Elizabeth Miller. Adjoins land of George Shreckhise, William Bull and others.
Levi Garber	104	553	3-15-1887	?	Cutting and opening ditches on the land of Mary Garber for the purpose of laying piping for the construction of a hydraulic water ram to convey water from the creek running through her lands to the premises of Levi Garber (dam not more than two feet high). Mary Garber was granted wagon right-of-way over Levi's land.
D. S. Garber and Lizzie M. (wife)	109	44	3-24-1890	145.75	Purchased from Levi Garber, for $8,000, Tract 1 $2547 down, conveyed with water rights.
Homer Garber & Sallie B. Reed (wife)	180	131	4-1-1915	141	Purchased from Daniel Garber for $10,162 cash (112, 27, & 2 acres) $963 down, bond $1700 payable to Annie R. Garber by 4-1-1916 (Paid 5-17-1921) and 15 payments of $500 each, totaling $7500
K. A. Harman	318	39	4-5-1943		Harman purchased the farm in 1928 from Homer Garber for about $10,000 but evidently the deed was not recorded until 4-5-1943 (Author's note)
John R. Kegley,	378	184	8-3-1950		Purchased from K. A. Harman, Sr., and Celia M. Blankenship
John R. Kegley, Sr. and Victoria M. (wife)	408	54	2-19-1955		Land adjoins W. C. Wampler, H. R. Shreckhise and others
John R. Kegley, Jr. and Ruth S. (wife)	809	459	12-28-1983	121.57	$128K Kegley, Sr., Died 7-18-1980

Source: The writer researched and typed the property deed history in January 2005 from the original deeds located in the deed books at the Augusta County Courthouse, Staunton, Virginia.

Early Glimpses of Family Life of Homer and Sallie Garber
Period of Time 1910-1930

The story began when Homer Garber and Sallie Reed fell in love and eloped in 1909. They drove a buckboard to Staunton, Virginia, and took a train to Hagerstown, Maryland, where they got married. Before their marriage, Sallie had been a seamstress in Staunton making clothes and curtains. Homer had been working on the farm for Daniel Garber, his father. In 1910, Homer and Sallie bought the Levi Garber family farm (the land was conveyed in 1915) from Daniel and Lizzie Garber, his parents. The farm was located 1.5 miles from Mt. Sidney, Virginia, on the Buttermilk Road. During the period 1910 to 1928, they lived on the farm, operated a typical farming operation with livestock, crops and apple orchard and reared their four children, Cleatis, Harold, Paul and Margaret. Their fifth child, Dolly, was born in the farmhouse, but was reared near New Hope, Virginia.

Homer and Sally Garber's Farmhouse, Built c1840

Homer and Sallie earned a living by growing corn, wheat, oats, clover and timothy hay for horses; maintaining horses to work the fields, raising cows and calves; selling calves/yearlings after weaning, keeping 6-10 milking cows and selling milk to the Staunton Creamery. In addition, the family had a 25-acre apple orchard, a one-acre vegetable garden and raised sheep from 1925 to 1928. The barn had stables for 14 horses, one hay mow and one wheat mow. In 1918, Homer bought one of the first tractors in the area, a Fordson tractor with a hand crank that would break one's arm if they were not careful. As a result of having a tractor, he reduced to three the number of horses he kept.

The family farmhouse was built before the Civil War of frame construction, had 14 rooms with end chimneys, fireplaces upstairs and down and a smokehouse on one end. Wood stoves were used to cook and coal stoves provided heat. Kerosene oil lamps provided lighting until 1917. The washhouse was a separate house still standing in 2007. Levi Garber, Homer's grandfather, and his daughter Becky lived independently in the left wing addition to the original farmhouse with Homer, Sallie and family in the main part of the house. After Levi died, the left wing was torn down, and Aunt Becky went to live with Joe and Barbara Garber Norford. Homer and Sallie sold the farm in 1928 to Kimmel A. Harman, who sold it in 1943 to John R. Kegley, Sr. The Kegleys allowed the kitchen part of the house to be torn down in the 1970s by Buddy Gordon, who used the logs for a cabin along Middle River. It is unknown what happened to the main part of the house.

The Garber Washhouse, c1840, Picture Taken Feb. 2004

Homer and Sallie's children grew up speaking English because neither Homer nor Sallie was allowed to learn any German. Through the fifth grade, the children attended the Centennial Elementary School, which was a half mile from the house on Buttermilk Road and the same school that Homer had attended. The kids walked to the Centennial School, but for the sixth grade, Cleatis and the boys drove a horse and buggy to the Mt. Sidney School. For the seventh grade, the boys walked to Knightly and then rode the school bus to the New Hope School. Daniel Garber, their grandfather, drove the school bus that was one of the first buses (about 1918) in Augusta County.

A big part of the family's social life was attending church and Sunday school at Middle River Church of the Brethren. Abraham Garber, Homer's great-great-grandfather, founded the church in 1824. The Garber Family Reunion was a July 4th picnic that was held at Gypsy Hill Park in Staunton or on various farms. The family did have a radio and occasionally Homer and Sallie would take the kids to Staunton to see a black and white silent movie. The movies cost 25 cents each, and everyone liked Westerns. The family also subscribed to the "Stockman Journal," a farm magazine with a serial story about Indian life in America. Homer was the best speller and reader, so he would read the stories to the family gathered in the front living room. There was little time for recreational pursuits like fishing and hunting (No county or state hunting/fishing regulations existed). In general, the family always had plenty to eat but no money.

Strict discipline governed the Garber household. Children were disciplined for minor infractions such as speaking out of turn and talking back to adults. The rules were "Do what you are told and don't ask questions." and "Children are to be seen, not heard, when in public." Sallie was a sometimes volatile and emotional parent, but Homer was more consistent. Cleatis' last switching was due to Sallie's insistence. Homer told Cleatis to go to the apple orchard and cut a shoot for a switch. Cleatis complied with the request and cut a large switch and notched it with his very sharp pocket knife. Homer began to administer the punishment behind the chicken house near the orchard, but the switch broke twice where it had been notched. Homer quickly figured out what Cleatis had done and began to laugh. That was the end of corporal punishment for Cleatis.

Household chores were assigned to various members of the family. For Cleatis, household chores started in 1918, when he was seven years old and Homer and Sallie were in bed with the flu epidemic. He helped manage the farm by feeding and currying the horses. Harold's routine chore was chopping wood and Paul's was washing dishes. Margaret was smaller and did very little, but all the children cleaned, mopped and dusted. Homer and Sallie tended the garden and Sallie prepared meals. Sallie also made the children's clothes when they were small. An outside woman washed the clothes using a tub and washboard and ironed the clothes. When nightfall came, the family went to bed after the dishes were done.

Traveling during the early 20th-century was not pleasant even though the family lived only 1.5 miles from Route 11, which they used to travel to Staunton and Harrisonburg. The Valley Pike (Route 11) was the first paved road in America and was macadamized about the 1850s. The nearest town was Mt. Sidney, which did not have any streetlights, sidewalks or parks. Cleatis remembers a trip to the Brethren Annual Conference in Hershey, Pennsylvania, in a Model T-Ford that took two to three days one way. The family also went to Blacksburg for a week every summer to visit the agricultural school and attend classes about farming. Homer and Sallie wanted the boys to understand how to farm profitably since the social hierarchy were landowners like the Garbers, tenant farmers and laborers. However, Cleatis, Harold and Paul found farm work boring, and they wanted to do something else in life. Cleatis would daydream about hunting when doing farm work.

Sallie always wanted the latest innovations of the day, whether or not Homer could afford them. They were the first in the area to have a party line telephone in 1910. At Sallie's insistence, they were one of the first area families in 1917 to have the house electrified for lights. Around 1920, they installed indoor plumbing and running water. These changes had the greatest impact on the family, community and country. Homer and Sallie were also one of the first to get a new car, a 1918 Model T-Ford. Homer usually drove the car since Sallie was a terrible driver and was known for her accidents. Her most spectacular accident was on Route 11 near Burktown, between Harrisonburg and Staunton, when she wrecked the Essex car, which had recently replaced the Model T-Ford, when carrying a load of baby chickens. It must have been quite a sight and quite a mess.

The family was definitely aware of the "Roaring Twenties" as flappers changed the social structure by raising dress hems and popularizing hats. Sallie had a sense of style and did not like the long skirts worn by most of the Mennonite and Brethren women, so she wore short skirts. She also liked hats, brightly colored clothes, facial powder and perfume water. The family was also aware of Prohibition, but it did not impact them since all Brethren were forbidden to drink. Sallie was a member of the Temperance Movement and carried a protest sign in a Staunton parade. The predominant hairstyle was a part down the middle and Homer cut the boys hair on the side with sheep shears. Montgomery Ward's mail order catalog store in Baltimore, Maryland, was used for many purchases to include shoes, socks, coats and the purchase of a 12-gauge, single barrel Iver Johnson shotgun for $10.

Cleatis has a number of family childhood memories. Around 1917, a woman committed suicide by wearing a big, full heavy skirt and jumping from the Knightly Bridge. The story was that she and her husband were not getting along well. The family rode to church in a horse-drawn road wagon with snow skids in place of the wheels due to a three-foot deep snowstorm that had paralyzed the area. During thunderstorms sparks would fly across the living room from the two brass bells on the front of the telephone. The family stayed cool in the summertime by sitting under a shade tree in the front yard and using hand fans. The family went to the Johnson Brothers store at Mt. Sidney or the Fretwell General Merchandise store at New Hope every Saturday night with eggs, chickens and rabbits that were converted to cash by the store. With the cash received, the family bought staples such as sugar, salt, coffee and spices. In the early summer, the cattle were taken to graze in the mountains east of Harriston, Virginia. Motten Marshall, a big bootlegger who was not discovered until the early 1930s, owned the grazing land.

A couple of Civil War stories were handed down in the family. The first story involved Federal troops that came to the farmhouse during a big snowstorm. One member of the family was very sick and the family was concerned that the troops might burn down the house. The sick person was wrapped in blankets and buried in a snowdrift to keep warm. Then in the 1880s, a five-gallon lard can full of flax was found in a secret attic of the house where it had been hidden during the Civil War. In the 1920s, Ada Garber Reed and Cora Garber made linen from the flax that had been grown on the Levi Garber farm. Cora stored the linen doilies in her hope chest where they remained until her death since she never married. Catherine Garber Crist found the doilies and gave one to Wayne Garber in December 1991.

In 1928, the farm was sold and the family moved to a new house in New Hope, Virginia. The children then walked to New Hope High School. The school operated 9:00 AM to 3:00 PM from September through May. Subjects offered included Civics, Geometry, Algebra, History, English and Latin. The school assigned lots of homework to include reading, math and book reports. Most of the boys wore overalls and casual clothes including knickers with long stockings. School holidays included Thanksgiving, Christmas, New Year's, Washington's and Lincoln's birthdays. The main rule at the school was "no fighting." School sports activities were limited to baseball and basketball. Cleatis and Paul played baseball, and Paul also played basketball. Harold was the studious type and did not play sports.

Source: The story line is based on an interview conducted on November 18, 2003, by Wayne Garber with Cleatis Garber, son of Homer and Sallie Garber, at his house in Waynesboro, Virginia.

Glimpses of Family Life of Homer and Sallie Garber
Period of Time 1930-1950

This part of the story began when Anna Lee "Dolly" Garber was born March 24, 1928, in the old Levi Garber farmhouse near Mt. Sidney, Virginia. Shortly after her birth, Homer and Sallie Garber, her parents, moved to a new homestead on Route 608 (Battlefield Drive) about one-quarter mile from New Hope, Virginia, beside Dolly's present home. Dolly's older siblings Cleatis, Harold, Paul and Margaret soon graduated from New Hope High School and left home to work in Washington, DC. Dolly was 13 years younger than her sister, Margaret, so she was reared like an only child.

When Homer and Sallie first moved to New Hope, their new house had not been completed, so they lived in the garage for nine months. The boys slept in the garage loft, a temporary kitchen was set up and the family existed with their furniture stored in the garage. The new house was built of frame construction on nine acres of land and had six rooms including three bedrooms and one and a half baths. The homestead also had a three-bay garage, a garden and a chicken house. The lawn was nicely landscaped with shrubbery, trees and a circular fishpond with a Little Black Sambo figurine fishing for goldfish.

The Great Depression era was a very tough time for most people in America; however, Sallie always wanted everything modern whether Homer could afford it or not. Dolly never knew poverty as evidenced by the fact that she was given piano lessons for eight years and a $2500 player piano so she could practice her lessons. After giving up farming, Homer supported the family from 1928 to 1941 by driving a flour truck for the Ft. Defiance Mill, which was owned by Joe Norford. Sallie rented Dolly's bedroom to Mr. Edmondson, a school-teacher at New Hope High School, so Dolly slept in a closet on a single bed when she was four and five years old. For spending money, Sallie raised chickens for 10 years. Dolly's chores were gathering eggs, feeding the chickens, washing dishes and locking the basement door because Sallie was afraid that someone might break

New Hope Home, Built 1928, Picture Taken c1945

into the house at night through the basement. The family's purchases often were previously-owned property. Dolly's first and only bike was a used bicycle that Homer bought for $10 from Frank Willberger's sister.

The Middle River Church of the Brethren was the center of the family's social life. The family's weekend routine was to run errands or work around the house on Saturday and go to church on Sunday. After church, Homer would take a nap before driving the family to Grandmother Amanda Shiflet Reed's house at Mt. Sidney near the railroad track on the Buttermilk Road. Sometimes they would go to Grandmother Lizzie Garber's house. The family social life also included Christmas celebrations, Garber Family Reunions at different Brethren churches and picnics in the summer.

Growing up as an only child was not easy for Dolly because there was not much to do. She did have a favorite toy, a doll and carriage, and a best friend, Mary Ellen Western (now married to Thomas Smiley). For entertainment at night the family would listen to Amos and Andy on the radio. Dolly had no pets and only one birthday party that she remembers - a wiener roast in the woods behind the house when she was about 13 years old. At age 16, she went to the movies in Staunton on Saturdays with her friend, Wanda Grove. Her favorite movie was "Gone with the Wind" and her heroes were movie stars. In the summer, the family would visit Clarence Garber at his Maryland cottage on the Chesapeake Bay where they boated and fished. Wanda Grove's family invited Dolly as a teenager to go with them to Virginia Beach. She also attended church camp for several summers.

Dolly has a number of vivid childhood memories. When Sallie had a hysterectomy, she remembers being shipped to Aunt Ada and Cora's house and learning their daily routine. They would listen in on telephone calls on the 20+ family party phone line, write in their diaries, stop everything at 10 minutes to 9:00 PM to watch the clock jump to nine o'clock and take warm rocks to bed to keep warm.

Sisters Ada Garber Reed and Cora Garber took care of Elizabeth "Lizzie" Garber, Dolly's grandmother. Lizzie was a 95-pound woman who wore long, out-of-style dresses and who would get on the floor and roll up into a ball because she was proud that she possessed the flexibility to do it at her advanced age. Every morning Lizzie drank a cup of warm water with salt in it. When they went to church, Lizzie would cut fresh flowers and put them in a bud vase on the dash of the 1925 Model T-Ford car that Cora drove. Lizzie always sat in the front seat and Ada in the back seat. Each of the ladies carried their pocketbooks in paper bags for protection and Cora took extra church shoes. The best part of staying at Ada and Cora's house was the whipped cream pies with ginger snap crust. When Dolly was 13, she remembers the bombing of Pearl Harbor and World War II being declared by President Franklin Roosevelt and the U.S. Congress.

As a child, Dolly had several memorable experiences with death. A major event happened in New Hope in 1934 when a boat sank on Middle River. Three men went over the Ft. Defiance Mill dam in a small boat during a flood. One man drowned and the body (found two weeks later) was Charles Early, Owen Harner's uncle. When Dolly was a little girl, she learned that dead bodies were taken to the funeral home for embalming. The body was then returned to the home for three days and someone sat with the body around the clock. Sitting with a dead body was a scary thought for her. As a 14-year-old girl, Dolly and two girlfriends were boating at Ft. Defiance Mill on Middle River, when they found the body of a retarded 15-year-old boy who had been missing for about a week. Dolly discovered the body by hitting it with her paddle.

Ft. Defiance Mill Dam, 2004

Dolly attended the New Hope School for elementary and high school. She walked one quarter mile to school. She liked history and disliked math. In high school, she played a rented trumpet in the band and performed at school functions. She also played on the basketball team. Her favorite clothes were skirts, sweaters and saddle shoes. Her dream was to be a swimmer like Esther Williams. She blames Cleatis and Paul for her not being able to swim because when she was trying to learn to swim at Clarence's cottage on the Chesapeake Bay, they would turn her loose and she would sink like a rock or the waves would fill her mouth with saltwater.

Dolly did not get into mischief very often. She was never spanked, but she did get several tongue lashings from Sallie for saying something in public. The main rules were to respect your parents, no sassing and one could not offer a different opinion. Homer and Sallie were also strict about dating. They had to know the boy's family and the family must have the "right name" for Dolly to be allowed to date him. Dolly learned an important lesson from Sallie that she has applied in later life; she has not dictated or dominated her children the way that Sallie did. An example is that Dolly wanted to be a nurse, but Sallie decided that she should be a schoolteacher. So Dolly attended Madison College for one and a half years and taught 4th and 6th grades at Crimora Elementary School from 1946 to 1948 because her mother wanted her to teach. She hated teaching, so she stopped and began a family. In 1977, Dolly fulfilled one of her dreams when she became a License Practical Nurse (LPN). She worked at King's Daughters Hospital and Oak Hill Nursing Home for four years.

In 1939, Paul Garber, her brother, returned from the Washington area where he had been a grocery store manager and had opened the first self-serve supermarket for Acme Foods. Homer and Paul bought the New Hope Grocery store and the business was called "H. F. Garber & Son, General Merchandise." Homer, Paul and Sallie operated the store for 11 years (1939 to 1951). In 1950, Homer and Sallie sold their New Hope house because Sallie wanted to go to Waynesboro due to some health concerns. Homer had ulcers that required three fourths of his stomach to be removed and Sallie had arthritis in her hands. Paul had bought 128 acres called "Green Acre Farm" three miles north of Waynesboro on the White Bridge Road and wanted to begin farming.

Homer and Sallie bought a white asbestos-shingle house on Wayne Avenue in Waynesboro. They began receiving Social Security payments from the federal government and did various things to earn extra income. Homer worked for Charlie Davis, a small housing contractor, as a finish carpenter. He also repaired furniture, made furniture and did small remodeling jobs. At age 65, Sallie taught herself how to paint birds and flowers and became a "Grandma Moses." She bought antique furniture, refinished it and sold it to antique dealers in the area. She also painted and sold pictures and collectibles and rented a room to George Nichols for many years. Sallie started a collection of antique salt and pepper shakers, mustache cups and glassware. In the wintertime, Homer and Sallie would pull a very small trailer to the Sarasota, Florida, area and spend the winter with Sallie doing handicrafts. She made handbags, decorated picture frames and made animals from seashells. Many of her handicrafts and works of art are proudly displayed in the homes of her descendants.

Source: The story line is based on an interview conducted with Anna Lee "Dolly" Garber Harner, the youngest daughter of Homer and Sallie Garber, on November 19, 2003, at her house on Route 608 near New Hope, Virginia.

Homer and Sallie Garber's Picture Story

Homer Franklin Garber, c1907

Homer F. Garber in North Dakota, c1908

Centennial Public School, where Homer and his Children Went to School, Built 1870

SOUVENIR

CENTENNIAL PUBLIC SCHOOL,
AUGUSTA CO., VA.

Oct. 21, 1907 - April 17, 1908.

Minor C. Miller, Principal,
Miss Edna M. Shover,
Assistant.

Names of Pupils.

Bessie Craig	William Campbell
Effie Campbell	William Foley
Martha Garber	Russell Miller
Ola Garber	Edward McCary
Belle McAllister	Earl Norford
Mary Miller	Everet Wampler
Rena Western	Cora Garber
George Crawford	Nannie Rhodcap
Minor Garber	Bertie Rhodcap
Charley Miller	Olive Wampler
Charley McAllister	Samuel Craig
Frank Wampler	Raymond Craig
Maud Foley	Dewey Garber
Sophia Manuel	Reeves Miller
Emma Rhodcap	Oscar Miller
Olga Whitmer	John Rhodcap
Minnie Wampler	Galen Whitmer
Thomas Craig	Wayman Western
Florence Craig	Roy Garber
Edna Early	Quinter Miller
Mary Garber	Marvin Miller
Evie Garber	Byron Wampler
Lydia McAllister	Emmert Wright
Florence Miller	

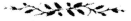

Centennial School Roster, 1908
The Roster Includes Cora, Dewey, Evie, Martha, Mary, Minor, Ola and Roy Garber.

Couples Dating, 1908

(L-R) Homer Garber, Sallie Reed, Ben and Lena Reed, Rena Western and Minor Garber

Note: Homer is pulling the camera string and all three men are smoking cigarettes.

Smoking Pipes, Homer and Minor Garber, c1910

(L-R) Homer and Sallie Garber, Minor Garber, Rena Western, Lena and Ben Reed, c1910

Homer Garber with Horse and Buggy, c1915

Back Yard Play (L-R) Cleatis and Harold Garber, 1912

Playing with the Dog, Harold and Cleatis Garber, 1923

Homer and Sallie Garber's Children

1913 1914 1915 1916 1917 Dolly - 1930 1920 1922 1923 1924 1925 1926 1927

The Garber Family Hauling Hay from the Field, 1922
Homer Garber Sits on the Horse and Sons Cleatis, Harold and Paul Ride the Hay Wagon.

Homer and Sallie Garber with Their Extended Family, 1942
Harold, Sallie, Isabelle with Freddie, Dolly, Ruby and Paul with Jan, Cleatis and Doris and Homer Garber

Four Garber Generations, 1938
Harold and Jan, Lizzie and Homer

Four Garber Generations, 1947
(L-R) Paul and Wayne, Homer,
Lizzie Holding Don Garber

Four Garber Generations, 1947
(L-R) Harold, Freddie, Homer and Jan
(Seated) Lizzie with DeNette Garber

Homer Garber's 70th Birthday Celebration
Gypsy Hill Park, August 1956

Homer and Sallie Garber, c1950

Homer and Sallie Garber's House, c1960
657 Wayne Avenue, Waynesboro, Virginia

Paul Wilson Garber & Ruby Elizabeth Sipe

Paul and Ruby Garber, April 25, 1986

Glimpses of Paul and Ruby Garber

Paul Wilson Garber, the third child and third son of Homer Franklin and Sallie Belle Garber, was born in 1913 in the farmhouse on the Levi Garber farm. As a boy growing up, he performed household chores and helped on the farm. After graduation from New Hope High School, he worked on the farm for about one year and then went to Washington, DC, to work in the grocery store business. Eight years later, he returned to the Valley and bought with his father, Homer, the New Hope General Merchandise Store, called "H. F. Garber & Son."

As a patient at Rockingham Memorial Hospital, he met Ruby Elizabeth Sipe, who was born in 1919 and was the daughter of Robert Sipe and Bertha Shifflett Sipe. They were married April 5, 1942, six months after Ruby became a Registered Nurse. Paul and Ruby renovated the New Hope Presbyterian Church in 1942-43 and made it their home where two sons Wayne and Don, were born.

In 1951, Paul and Homer sold the store and Paul and his young family moved to "Green Acre Farm," a grassland and cattle operation near Waynesboro, Virginia. Paul and Ruby's daughter, Carolyn, was born May 27, 1952, the day the family moved to the farm. For the next 37 years, they worked very hard, raised cattle and chickens, made and sold hay and worked outside jobs. For a few years they operated a Grade B dairy and a chicken (laying hen) business. Economic times were tough, so Paul became the Dog Warden (second full-time warden in Virginia) for Augusta County and Ruby became an Industrial Nurse for the local DuPont plant.

In 1989, Paul and Ruby sold the farm and built a new house in Stratford Estates near Waynesboro, Virginia. The retired couple enjoyed life by spending winters in their Florida condo, playing a lot of bridge, hosting family get-togethers and traveling to Europe, California and South America. Paul was a life long member of the Church of the Brethren and he and Ruby were very active in the church during their married life. After Paul died on July 16, 2001, Ruby sold their Florida condo and their lovely home in 2002 and moved to the Bridgewater Retirement Community.

To Paul and Ruby Garber were born two sons and one daughter to include:

1. Wayne Edward Garber b 1944 m 1966 Gail Twombly b 1946. Two children.

2. Don Paul Garber b 1945 m 1971 Roxanne Kaiser, m 1976 Michelle Montesclares, m 1996 Jana Kiena. Two children.

3. Carolyn Ann Garber b 1952 m 1973 David Homer Pettit b 1952. Three children.

A Good Rich Life: 1913 - 2001

Paul Wilson Garber was born December 31, 1913, and was the third child born in three years to his parents, Homer and Sallie Garber. His older brothers were Cleatis, born 1911, and Harold, born 1912. Cleatis was the adventurous type who once climbed a tree, stuck his hand in a squirrel hole and got a severe squirrel bite and a broken finger. Harold was the studious type and enjoyed reading. Paul was a doer and an experiential learner. Being the youngest of three boys, he was smaller and always trying to keep up with Cleatis and Harold. The boys were good friends, but Cleatis and Harold probably had the closest relationship. However, one day Harold and Paul started calling Cleatis names. Cleatis got angry and wanted to beat up his brothers. He knew he could not win a fight against both Harold and Paul, so he first threw Paul off the barn bridge, a drop of 10 feet and then proceeded to beat up Harold. Both Paul and Harold survived without serious injuries and probably did not call Cleatis a "hang down" again. In general, the boys played well together, liked to hunt rabbits and foxes for bounty money and liked to skate on the farm pond in the winter. Since Paul was the youngest, he was often assigned house chores like washing dishes, dusting and sweeping. Cleatis and Harold were more likely to be assigned chores at the barn or in the fields.

Paul did not particularly like school, but he did his homework and passed each grade. Through the fifth grade, he walked the half-mile to Centennial Elementary School where he was always the youngest and one of the smallest kids in the class since he started school when he was four years old. For the sixth grade, Paul attended the Mt. Sidney Elementary School, and Cleatis drove the boys to school in a horse and buggy. The horse was named Pet and was a very fast buggy horse because it was a former racehorse. Unfortunately, Pet slipped on ice going down the hill in front of Johnson Brothers store on Route 11 in Mt. Sidney and broke her hind leg. As a result, Pet was put down with Homer's shotgun, which was later inherited by Wayne Garber from his father, Paul. This was a very sad day for the boys. Starting with the seventh grade, Paul walked through the fields and climbed the bluff to Knightly and then rode the school bus to the New Hope School. Daniel Garber, his grandfather, drove one of the first school buses in Augusta County. Paul enjoyed sports and played on the New Hope High School basketball and baseball teams. He was also a member of the cast in a school comedy drama entitled "Wild Ginger." Paul worked one summer during high school for his uncle Minor Garber, who owned and operated the Knightly Mill, which generated electricity for the Mt. Sidney, Ft. Defiance and New Hope areas. Paul planted electrical poles from the mill to New Hope.

WILD GINGER

A Comedy Drama presented by

New Hope High School

Thursday Evening, Dec. 11, 1930

At 8 o'clock

In the

HIGH SCHOOL AUDITORIUM

Cast of Characters

Jake Tallman	Harold Via
Geoffrey Freeman	Sheldon Baber
Sanford Lakey	Nelson Burkholder
Marwood Lakey	Thomas Simpson
Wuxy Walker	Paul Garber
Mr. Peterson	Clyde Via
Virginia Tallman	Bernice Sandridge
Miss Rachel Lee	Alma Gordon
Miss Stanley	Lucille Garber
Mix Walker	Louise Davis
Bonita Lakey	Eunice Swisher

☛ **Music by the famous Higgins Sisters between acts.**

Admission   —   25c and 35c

Paul Garber Was a Cast Member, 1930

After high school graduation, Paul worked on the farm for Homer for one year before going to Washington, DC, to join Cleatis and Harold. Paul worked for Acme Food Stores as a grocery store clerk and store manager in Washington, DC, and Chevy Chase, Maryland. Upon promotion to Store Manager at age 20, Paul was the youngest Acme manager and had eight people working for him. While working for Acme, he opened and managed the Washington area's first self-serve super market. Initially, Paul lived with Cleatis, but when he was transferred to a store in Chevy Chase, he rented a room from Clarence Garber, his uncle, who lived at 18th Street, NW, near Catholic University. Clarence liked the seashore and owned a cottage on the Chesapeake Bay where they boated and fished. One winter Clarence built a powerboat in his basement and had to tear down the basement wall to get the boat out of the house. The boat was outfitted with a Hudson engine.

Paul Garber, Manager, (on left) with his Washington Grocery Store Staff, c1934

Paul traveled by foot or bus his first four years in Washington. After he was promoted to store manager, he earned about $40 per week, which was a very good salary during the Depression era. He saved his money and bought a new 1937 black Ford sedan; later he owned a 1938 blue Oldsmobile convertible. He learned a lesson when he loaned it to a friend who wrecked the car. The car was a total loss and the friend did not reimburse him for its value. Paul's good salary also allowed him to play golf at East Potomac Golf Course, to be a sharp dresser and date many young ladies.

In 1939, Paul returned from the Washington area to own and operate his own business. He and his father Homer bought the New Hope grocery store and called it "H. F. Garber & Son, General Merchandise – Notions and Groceries, Fresh and Cured Meats a Specialty." Paul's mother Sallie and sister Dolly clerked in the store. They sold canned goods, work clothes, needles and thread, gasoline and kerosene, pickled fish, meats and cheese, ice, candy and ice cream and homemade sandwiches. The store was a very successful business during the war years. Paul and Homer each made about $14,000 per year, which was very good money at the time. Due to the war effort, many things were in short supply. They went to Richmond and bought used tires with bald spots and resold the tires to customers who commuted to Waynesboro to work. They butchered five beeves a week and sold the meat. Due to gasoline rationing, they were able to sell all the gasoline they could get.

About 1941, the Staunton Draft Board selected Paul for a physical, but he was rejected for the Army due to a heart murmur. The murmur was caused by undulant fever but doctors did not discover this for six years. During the next few years, unknown citizens reported him several times to the draft board as someone who should be serving in the military. The Board called him up three additional times, and each time he was rejected. At the beginning of World War II, Cleatis worked for the General Accounting Office in the Office of Investigations and made the personal decision to serve in the Army. Cleatis was one of the first members of the

Homer F. Garber & Son, New Hope General Merchandise Store Built in 1804
Picture Taken 1954

Middle River Congregation of the Church of the Brethren to not become a conscientious objector, a person who objects to warfare and refuses to perform in the military. Brother Harold received a deferment because he was married and had a child.

Shortly after buying the store, Paul developed undulant fever from drinking unpasteurized milk and was sick for 20+ years until he began taking a vaccine to control the ailment. During one of his hospital stays at Rockingham Memorial Hospital, he met Ruby Elizabeth Sipe, a student nurse. Paul was smitten with Ruby and pursued her aggressively. Ruby's schedule varied greatly, so they had morning, afternoon and evening dates. Paul asked Ruby to marry him when they were parked in his black 1940 Ford. They were married April 5, 1942, six months after Ruby became a Registered Nurse. Ruby worked at Waynesboro Hospital and also worked as a private duty nurse.

H. F. Garber & Son Store Calendar, 1947

In 1942, Paul and Ruby bought the vacated New Hope Presbyterian Chapel for $800. It was located two blocks from the store. The New Hope Presbyterian Chapel was started by the Old Stone Presbyterian Church at Ft. Defiance. The property consisted of two rods and three poles, and was located adjacent to properties of John C. Scott, John L. Patterson and others. *The Staunton News-Leader* article, "Augusta Stone Church to Sell Real Estate in New Hope for $800," dated August 1, 1942, stated, "In the court order permitting and confirming the sale, Judge Crosby stated that the trustees of the church had presented the congregation's wish to sell the property before the court, trustees being R.S. Sites, Ira W. Whitmer, J.C. McCue, W. M. McCutchan, John D. Palmer, E. M. Sites, W. S.

New Hope Presbyterian Chapel, Built 1890s

Robinson and Chas. S. Roller, Jr. The order states further that the decision to sell was taken through resolutions adopted at a congregational meeting held on August 1, 1941, the Rev. J. M. McBryde, moderator of the congregational meeting, presided. The congregation further expressed a desire to use $450 of the sale price for the construction of a wall around the old cemetery of the church at Ft. Defiance."

It is believed that the chapel was built in the early 1890s. Ruth McBryde Gill, daughter of the late Rev. McBryde, who was pastor at Old Stone Church in the 1930s–40s, remembers coming to the New Hope Chapel with her father in the late 1930s. Services were held every other Sunday night until poor attendance caused the services to be discontinued in 1939.

Paul and Ruby Garber House, Rebuilt 1942
Picture 2005

During World War II, Paul and Ruby rebuilt the New Hope Presbyterian Chapel into a house. Because of the shortage of building materials, one could not obtain a permit to build a new residence, but they were given a permit to renovate. The preliminary renovation plans, based on a house in Waynesboro, were drawn on a box cover. The chapel was located on a ¾-acre lot, and since the structure was a long building, it was cut in half. The house was built with day labor; carpenters were paid 50 cents an hour and laborers 35 cents per hour. The basement was dug out by hand, a coal furnace was installed, the tin roof was sold and asphalt shingles were installed. The wide pine flooring was re-laid and refinished and the new house was built around the 4 ½ foot bathtub. The tub, pipes, hardware, windows and doors were bought from Montgomery Wards in

Staunton. The gas stove was an apartment model and the refrigerator had a dent in it. The house cost $5,000 to renovate and sold for $10,000 in 1952. The Garbers occupied their new house in 1943 and started a family. Their first child Wayne was born on September 11, 1944, and Don was born on April 18, 1946.

In 1945, World War II ended. Shortly thereafter, the veterans returned home, and the country prepared for a period of rapid change and growth. The returning veterans married, began families and built new houses. Paul realized that self-service supermarkets would be coming to the Waynesboro area soon, so he and Homer began to make plans to sell the store business. In 1948, Paul bought from Vernon McCune a 128-acre tract of land that was located on the White Bridge Road across the road from his brother Harold's farm. The land was fertile but erosion had created many deep gullies in the fields. Paul began filling in the gullies and building fences, a new barn and a new house.

In 1950, Homer and Sallie sold their New Hope house because Sallie wanted to move to Waynesboro due to some health concerns. In 1951, the store was sold for $11,000 to C. William Garber and about 1957 was sold to Nelson G. Hinebaugh. Then the store passed through several owner-operators until it went out of business about 1975, due to competition from self-service super markets. Although the New Hope General Merchandise Store was one of the oldest brick structures in Augusta County, it was bulldozed in 1980 by Jefferson National Bank to make more parking available for the bank.

Paul moved the family to "Green Acre Farm" and began a cattle and hay operation. Carolyn was born May 27, 1952, the day the family moved to the farm. After a severe drought the first year, Paul started a Grade B

Paul & Ruby Garber's Green Acre Farm, 1988

milking operation and also purchased a flock of sheep. After the second severe drought in four years, Paul was not able to support the family and pay interest on the farm and house loans. In 1956, he discontinued the dairy, sold the sheep and accepted a job with Augusta County as Virginia's second full-time dog warden. Ruby accepted a job as an industrial nurse at the Waynesboro DuPont Plant. In the mid 1950s, Paul was asked to join the Board of the New Hope Bank as a Director. The Bank was later sold to Jefferson National Bank in Charlottesville, and he continued on the Advisory Board until the early 1990s when Wachovia Bank acquired the bank. Paul continued a part-time farming operation raising feeder steers and selling hay until his retirement from Augusta County in 1974.

Paul was now 61 years old, his children were grown and nearly educated and he began to enjoy life by doing what he liked to do, which was farming and traveling. In 1978, Ruby retired from DuPont and they began taking some trips in their 24' travel trailer and took a tour to South America. Paul loved Florida, so they took the trailer down for the winter. After being there a few weeks, they sold the trailer and bought a two bedroom garden condo on the west coast of Florida at Fort Myers and spent the next 23 winters in Florida. They would leave the Shenandoah Valley the day after Christmas and return about April 1. Paul enjoyed himself by playing shuffleboard, shooting pool, playing poker and bridge, picking tomatoes, buying and squeezing oranges, grilling T-bone steaks and visiting Sanibel Island for cook-outs and sunbathing. At age 76, Paul decided it was time to sell the farm and auction off the farm equipment. In 1989, Paul and Ruby built and moved into a new house in Stratford Estates near Waynesboro, Virginia. They celebrated their 58th wedding anniversary in April 2000.

Paul was 5'9" tall, medium build 165 lbs. with small shoulders, black hair and brown eyes. He smoked cigarettes (Lucky Strikes, Pall Mall and Old Gold Spin Filters) until his heart attack at age 48, when he quit smoking cold turkey. As a young man, Paul had developed undulant fever from drinking unpasteurized milk and was sick for 20+ years until he began taking a vaccine to control the ailment. Paul never cursed, enjoyed reading the newspaper, never wrote letters, rarely told jokes, was a good conversationalist, loved to play bridge and shoot billiards and liked to visit family and friends. His favorite foods were fried oysters, sugar-cured ham, macaroni and cheese, mashed potatoes and gravy, all beef hot dogs and Snickers candy bars for dessert. His favorite drinks were Cokes, coffee, iced tea and an occasional shot of Old Crow whiskey mixed with Wink.

Paul was a good money manager and businessman and was thrifty. He worried about finances, droughts and bad weather. He liked raising cattle but did not have time for pets, worked hard and long hours on the farm, did not like thistles and had disdain for most of the trees in his fields. He was not particularly hard to please but expected his children to be responsible, do the job right the first time and not complain. His philosophy was that, "A job worth doing is worth doing right," and "If you cannot say something nice, then don't say anything at all." Paul was a neat dresser; his favorite color was blue so he wore a lot of it. He was a logical thinker, often literal minded, sometimes argumentative and stubborn, even-tempered, seldom moody or gruff, energetic and a very responsible individual. Paul had no creative or artistic talents, but he possessed a strong faith in God. Paul was a life long member of the Church of the Brethren, and he and Ruby were very active in the Church during their married life. He was generally serious but often relaxed and cheerful, frequently hurried, rarely stern or angry, rarely egotistical, often humble, very honest, even-tempered and modest.

Paul liked to speculate on land and he and Ruby owned the following properties:

- New Hope, Virginia, house (1942) and lot

- Two lots near Verona (built a house on one lot in the late 1940s)

- Green Acre Farm (1948) which had 156 acres of farmland. Built house and two barns.

- Guy Brower Farm (about 1960) and house at Hermitage, Virginia

- Apartment house (about 1961) (old brick school) at Harriston, Virginia

- Part of Hensley Farm (1963) at New Hope, Virginia

- House (late 1960s) on King Avenue in Waynesboro, Virginia

- Lookabill Farm (1976) at Greenville, Virginia

- Herbert Fauber Farm (1977) at Greenville, Virginia

- Condo (1978) at Fort Myers, Florida

- House (1989) on Berkeley Drive in Waynesboro, Virginia.

Paul loved life and was in disbelief when the doctor told him he had lymphoma of the stomach. He expected to live into his late nineties and fought hard to survive. Paul lived 87 years and six months and died on July 16, 2001. When the viewing was held at the Reynolds Funeral Home in Waynesboro, Virginia, the line of people to view the body and pay their last respects wound its way down the hallway and out of the building. Over 300 people came to the viewing and 150 to the funeral the next day. Paul and Ruby had earned the respect of many people, who came to honor and celebrate their good rich life together.

Obituary for Paul W. Garber, *The News Leader,* **Tuesday July 17, 2001**
Waynesboro – Paul Wilson Garber, 87, of 11 Berkeley Drive, died Monday (July 16, 2001) at his residence. He was born December 31, 1913, at Mount Sidney, a son of Homer F. and Sallie Reed Garber.

He was a graduate of New Hope High School and was a lifetime member of the Brethren Church, where he held the office of deacon, as well as many other positions throughout his church life. He operated New Hope Grocery from 1939-1951 and from 1948-1988 he owned and operated Green Acre Farm. He also worked for Augusta County as an Animal Control Warden from 1956-1974 and was a member of the Jefferson National Bank Advisory Board.

In addition to his parents, he was preceded in death by one sister, Margaret Garber Woodside. In addition to his wife of almost 60 years, Ruby Sipe Garber, survivors are two sons and daughters-in-law, Wayne E. Garber and his wife Gail of Williamsburg, Virginia; Don Paul Garber and his wife Jana of San Diego, California; a daughter and son-in-law, Carolyn Garber Pettit and her husband David of Charlottesville; two brothers, Cleatis F. Garber and Harold L. Garber of Waynesboro; a sister, Dolly Garber Harner of New Hope; seven grandchildren, Marc and Holly Garber, Alisa and Chase Garber, and Allan, Drew and Brooke Pettit, as well as two step grandchildren, Joel and Lisa Friedman.

A private burial will be held at the Middle River Church of the Brethren Cemetery. Memorial services will follow at 11 a.m. Thursday at the Waynesboro Church of the Brethren, conducted by the Rev. William Eicher and assisted by the Rev. Earl Hammer. Honorary pallbearers will be Lyle Palmer, Bill Moyer, Marvin Stoner, Linwood Adams, Joe Early, Dick Mimmack, Bradley Myrtle, Don McClure, William Shuler, Earl Burcham and Lowell Palmer.

The family will receive friends from 7:30-8:30 p.m. Wednesday at Reynolds Funeral Home, Waynesboro. Memorials may be made to the Waynesboro Weekday Religious Education Program, P.O. Box 613, Waynesboro, Virginia 22980 or to the Waynesboro Church of the Brethren Memorial Fund, 364 Bridge Avenue, Waynesboro, Virginia 22980.

Paul Wilson Garber Eulogy

A Celebration of His Life

As we gather today to bid farewell to our husband, father and friend, we wish that you would not look upon this day with sadness but with a joyful heart. Take comfort with us in knowing he no longer will suffer from the incurable illness which plagued him this past year. He was a man who greatly loved: his God, his family and home, his community, his many friends, his church and his country. The wonderful memories he has left us will sustain us through the years. Share with us today the joy of knowing that he passed our way. Share with us the joy of knowing that although his body is gone from us, his spirit will dwell with kings.

Strong Hands

We are so glad that you are here today to help us celebrate our father's life. If you have memories and special events that you want to share about Dad, we would love to hear them after the service in the Fellowship Hall. I am Carolyn. The thoughts that I share with you today are the collective thoughts of Wayne, Don and me. When we think about Dad, we think about his hands because they tell the story of who he was. Dad's hands were large with short fingers and a flat thumb. We teased him that someone must have hit his thumb with a hammer when he was young because it was so flat. We have often laughed that in some future generation an unsuspecting mother will find this thumb on her newborn child and wonder where it came from.

Dad's hands told the story of a man who worked hard and was strong, although not a big man. His hands were callused and cracked at times with the work from the farm but were always soft and kind when a gentle touch was needed. Farm work is never ending. In the winter, it is necessary to feed cattle, cut ice and plow snow. Spring brought with it birthing of calves, fixing fences, making hay, picking rocks and digging thistles. All three of us remember many days and evenings having to go out with Dad to dig the dreaded thistles up by their roots. He was most proud that few thistles survived on his farm and most annoyed whenever he saw a thistle going to seed that a breeze could carry his way. When we did a task with Dad, even one we might not have liked, he would often remind us that, "If a job is worth doing, it is worth doing right."

When he shook your hand, it was a strong handshake and he would always look you in the eye. For Dad it was a mark that he respected you and that he was an honorable and trusting individual. He was never one to talk about others and lived by the motto, "If you can't say anything nice, then don't say anything at all." Dad's hands, as many of you here know, were used to play many card games. Bridge was a card game that Dad played for most of his life, and it brought him much joy as well as frustration because he always wanted to win. When he wasn't playing bridge, he was playing Rummy Q with Ruby or his grandkids.

Dad would have liked to be here today. He liked a party and church socials, especially for the food. If he had designed the menu for today's social, it would have consisted of country ham, macaroni and cheese, fried oysters, all-beef hot dogs and Snickers candy bars for dessert. He would have then gone home and watched his favorite TV programs to include the Wheel of Fortune and the Price Is Right.

Paul was a humble man with simple tastes. In retirement, he liked growing tomato plants, mowing the yard and watching his bluebirds. He also loved the warm winters and their friends in Florida. A life long baseball fan, he loved watching the Baltimore Orioles or the Atlanta Braves, whichever team happened to be winning. He liked new things and had little sense of tradition or history except for the Fashion clock, which he inherited from his parents.

Dad walked hand in hand with God. He was a man of strong faith and lived what he believed. He was a good father, a good provider, loved his children and grandchildren and our Mother. Mom, we want to thank you for the strength, love and devotion that you showed Dad during your 60 years of marriage and particularly during the last ten months. You were his friend, nurse and confidant. He leaned on you and drew upon your strength and love.

I (Carolyn) recently received from a friend a saying that we would like to share with you that reminds us of the values Dad passed along to his children:

"I wish you enough sun to keep your attitude bright.

I wish you enough rain to appreciate the sun more.

I wish you enough happiness to keep your spirit alive.

I wish you enough pain so that the smallest joys in life appear much bigger.

I wish you enough gain to satisfy your wanting.

I wish you enough loss to appreciate all that you possess.

I wish enough Hellos to get you through the final Good-bye."

Friends and family, Dad would wish you enough. Thanks for honoring Dad and us with your presence today.

Source: Paul Wilson Garber's three children, Wayne Garber, Carolyn Garber Pettit and Don Garber, wrote this tribute for his memorial service: Carolyn Garber Pettit presented it on July 19, 2001, at the Waynesboro Church of the Brethren.

Paul Garber's Footstone at Middle River Cemetery, New Hope, Virginia.

Paul and Ruby Garber's Picture Story

Paul Garber, Age 2, 1915

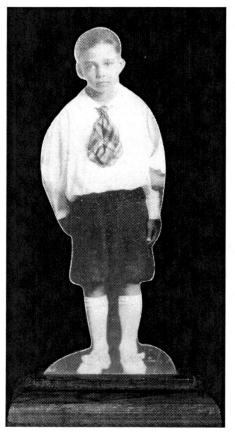

Paul Garber, Age 9, c1922
Mounted on wood cutout.

Paul Garber, Age 29, 1942

Ruby Sipe, Paul Garber and Eleanor Sipe (sister) at VA Beach, 1941

Ruby in Nurses Training, 1941

Ruby in Her Wedding Clothes, 1942

Paul on His Honeymoon, 1942

Three Brothers, Paul, Cleatis and Harold Garber, c1943

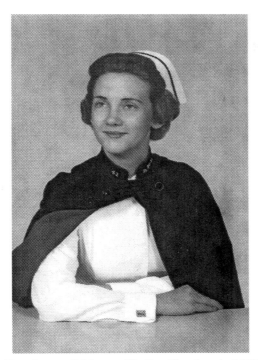

Registered Nurse Ruby Garber, c1950

(L-R) Don, Ruby, Carolyn, Paul and Wayne Garber, 1956

Carolyn Garber on Her Pony, c1965

Carolyn Feeding a Fawn from a Bottle, 1968

Ruby and Paul Garber's 30th Wedding Anniversary, 1972

(L-R) Paul and Ruby Garber's 50th Anniversary, 1992
(Back Row, L-R) Wayne, Carolyn and Don Garber

Green Acre Farm on the White Bridge Road near Waynesboro, 1988

Paul and Ruby Garber's Home in Stratford Estates, Waynesboro, Virginia
Built 1989, Picture Taken 2000

Paul and Ruby Garber on a Cruise, 1998

Other U.S. No. 7 Generation Family Pictures

The Cleatis Garber and Doris Miller Family

Riding Camels on the Giza Plateau (Egypt), 1962
(L-R) Doris, Cleatis, Barbara and David Garber

The Harold Garber and Isabelle Fisher Family

Isabelle and Harold Garber
Wedding Day, February 25, 1937

Isabelle and Harold Garber, 1987
50th Anniversary

Picture Taken at Harold & Isabelle's House in Fairway Hills, Waynesboro, VA, 1965
(L-R) Fred and Donna, Sallie and Homer, Hazel and John DeGroff (Donna's Parents), Isabelle with
Kimberly and Harold, DeNette, Jan and Anita Leavell Garber with Trey

The Paul Garber and Ruby Sipe Family

Family Gathering at Farmington Country Club, September 1986
(L-R Standing) Marc, Wayne, Don Garber and David Pettit
(L-R Seated) Gail, Holly, Ruby, Paul, Chase, Michelle, Alisa Garber and Carolyn Garber Pettit with Brooke, Allan and Drew Pettit

The Walter Woodside and Margaret Garber Family

Margaret and Woody Woodside, 1938

(L-R) Donna Ray, Susann Jean and Walter Woodside, 1953

The Owen Harner and Dolly Garber Family

Family Gathering at Owen and Dolly's New Hope House, 1990
Standing (L-R) Jimmy, Michael, Owen Harner and Sharon Harner Dyer
Seated (L-R) Teresa Harner Barr, Susan Harner Coffman and Dolly Garber Harner

Owen and Dolly's Extended Family at New Hope House, 1998
Standing (L-R) Michael Harner, Alisan and Brant Mackaw, Johnnie and Teresa Barr, Matt Coffman, Lindsey
Barr, Tim Bergman, Jimmy Harner, Tom Dyer, Tasha Harner, Amye Bergman, Susan and Jerry Coffman,
Chris Tuttle, Heidi Binko, Andy Dyer and Sharon Dyer
Seated (L-R) Lavanne Harner, Owen Harner, Nicolas Bergman, Dolly Harner, Ariana Harner,
Amanda Barr, Connie Harner
Kneeling (L-R) Kristine Harner, Nicole Tuttle, Angela Harner, Dillon Harner and Bradley Harner

Garber Family Celebration Picture Stories

Garber Gathering at Black Rock Spring, August 24, 1909

Black Rock Spring, August 24, 1909. Hotel Burned November 1909

Paul and Ruby's New House, Summer 1952
(BR) Sallie Garber, Doris Miller Garber, Homer Garber
(FR) Ruby and Carolyn, Barbara with Doll, David, Paul, Wayne and Don Garber

Christmas 1953, Family Gathering at Homer and Sallie's
Wayne Avenue, Waynesboro, VA
(BR) Isabelle, Harold, Homer, Sallie, Paul Garber (MR) Ruby and Carolyn, Dolly Harner and Teresa,
Sharon Harner, Jan and Don (FR) Freddie, Wayne and Denette Garber and Susan Harner

Gathering at Harold and Isabelle Garber's Pool, 1962
(BR) Wayne, Ruby, Dolly, Harold, Anita and Jan Garber
(MR) Doris, Homer, Sallie, Carolyn, Isabelle, Don and David Garber
(FR) DeNette Garber, Sharon, Teresa, Susan and Jimmy Harner

Sallie Belle Garber's 95th Birthday Celebration, 1982
Family Celebrates at Green Acre Farm

Homer and Sallie Garber's Children, July 1, 1995
Picnic at Carolyn Garber Pettit's Home
(L-R) Dolly Garber Harner and Paul, Harold and Cleatis Garber

Homer and Sallie Garber's Children and Spouses, 2002
Teresa and Johnnie Barr's Home at Barron Ridge, Virginia
(BR) Owen and Dolly Garber Harner, Ruby Garber (FR) Nancy and Cleatis Garber

Homer and Sallie Garber's Grandchildren, 2002
Picnic at Johnnie & Teresa Barr's Home
(BR) Teresa Harner Barr, Susan Harner Coffman, Sharon Harner Dyer, Barbara Garber Austin,
David Garber
(MR) Suzie Woodside, Fred and Jan Garber, Carolyn Garber Pettit, Wayne Garber
(FR) Jimmy and Mike Harner

Homer and Sallie Garber's Great Grandchildren, 2002
Picnic at Teresa and Johnnie Barr's Home
(BR) Thomas and Michael Garber
(2nd Row) Lindsey Barr, Matt Coffman, Amanda Barr, Ariana Harner, Nathan Austin, Brooke Pettit
(3rd Row) Kristine Harner, Tasha Harner, Nicole Tuttle, Kristin Keating, Kimberly Womer
(FR) Trey Garber, Dillon Harner, Angela Harner, Brad Harner, Kevin Garber, Amye Bergman,
Alison Markow

Garber Family Reunions

Garber Family Reunion at Home of J.C. Garber, Minister of Staunton COB, August 1927

Reunions

Have you thought of the good times and fun our ancestors must have had prior to the days of computers, television, popularity of automobiles, radios and telephones, with dreams of some day flying in an aero plane? Well, Calvin Garber remembers some of those days. He says that, "Garber family celebrations were held for a long time in people's homes. It was a big affair because there wasn't much else to do. I remember going to Ira Garber's home in Weyers Cave and to John Garber's home in Staunton. They took a group picture of the gathering of people."

Based on the author's research, it appears that Garber family celebrations started about 1909 by getting together in local homes to celebrate the birthday of Elder Levi Garber. The celebrations were always held on August 21, the day that Levi was born in 1828. They stayed all day, with dinner at noon followed by games and activities in the field and then supper. Friends, relatives and neighbors brought baskets of food and joined in the fun. What did they do? "Talks on family ties… a basket dinner… peanut shower… kodaking… scripture reading… prayer… impromptu speeches… hymn sings." In 1924, the Garber celebration was held at the home of Homer F. Garber (former home of Elder Levi Garber), and a motion was proposed and passed to make this a Garber Reunion instead of a celebration of Levi's birthday. Recorded minutes of the Annual Garber Reunions are on file for each year subsequent through 2005. A brief synopsis of each reunion is presented below:

Date	Location	Comments
1909 – 1922	Middle River Church	The Levi Garber family held birthday celebrations, which were private reunions.
July 1, 1922	Nancy Cline's Home	
August 21, 1923	Enos & Becky Garber's	95th Anniversary of Levi Garber's Birth. D.S. Garber talked about his family relations. First minutes that we have on record. Social time included a peanut shower and kodaking.
August 21, 1924	Homer F. Garber Home	Reunion motion passed.
August 24, 1925	Milton & Barbara Shavers	1st Garber Reunion, Celebrated Ancestry. B.B. Garber gave an address in which he urged the young to follow the steps of our forefathers and not betray our heritage.
August 21, 1926	B. B. Garber (rained out)	No minutes on file.
August 23, 1927	Minister J.C. Garber Home	Peter Garber gave an address entitled, "Our History."
August 21, 1928	Middle River Church	100th Anniversary of Levi Garber's Birth. Program was history of the Middle River Church by B.B. Garber.
August 22, 1929	Luther D. Garber Wampler	Discussed Family Tree.
August 21, 1930	Middle River Church	An address by B.B. Garber & H.C. Early.
August 21, 1931	Garber Homestead	Near Green Mount.
1932	No Reunion	
August 17, 1933	Middle River Church	
August 21, 1934	Garber's Church	An address by Dr. J. W. Wayland.
1935	No Reunion	
August 21, 1936	Pleasant Valley Church	An address by S.D. Miller.
August 24, 1937	Middle River Church	No minutes on file.
August 18, 1938	Garber's Church	Special music was presented by the Ben Garber family quartet, Pleasant Valley Church. Dr. J.W. Wayland gave the address of the morning.

Garber Family Gathering at Enos and Becky Garber's Farm, 1923

First Public Garber Reunion at Milton H. Shavers Home, the Peanut Shower, 1925

Garber Family Reunion at Home of J.C. Garber, Minister of Staunton COB, August 1927

Date	Location	Comments
August 16, 1939	Middle River Church	Talks were given by Rebecca Kindig, H.C. Early, Gordon Garber, George Garber, Merle Hamilton and Dr. J.S. Flory. Children enjoyed a peanut shower.
August 9, 1940	Pleasant Valley Church	An address by Dr. J. Adam Garber.
August 21, 1941	Middle River Church	An address by Rev. J.C. Garber.
1942 – 1945	No Reunions	World War II
August 24, 1946	Garber's Church	Afternoon was spent renewing acquaintances and greeting friends and relatives. Talk by Clark M. Garber, historian.
August 29, 1947	Pleasant Valley Church	Talks by Dr. Burkeholder and Merle Hamilton.
August 22, 1948	Middle River Church	Music, devotion and memorial service.
August 21,1949	Greenmount Church	Music, devotion and memorial service and talk by John Adam Garber entitled "We Leave Our Mark in the World."
August 20, 1950	Pleasant Valley Church	Music by Casper Garber.
August 26, 1951	Garber's Church	Music and devotions.
August 24, 1952	Middle River Church	Music, devotion and memorial service.
August 23, 1953	Greenmount Church	Music, devotion and memorial service.
August 22, 1954	Pleasant Valley Church	Music and devotions.
August 21, 1955	Middle River Church	Music and devotions, peanut scramble.
August 26, 1956	Dayton Church	Music and open forum.
August 25, 1957	Arbor Hill Church	Music.
August 24, 1958	Pleasant Valley Church	Music and memorial service.
August 23, 1959	Greenmount Church	Music and talk on values of family heritage.
August 28, 1960	Gypsy Hill Park	
August 27, 1961	Gypsy Hill Park	Special recognition of older folks.
August 26, 1962	Dayton Church	Music and memorial service, peanut scramble.
August 25, 1963	Greenmount Church	Music and memorial service, peanut scramble.
August 23, 1964	Pleasant Valley Church	Peanut scramble.
August 22, 1965	Arbor Hill Church	Music and memorial service.
August 28, 1966	Middle River Church	Dr. Paul L. Garber and Dr. John Adam Garber spoke regarding Garber traditions and history.
August 27, 1967	Pleasant Valley Church	Music and memorial service, peanut scramble.
August 25, 1968	Dayton Church	
August 24, 1969	Greenmount Church	Sharing time regarding family history.
August 23, 1970	Pleasant Valley Church	Poems from Gordon Garber.
August 22, 1971	Garber's Church	Music, devotion and memorial service.
August 27, 1972	Greenmount Church	Music, devotion and memorial service.

Date	Location	Comments
August 26, 1973	Pleasant Valley Church	Memorial service for departed cousins and friends.
August 24, 1974	Dayton Church	Heirlooms from the A.D. Garber family were shared.
August 24, 1975	Greenmount Church	
August 22, 1976	Harrisonburg Church	Various families told of old reunions and memories.
August 28, 1977	Pleasant Valley Church	Music, devotion and memorial service.
August 27, 1978	Greenmount Church	Music, devotion and memorial service.
August 26, 1979	Pleasant Valley Church	
August 24, 1980	Harrisonburg Church	Music and memorial service, peanut scramble.
August 23, 1981	Garber's Church	Interesting exhibits and history of Garber's Church.
August 22, 1982	Pleasant Valley Church	Devotion and memorial service.
August 27, 1983	Greenmount Church	Memorial service.
August 26, 1984	Nokesville Church	Memorial service.
August 25, 1985	Harrisonburg Church	Memorial service.
August 24, 1986	Pleasant Valley Church	Sophie Miller presented Garber Book with Abram and Sophie Garber letters and pictures.
August 23, 1987	Greenmount Church	Music and memorial service.
August 28, 1988	Harrisonburg Church	Music and memorial service, peanut scramble.
August 27, 1989	Pleasant Valley Church	Music, entertainment and memorial service.
August 26, 1990	Middle River Church	Memorial service.
August 25, 1991	Harrisonburg Church	Harold L. Garber presented "Garber Highlights" and discussed Garber museum at Middle River COB.
August 16, 1992	Greenmount Church	Memorial service: Harold L. Garber presented Middle River Historical Museum and Garber History.
August 15, 1993	Greenmount Church	Memorial service: brainstorming discussion about creating more interest in Garber Family Reunions.
August 21, 1994	Dayton Church	Harold Garber presented history of Garber family, coat of arms and German Garber families.
August 20, 1995	Waynesboro Church	Music and memorial service.
August 21, 1996	Pleasant Valley Church	Music and memorial service, History of Garber Family Celebrations and Family Reunions.
August 17, 1997	Dayton Church	Harold Garber presented framed family tree of Jacob Garber Family.
August 16, 1998	Greenmount Church	Memorial service, copies of Jacob Garber family descendants available for sale.
August 15, 1999	Greenmount Church	Music and memorial service.
August 20, 2000	Waynesboro Church	Memorial service.
August 19, 2001	Middle River Church	Tour of Garber Historical Room.
August 18, 2002	Dayton Church	Memorial service.
August 17, 2003	Pleasant Valley Church	Memorial service.
August 15, 2004	Garber's Church	Toured Brethren-Mennonite Heritage Center.
August 21, 2005	Flat Rock Church	80th Garber Reunion.
August 19, 2007	Gypsy Hill Park	Wayne Garber introduced this book, *Johannes "John H." Garber* and Owen Harner introduced his new book, *The History of New Hope, Virginia*.

Source: In 2005, Mildred Renalds Wittig of Broadway, Virginia, allowed the writer to research original "Jacob Garber Family Reunion Minutes" and provided the first and second photographs.

Garbers Buried at Middle River Cemetery

Middle River Cemetery

Middle River Cemetery

The cemetery is located at the Middle River Church of the Brethren, which is two miles northwest of New Hope, Virginia, Augusta County on Route 778. This is a well-kept cemetery and has many interesting epitaphs. The earliest date is 1829, and some of the dates are written differently from any found elsewhere. One Civil War veteran killed at the Battle of Piedmont is buried here. There are many German names and names which were changed at various times from the original spelling. Below is a listing of the many Garbers buried in the cemetery.

First Name	Middle Initial	Year of Death	First Name	Middle Initial	Year of Death
William	J.	1950	Hallie	D.	?
Mamie	L.	1959	Florence	E.	1968
William	H.	1925	Luther	M.	1950
Sallie	M.	1933	Sallie	A.	1929
			Paul	W.	1905
Clifford	B.	1937	Samuel (son of Abraham)		1892
Josie		1944	Anna		1900
Lucy	I.	1981	Mary	E.	1946
Barbara	A.	1925	Benjamin	B.	1951
Ella	C.	1951	Kattie	A.	1916
Fannie	V.	1941	Lida	R.	1955
			Elizabeth	H.	1903
Joseph	M.	1923	Eli		1884
Minor	F.	1887	Susannah		1863
Elizabeth		1890	John	C.	1863
John	D.	1889	Florence	E.	1878
Mary	E.	1891	Benjamin		1858
Sylvester	M.	1887	Anime	L.	?
Elizabeth	C.	1902	Catherine	R.	1857
Noah		1904	John (Rev., son of Abraham))		1854
Virginia	C.	1919	Abraham (founder)		1848
Enos	F.	1934	Elizabeth	H. (wife of founder)	1838
Anna	R.	1940	Nancy (Arnold)		1868
Leta	B.	1965	Jacob (son of Abraham)		1876
Samuel	L.	1936	Ansle		?
William J.		1959	Oscar (Jr.)		?
Jane A.		1969	Catherine		1857
Bettie	C.	1955	William	A.	1914
Elizabeth	F.	1921	Susan	A.	1932
Daniel	A.	1908	Jacob	W.	1908
Maggie		?	Cornelia	C.	1903
John	D.	1912	Benjamin	J.	1924
Fleeta	E.	1916	Nettie	C.	1876
			John	R.	1938
			Mattie	L.	1952
			Nancy	R.	1894

First Name	Middle Initial	Year of Death	First Name	Middle Initial	Year of Death
Henry		1872	Eli	Abraham	1908
Reuben	A.	1884	Minnie	I.	1907
Mary		1898	Sallie	E.	?
Fannie		1909	Cora	V.	1985
Joel		1884	Ethel	B.	1958
Daniel (son of Abraham)		1883	Charles	W.	1927
Elizabeth		1880	Lola	Belle	1918
Charles (Jr.)	W.	1968	Catharine		1877
Everett	M.	1974	Lorena	R.	1928
Infant Son		1925	Joseph	N.	1893
Infant Child		1961	Walter	L.	1894
Cora	B.	1962	James	W.	1871
Everett	M.	1942	Robert	R.	1874
Nancy	J.	1927	John	H.	1841
William	B.	1920	Susan		1894
George	W.	1922	Susan		1852
Samuel	F.	1885	Samuel	M.	1896
Sallie	V.	1885	Sarah	F.	1915
Mertie	L.	1885	Samuel	P.	1890
William	L.	1870	Encert	D.	?
Elizabeth	M.	1890	Abie		1873
			Arthur		1880
Nathaniel	B.	1941	Levi	J.	1864
Mary	C.	1946	James	W.	1871
Ceil	E.	1951			
			Pauline	E.	1961
Addie	M.	1976	Barbara	L.	1961
Carson	G.	1953	Pearl	E.	1956
			Huge	E.	1954
Edythe		1967	Everett	F.	1937
Frank	G.	1980	Benjamin	F.	1938
Bettie	M.	1989	Mary	E.	1924
			John	J.	1921
Sarah	C.	1931	Effie	C.	1937
Christene	S.	1938			
Coray	B.	1937	Minor	W.	1966
Ira	Levie	1941	Rena	B.	1982
Elizabeth M.		1943			
Daniel S.		1923	Homer	F.	1973
James	E.	1908	Sallie	B.	1989
Nancy	J.	1890			
Levi (Elder)		1914	Paul	W.	2001
Barbara		1878			
Elizabeth R.		1877			
Mary E.		1895			
Elizabeth		1874			

Source: Information provided by the Middle River Church cemetery caretaker in 2005.

Garber Family Artifacts

The artifacts shown in this section illustrate that many family members are preserving our Garber Family History and that some make interesting exhibits, particularly if the history is known.

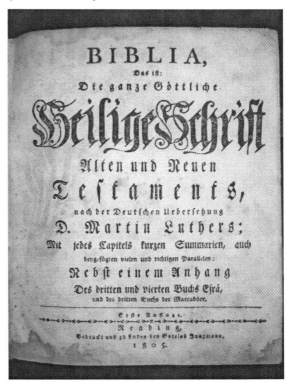

Jacob Garber Bible, Contains Old and New Testaments, Printed in German, 1805

Owner and Marriage pages of Jacob Garber Bible

Left-side page states that Jacob Gerber was the son of Abraham Gerber. The Bible was probably presented to Jacob when he got married. It is interesting that the family was still using the surname Gerber. Right-side page is the family register of the marriage of Jacob Gerber on March 10, 1823, to Nancy Arnold.

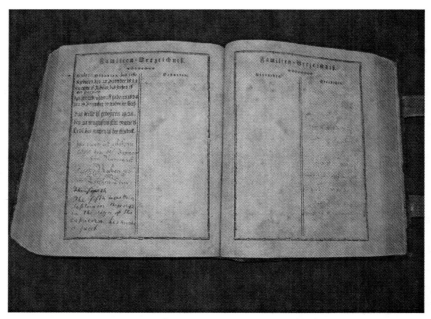

Jacob Garber Bible, Family Register of Children Born

The left-side page is the family register of children born to Jacob and Nancy as follows:

Rebecca	December 27, 1823
Abraham	December 19, 1824
Levi	August 21, 1828
Ruben	January 26, 1836
Jacob	September 11, 1842

The first four births are recorded in German and the fifth birth in 1842 is recorded in English, an indication that the Garbers were beginning to speak and write the English language.

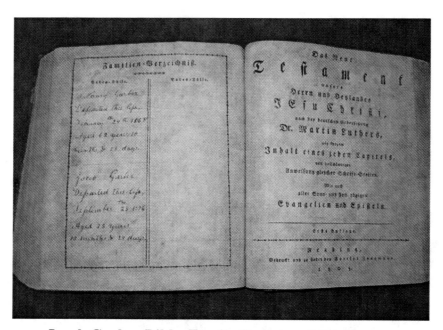

Jacob Garber Bible, Family Register of Deaths

The left-side page states in English that "Nancy Garber departed this life February 29, 1868, at age 62 years 10 months 18 days." It also states that "Jacob Garber departed this life September 25, 1876, aged 78 years 10 months 27 days." The right-side page is the beginning of the New Testament. The Bible was given to Elizabeth Garber Renalds (deceased) and is now in the possession of her daughter, Margaret (Renalds) Witmer, of Oxford, Ohio.

Garber Family Artifacts

Levi Garber Bible, 1830

Levi Garber's entire ministerial life of more than 55 years was devoted to serving the Middle River Congregation. The Levi Garber Bible was used by him and his wife, Barbara Miller Garber. This leather-bound Bible was printed in 1830. Levi and Barbara spoke German, and the Bible was printed in the German language. The Bible was given to Harold Garber by Cora Garber and Ada Reed and Harold gave it to his son, Frederic C. Garber, who retains possession.

Bookmark

This bookmark was found in the Levi Garber German Bible. Barbara Miller was the wife of Levi. She made the bookmark in 1831, when she was six years old.

Levi Garber's Shoes, 1830

These handmade leather shoes and laces were worn by Levi as a very young boy. The shoes have petrified from dryness over time. Frederic C. Garber has possession of the shoes.

Levi Garber's Pocket Watch

This late 1800s pocket watch belonged to Levi Garber. It is in the possession of Frederic C. Garber.

Linen Doily

Flax was grown and spun on the Levi Garber farm family homestead near Mt. Sidney, Virginia. In the 1880s, a five-gallon lard can of flax was found in a secret attic of the house where it had been hidden during the Civil War. In the 1920s, Ada Garber Reed and Cora Garber spun the flax and made linen doilies. This doily was found in Cora's hope chest and was given to Wayne Garber in December 1991 by Catherine Garber Crist.

Levi and Barbara Garber's Cherry Drop-Leaf Table, c1850s

This handmade cherry drop-leaf table belonged to Levi and Barbara Garber and dates to the 1850s. It was then used by Daniel and Lizzie Garber's family as a dining room table. After sixty years of heavy use by two families, it was placed on the back porch and Homer and Sallie Garber stored crocks of milk, cream and garden seed on the table. In 1951, Ruby Sipe Garber traded a new mahogany drop-leaf table to Sallie Garber for the cherry table and had it refinished. It is now in the possession of Wayne Garber.

Levi Garber's Blacksmith Vise

The blacksmith leg vise was an important tool on a farm and in blacksmith shops. This 40-pound English vise with 4" jaws belonged to Levi Garber and was used to make horseshoes and hold hot iron while it was hammered, chiseled or twisted. This leg vise probably dates back to the 1840-50s and was used by Levi, Daniel, Homer, Paul and Wayne Garber on their farms. Wayne now uses it in his garage in Williamsburg, Virginia.

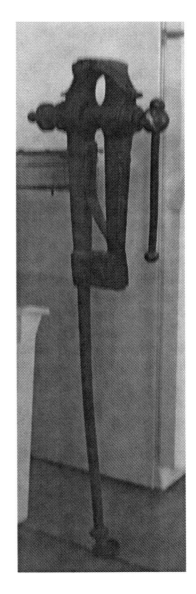

Levi Garber Handmade Table, c1870

This drop-leaf table with drawer belonged to Levi Garber. It was used by Levi and his daughter, Rebecca Garber. Minor Garber, Levi's grandson, bought the table at Daniel's sale in 1924. The table was recently sold to Wayne Garber by William "Bill" Crist, son of Catherine Garber Crist and grandson of Minor Garber.

Daniel Garber Bible, 1880

This English translation of the Old and New Testaments was printed in 1880 by the A. J. Holman & Co., Philadelphia, Pennsylvania. Shown is the family register where the marriage of Daniel Garber and Elizabeth Glick is recorded. The Bible states that "This certifies that the rite of Holy Matrimony was celebrated between Daniel S. Garber of Augusta County and Elizabeth M. Glick of Augusta County on the 9th day of March 1879 at Samuel Glick's by Rev. A. D. Garber." The Bible was given to William Ray Crist in August 1979 with the following note "Your great grandfather's family Bible. Hope you will treasure it. (It is) given by your great Aunt, Cora Garber."

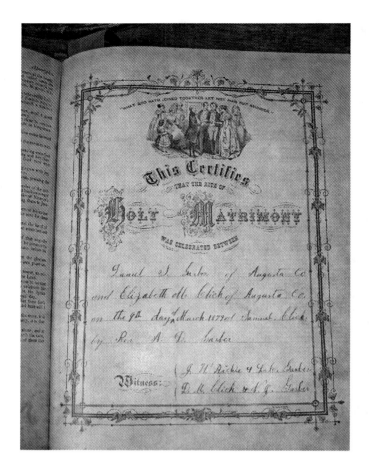

Glass Pitcher, Cup and Tray

This cut-glass pitcher, cup and tray were a wedding present to Daniel and Lizzie Garber, who were married March 9, 1879. They used them on their bedside table. They were given to Dolly Garber Harner, who displays them in her china cabinet.

Daniel S. Garber Fashion Clock, c1880

Daniel Garber bought this Fashion clock number four from a peddler selling clocks from a covered wagon. The clock was sold by the Southern Calendar Clock Company of St. Louis, Missouri, and manufactured for Southern by Seth Thomas Clocks. The clock works were patented December 28, 1875, and the calendar works were patented March 3, 1879. Minor Garber bought Daniel's clock at Ada Garber Reed's sale in 1963 for $115. The clock has the original finish and is in the possession of William Crist.

Pie Safe, c1880

This white walnut pie safe belonged to Daniel and Lizzie Garber. It was kept in the pantry of their Knightly home and used to store pies, bread and cookies. Catherine Garber Crist acquired the safe at Ada Garber Reed's sale in 1963 for $25. Catherine died in October 2005 and requested that Lecher "Dude" Western of New Hope have the safe.

Burk H. Kart Spindle, c1870

This flax wheel belonged to the Samuel T. Glick family and was used by Lizzie Glick Garber and her daughters, Ada and Cora, for many years to twist flax fibers and make linen. The flax wheel was patented in 1868 and was made in New York by Mankins Bros. Frederic C. Garber has possession.

Chest of Drawers

This handmade chest of drawers belonged to Daniel and Lizzie Garber and resided in their bedroom. The chest of drawers came from the Samuel Glick family and dates to the early 19th century. The chest was given to Dolly Garber Harner by Cora V. Garber in 1985.

Lizzie's Spinning Wheel

A spinning wheel was used to make yarn or thread from flax and wool. This spinning wheel belonged to Lizzie Glick Garber and was used to spin the yarn for the linen doily displayed on a previous page. Harold Garber bought the spinning wheel from Ada Garber Reed and Cora Garber in the 1950s. It is now in the possession of Frederic C. Garber.

Lizzie's Bonnet

Black bonnets were commonly worn by women in the late 19th and early 20th century for dress occasions. This bonnet was worn by Lizzie Glick Garber shortly before her death in 1949. It is in the possession of Frederic C. Garber.

Edison Phonograph

This Edison GEM Phonograph was the property of Daniel and Lizzie Garber. It was made in Orange, New Jersey, by the Thomas A. Edison Company. The Serial No. is 284341 and the patents run from 1901 to 1905. The phonograph and its 200 cylinders of music are in the possession of Frederic C. Garber.

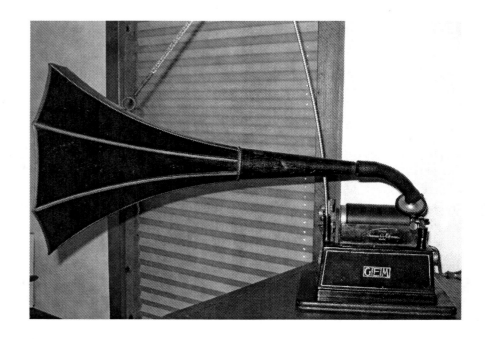

Lizzie Garber's Rocking Chair, c1879

This rocking chair belonged to Lizzie Glick Garber, wife of Daniel S. Garber. She acquired the chair shortly after her marriage in 1879 and used it her whole life. This rocking chair is in the possession of Wayne Garber.

Aunt Becky's Rocking Chair, 1880s

This rocking chair was used by Aunt Becky Garber throughout her life. She was an "old maid" until she married at age 59 to her second cousin Enos Garber, age 60. This rocking chair is in the possession of Marc W. Garber.

Cora Garber's Toys

When Cora Garber was a little girl about 1900, she played with these toys. Dolly Garber Harner has these toys displayed in her home in Barren Ridge, Virginia.

Cora's Doll

This three-foot doll belonged to Cora Garber (1889 to 1985) and dates to the very early 20th century. The doll is in the possession of Frederic C. Garber.

Milk Churn Table, 1954

Homer was a carpenter by trade and he made book cases, dividers and built-in cabinets. This is an example of his creativity: he took an old milk churn and made it into a table. The table is in the possession of Don P. Garber.

Baby Bonnet, 1912

This handmade baby bonnet was worn by Harold L. Garber. It is in the possession of Denette Garber Steverson.

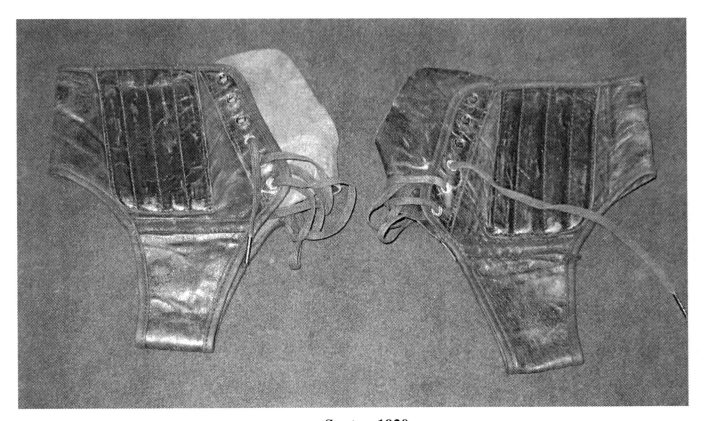

Spats, c1920

This pair of spats was worn by Harold L. Garber as a boy. A spat is a short gaiter worn over a shoe and fastened underneath with a strap. These are in the possession of Denette Garber Steverson.

Dismantled Abraham Garber House

Items stored in the remains of the chicken house.

A. Garber Floor Joists

A. Garber House Trim

Garber Family Artifacts

A Garber House Door

A. Garber House Mantle

A. Garber Step Treads

According to the book *After The Backcountry, Rural Life in the Great Valley of Virginia, 1800-1900* by Kenneth E. Koons and Warren R. Hofstra, the Valley had a system of town-centered settlements, but not all retail distribution was issued from towns. During the 19th century, peddlars carried various manufactured items, especially tin-ware, clocks and Bibles. They traveled through the countryside by horse and wagon offering their wares for sale to farmers and competed intensely with town merchants. These peddlars filled an important niche in the farm economy by saving the farmer a trip to the nearest town. Northern manufacturers used towns like Winchester, Virginia, as warehouse and distribution centers, where peddlars could replenish their inventories.

Fashion Clock

This Fashion Clock was bought from a clock peddlar who sold clocks in the Shenandoah Valley from his covered wagon. The clock was purchased about 1880 by Daniel M. Glick, who at the time lived near Trevillians, Virginia, in Louisa County. The clock was sold by the Southern Calendar Clock Company of St. Louis, Missouri, and manufactured for Southern by Seth Thomas Clocks. The Southern Calendar Clock Company sold nine different models of Fashion clocks during the period from 1870 to 1889 and then went out of business. This clock is called a Fashion number four.

After 50-60 years of ownership and use, in the 1930s Daniel Glick, a missionary, gave the clock to his nephew, Homer Franklin Garber, third oldest son of Daniel S. Garber of New Hope, Virginia. Homer gave the clock to his third oldest son, Paul Wilson Garber of Waynesboro, Virginia, about 1965. Paul died in July 2001 but left instructions for the clock to be given to his oldest son, Wayne Edward Garber of Williamsburg, Virginia. Paul's widow, Ruby Sipe Garber, gave the clock to Wayne in January 2002 with a request that it be kept in the Garber family.

Samuel Glick Family Bible

Peddlers also sold Bibles written either in English or German. The Bibles were often leather bound and had a family register for births, marriages and deaths. The author has the leather bound Samuel T. Glick Family Bible (Samuel was Lizzie Glick Garber's father) that dates to 1869. This item came from Cora Garber.

Daniel Garber's Pocket Watch

The pocket watch under the glass dome belonged to Daniel Garber and was made by the Walthan Watch Company. The "Church" or 1883 model watch has 15 jewels, a swing out case and features stem winding. Its monetary value is low. The watch is in the possession of Wayne Garber.

Homer Garber's Shotgun

The 12-gauge single barrel shotgun was made by the Iver Johnson Cycle & Arms Works in Massachusetts. Homer F. Garber purchased the shotgun from Montgomery Ward's mail-order catalog store in Baltimore, Maryland, for $10 about 1910. Montgomery Ward's catalog was used for many purchases to include shoes, socks and coats. As teenage boys, Cleatis, Harold and Paul Garber used the shotgun for squirrel and rabbit hunting on the farm. The shotgun was given to Paul by his father Homer when Paul moved to Green Acre Farm near Waynesboro, Virginia, about 1951. Paul used the gun on the farm and gave it to his son Wayne in the early 1970s.

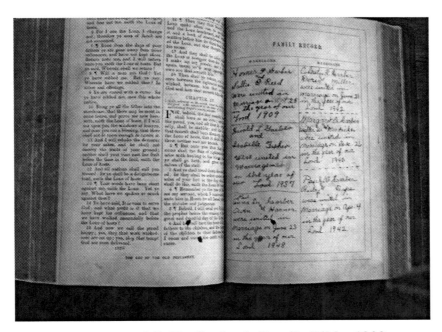

Homer and Sallie Garber's Family Bible, 1909

This family Bible was a present from Daniel S. Garber to Homer and Sallie Garber at the time of their marriage in 1909. The Bible was given to Wayne Garber by Dolly Garber Harner, daughter of Homer and Sallie.

Sallie Belle Reed Garber's Artwork - 1

Sallie Garber was an artist who loved to paint. She would go to antique sales or auctions and buy old obsolete items (trays, buckets, flat irons, utensils, etc.) which some people viewed as junk but she viewed as treasure. She would refinish the item by sanding and cleaning and often painting it with black gloss enamel. Then Sallie would do her magic by decorating the item with flowers and/or birds. All of these items are in the possession of Wayne Garber.

Sallie Garber's Artwork - 2

Examples of Sallie Garber's artwork include a floral painted tray and muffin pan of song birds. This art work is in the possession of Frederic C. Garber.

Sallie Garber's Artwork - 3

This varied and beautiful array of artwork is in the possession of Dolly Garber Harner. It demonstrates Sallie's talent at taking old items and bringing them back to life for future use.

In my opinion, the bird scenes above represent some of Sallie's best work. These beautiful items are in the possession of Don P. Garber.

Garber Family Tree

Around 1980, Harold L. Garber drew several of these Garber Family Trees and presented them to family members. This family tree is displayed in the home of Wayne Garber.

Bibliography and Sources

1. Bushman, Katherine Gentry, "Katherine Gentry Bushman Papers" at the Library of Virginia, Richmond, Virginia.

2. Coffman, W. Paul, *A History of Middle River Congregation, Church of the Brethren*, 1964.

3. Garber, Allan A., *The Descendants of Christian S. and Anna Garber of Lancaster County, Pennsylvania*, 1985.

4. Garber, Clark M., *The Garber Historical and Genealogy Record*, Volume III, 1964.

5. Garber, Dr. John A., "Inter-Virginia Romance and Marriage, Garber-Arnold," 1822-23.

6. Garber, Wayne E., "Early Glimpses of Family Life of Homer Franklin and Sallie Belle Garber, 1910-1930," Interview with Cleatis Garber, 2003.

7. Garber, Wayne E., "Glimpses of Family Life of Homer Franklin and Sallie Belle Garber, 1930-1950," Interview with Anna Lee "Dolly" Garber Harner, 2003.

8. Garber, Wayne Edward and Harner, Owen Early, *The History of New Hope Virginia, The Past Two Hundred Years*, "Humbert-Knightly Mill," 2006.

9. Garber, Wayne E., "Jacob Garber Farm Deed from the Lottery," Augusta County Courthouse.

10. Koons, Kenneth E. and Hofstra, Warren R., *After the Backcountry, Rural Life in the Great Valley of Virginia, 1800-1900.*

11. Mason, Floyd, *John H. Garber & Barbara Miller of Pennsylvania, Maryland and Virginia*, 1998.

12. May, C. E., *Life Under Four Flags In North River Basin of Virginia*, 1976.

13. May, C. E., *My Augusta*, 1987.

14. Mc Cleary, Ann, *Eighteen Century to the Present, Historic Landmarks of Virginia*, 1982.

15. Mitchell, Floyd H., "A Message from a Flower," 1949.

16. Obituary for Daniel S. Garber from *Staunton News-Leader*, 1923.

17. Obituary for Homer F. Garber from *Waynesboro News-Virginian*, October 16, 1973.

18. Obituary for Levi Garber from *Staunton News-Leader*, 1914.

19. Obituary for Sallie Belle Garber from *Waynesboro News-Virginian*, April 14, 1989.

20. Peyton, I. Lewis, *History of Augusta County, Virginia.*

21. "The Clifton B. Garber Family Record," 1989.

22. Wayland, John W., *The Virginia Magazine of History and Biography*, "The Germans of the Valley," October 1902.

23. Wine, Jacob David, *A History of Flat Rock, Church of the Brethren*, 1962.

24. Wittig, Mildred Renalds "Jacob Garber Family Reunion Minutes," 1922 – 2005.

Gail and Wayne Garber, 2007

About the Author

As a native of Virginia's Shenandoah Valley near Waynesboro, Virginia, Wayne Garber is a descendant of John H. Garber (1732 – 1787), who lived at Flat Rock near New Market in Shenandoah County, Virginia. Wayne lived in New Hope, Virginia, until he was eight years old and was a member of the Middle River Church of the Brethren until he was 11 years old. He is a graduate of Woodrow Wilson High School, Class of 1962 and has a Bachelor's Degree in Business Administration from Virginia Tech, 1966. In 1965, he met Gail Twombly of Vienna, Virginia, on a blind date; they were married in 1966. Wayne and Gail have two children, Marc Wayne Garber, born 1971, and Holly Michelle Garber, born 1980. Wayne maintained his roots in the Valley by owning a cattle farm near Greenville, Virginia, from 1977 to 1987. He is a former Human Resources Management professional in the management consulting industry and founder/owner of Wayne Garber & Associates (1995 – 2001), a retained executive search firm. Wayne is now retired and lives in Williamsburg, Virginia, where he enjoys playing tennis, traveling in his motor home and genealogy research. He is the co-author with Owen Early Harner of *The History of New Hope Virginia, The Past Two Hundred Years*, 2006.

U.S. Generation No. 1

[1] JOHANNES "JOHN H."[5] GARBER *(JO HANNES[4] GERBER, NICLAUS[3], CHRISTIAN[2], ULRICH[1])[1]* was born Abt. 1732 in Chester, PA (probably)[1] and died November 1787 in Moore's Store, Shenandoah Co., VA[1]. He married BARBARA MILLER[2] 1752 in York Co., PA[3] daughter of MICHAEL MILLER and SUSANNA BERCHTOL. She was born 1733 in Chester, PA (probably)[3] and died 1808[3].

Notes for JOHANNES "JOHN H." GARBER:
John Garber bought 200 acres of land in 1751 near Codorus in York County, PA. They lived there until 1768 when they moved to some land on Beaver Dam Creek in Frederick County, MD. In 1775, they moved to Flat Rock in Shenandoah County, VA. He lived there until 1787 when he died. He is buried in a small graveyard on his farm.

More about JOHANNES "JOHN H." GARBER:
Burial: Garber Cemetery, Flat Rock, Rockingham Co., VA[3]
Religion: John became the first minister of the Church of the Brethren in the Shenandoah Valley of VA in 1775.
Residence: 1775, Settled in York Co., PA. He moved to Frederick Co., MD in the spring of 1768 and from there to Shenandoah Valley of VA in 1775. Founded the Flat Rock Congregation at Linville's Creek in what is now Rockingham Co.

Children of JOHANNES GARBER and BARBARA MILLER are:
[2] 3-1 SAMUEL[6] GARBER, b. 1756, York, PA, d. 1814.
[3] 3-2 JOHN H. GARBER, JR., b. Aft 1758, York, PA, d. 1819.
[4] 3-3 ABRAHAM GARBER, b. November 10, 1760, York Co., PA, d. February 16, 1848, New Hope in Augusta Co., VA.
[5] 3-4 MARTIN GARBER, b. 1761, York, PA, d. 1824, Flat Rock, Shenandoah Co., VA.
[6] 3-5 ANNA GARBER, b. 1762, Shenandoah, VA, d. 1837, Rockingham Co., VA.
[7] 3-6 JACOB G. GARBER, b. December 31, 1766, York, PA, d. September 05, 1836.
[8] 3-7 DANIEL GARBER, b. 1769, Frederick Co., MD, d. 1849.
[9] 3-8 CATHERINE GARBER, b. March 15, 1771, Frederick Co., MD, d. September 18, 1838, Rockingham Co., VA.
[10] 3-9 JOSEPH GARBER, SR., b. August 10, 1773, Beaver Dam, Frederick Co., MD, d. October 04, 1854, Montgomery Co., OH.
[11] 3-10 MAGADALENE GARBER, b. June 14, 1774, Beaver Dam, Frederick Co., MD, d. July 20, 1832, Ottobine Rock, VA.

Note:
Numbers in brackets refer to End Notes.
Numbers separated by dashes refer to U.S. Generations and birth position within each family. Because Johnannes "John H." Garber was the third child in his generation and he represents U.S. Generatiion No. 1, all of these numbers start with a 3. Each dash separates a generation. So each descendant has a unique set of numbers which helps to make it easier to track the specific ancestors for each person, even though many may have names in common with cousins within the same generation.

U.S. Generation No. 2

[2] SAMUEL[6] GARBER *(JOHANNES "JOHN H."[5], JO HANNES[4] GERBER, NICLAUS[3], CHRISTIAN[2], ULRICH[1])[4]* was born 1756 in York, PA[5], and died 1814[6]. He married MARY "MOLLIE" STONER[6], daughter of JACOB STONER and LENAH. She was born 1760.

Notes for SAMUEL GARBER:
They lived at Beaver Dam, Frederick County, MD, until 1782, when they moved to Flat Rock, Shenandoah County, VA. They lived on some land on Fort Run, near Timberville, Rockingham County, VA, that was inherited by Mary from her father, Jacob Stoner. In the year 1811, Samuel Garber and his brother Joseph went to TN as missionaries. Samuel died in TN and was buried there. Joseph went from TN to OH and settled in Montgomery Co. Samuel and Molly were the parents of eleven children; most were born in the Beaver Dam area of MD. Before going to TN, Samuel had moved his family into Shenandoah County, VA, where he settled on land near his father's homestead. Of his eleven children, son John became the progenitor of the large family group.

Children of SAMUEL GARBER and MARY STONER are:
[2]	3-1-1	SAMUEL[7] GARBER, b. Abt. 1774.
[3]	3-1-2	HENRY GARBER, b. Abt. 1775.
[4]	3-1-3	SUSANNA GARBER, b. Abt. 1776.
[5]	3-1-4	MARY GARBER, b. Abt. 1777.
[6]	3-1-5	ABRAHAM GARBER, b. Abt. 1778.
[7]	3-1-6	ELIZABETH GARBER, b. 1779.
[8]	3-1-7	DAVID GARBER, b. 1780, m. SALOMA ZETTY.

More about DAVID GARBER:
Residence: They lived near Lacey Springs, Rockingham County, VA.

[9]	3-1-8	SOLOMON GARBER, b. 1781.
[10]	3-1-9	HANNAH GARBER, b. 1782.
[11]	3-1-10	NOAH GARBER, b. 1783.
[12]	3-1-11	JOHN GARBER, b. November 29, 1784, d. October 03, 1856, OH, m. M. NANCY ERBAUGH.

Notes for JOHN GARBER:
John became progenitor of the large Garber family in OH.

CATHERINE GARBER m. JACOB RIFE 1817.

[3] JOHN H.[6] GARBER, JR. *(JOHANNES "JOHN H."[5], JO HANNES[4] GERBER, NICLAUS[3], CHRISTIAN[2], ULRICH[1])[7]* was born Aft. 1758 in York, PA[8] and died 1819[9]. He married (1) BARBARA ZOOK[10]. She died 1808[11]. He married (2) FANNIE.

Notes for JOHN H. GARBER, JR.:
Some think that when the family moved to VA in 1775, John lived with his brother Martin until about 1780, when, as a young minister in the Church of the Brethren, he began his pioneer missionary journey. There is some evidence that he went to Somerset or Bedford County, PA. He is believed to be the John Garber who was ordained at Stony Creek, Brothers Valley, PA, in 1771. The birth of his children places the family at Botetourt County, VA, and then they went with some of the early migrations of Dunkers to

Muhlenbery Co., KY, and into OH. About 1786, he returned to Flat Rock, VA, and in 1787 attended annual conference of the Church of the Brethren at Pipes Creek, MD. At this time, he attended his father's funeral. After this conference and the funeral, he is believed to have journeyed to southern OH and was one of the early ministers who helped organize the Stonelick Church. He lived in Clermont Co. until 1802, when they moved to fertile lands west of Springfield, OH, which was then Champaign Co., OH, where he lived the remainder of his life. He left his will made December 11, 1813, and recorded June 3, 1814. He traveled widely during these years ministering to the churches in MD, VA, KY, IN and OH.

Children of JOHN GARBER and BARBARA ZOOK are:

	3-2-1	NANCY[7] GARBER[11], b. 1770, Botetourt, VA.
	3-2-2	JACOB GARBER[11], b. 1772, Botetourt, VA.
	3-2-3	BARBARA GARBER[11], b. 1774, Botetourt, VA.
	3-2-4	JOSEPH GARBER[11], b. 1776, Botetourt, VA.
	3-2-5	ABRAHAM GARBER[11], b. 1778, Botetourt, VA.
	3-2-6	ELIZABETH GARBER[11], b. 1780, Botetourt, VA.
[12]	3-2-7	MARY GARBER, b. 1782, Botetourt, VA, d. Lexington, KY.
[13]	3-2-8	MAGDALENE GARBER, b. 1784, Botetourt, VA.
	3-2-9	SAMUEL GARBER[11], b. 1800, OH.

[4] ABRAHAM[6] GARBER (JOHANNES "JOHN H."[5], JO HANNES[4] GERBER, NICLAUS[3], CHRISTIAN[2], ULRICH[1])[12] was born November 10, 1760 in York Co., PA[13], and died February 16, 1848, in New Hope, Augusta Co., VA[13]. He married ELIZABETH HUMBERT[14] 1790, in Augusta Co., VA[14], daughter of JACOB HUMBERT. She was born 1760, in Augusta Co., VA, and died 1838 in New Hope, Augusta Co, VA[15].

More about ABRAHAM GARBER:
Burial: 1848, Middle River Church of the Brethren in Augusta Co., VA[16]
Will: Dated 1843, the will is lengthy and detailed.

More about ELIZABETH HUMBERT:
Burial: Middle River Church of the Brethren in Augusta Co., VA

Children of ABRAHAM GARBER and ELIZABETH HUMBERT are:

[14]	3-3-1	JOHN[7] GARBER, b. July 14, 1792, New Hope, Augusta Co., VA, d. July 16, 1854.
	3-3-2	SARAH "SALLIE" GARBER[17], b. Abt. 1793, New Hope, Augusta Co, VA[18]; m. CHRISTIAN WHITMORE[19].
	3-3-3	DANIEL GARBER[20], b. October 23, 1793, New Hope, Augusta Co, VA[20]; d. 1883[21]; m. ELIZABETH DUNSTON[22], April 19, 1824, (Bond), b. 1800[22]; d. 1880[22].

More about DANIEL GARBER:
Burial: Middle River Church of the Brethren in Augusta Co., VA[23]
Occupation: Farmer

More about ELIZABETH DUNSTON:
Burial: Middle River Church of the Brethren in Augusta Co., VA

| [15] | 3-3-4 | JACOB W. GARBER, SR., b. October 28, 1797, New Hope, Augusta Co., VA; d. September 25, 1876, Mt. Sidney, VA, in Augusta Co. |
| [16] | 3-3-5 | MARY GARBER, b. 1805, New Hope, Augusta Co, VA, d. 1864. |

[17] 3-3-6 SAMUEL GARBER, b. September 22, 1806, New Hope, Augusta Co, VA, d. January 18, 1892.

[18] 3-3-7 ESTHER GARBER, b. Abt. 1813, New Hope, Augusta Co., VA, d. 1879.

[5] MARTIN[6] GARBER *(JOHANNES "JOHN H."[5], JO HANNES[4] GERBER, NICLAUS[3], CHRISTIAN[2], ULRICH[1])[24]* was born 1761, in York, PA[25], and died 1824, in Flat Rock, Shenandoah Co., VA[26]. He married REBECCA STONER[26], daughter of JACOB STONER and LENAH. She was born 1764.

More about MARTIN GARBER:
Burial: Wolfe's Cemetery, Pipe Creek congregation
Occupation: He was a farmer and Church of the Brethren Bishop of MD, VA and WV.
Property: He owned land in Rockingham Co., Shenandoah Co., VA, and Hardy Co., WV.
Religion: Church of the Brethren
Residence: They lived in Beaver Dam, Frederick Co., MD, until 1782 when they moved to Flat Rock, Shenandoah Co., VA.

Children of MARTIN GARBER and REBECCA STONER are:
[19] 3-4-1 ELIZABETH[7] GARBER, b. 1783, d. 1866.
[20] 3-4-2 JACOB GARBER, b. 1785, d. 1873.
[21] 3-4-3 CATHERINE GARBER.
[22] 3-4-4 REBECCA GARBER, b. 1790, d. 1866.

[6] ANNA[6] GARBER *(JOHANNES "JOHN H."[5], JO HANNES[4] GERBER, NICLAUS[3], CHRISTIAN[2], ULRICH[1])[27]* was born 1762 in Shenandoah, VA[27], and died 1837 in Rockingham Co., VA[27]. She married DANIEL MILLER[28], son of LODOWICH MILLER and BARBARA LONG. He was born 1752, in Shenandoah, VA[28], and died 1820 in Shenandoah, VA[28].

Notes for ANNA GARBER:
Eleven children

More about DANIEL MILLER:
Occupation: He was a farmer and Church of the Brethren minister.
Property: Bought 107 acres of land in 1783, in Shenandoah Co, VA. He then bought land and moved to the head of Cook's Creek in Rockingham Co., VA, in 1807.
Residence: Bet. 1752 - 1828, Shenandoah and Rockingham Counties

Children of ANNA GARBER and DANIEL MILLER are:
     3-5-1 JOHN[7] MILLER, d. died young m. SUSAN LEEDY, d. young.
     3-5-2 KATIE MILLER, m. JACOB RIFE.
[23] 3-5-3 MICHAEL MILLER, d. 1838.
[24] 3-5-4 DANIEL MILLER II, b. 1784, d. 1847.
[25] 3-5-5 BARBARA ANN MILLER, b. 1785, d. 1861.
[26] 3-5-6 JOSEPH MILLER, b. 1787, d. 1851.
[27] 3-5-7 JACOB MILLER, b. 1789, d. 1849.
[28] 3-5-8 SAMUEL MILLER, b. 1793, d. 1861.
[29] 3-5-9 ABRAHAM MILLER, b. 1796, d. 1862.
[30] 3-5-10 SUSANNAH MILLER, b. 1798, VA, d. 1862.
[31] 3-5-11 MARTIN MILLER, b. 1800, d. 1872.

[7] JACOB G.[6] GARBER *(JOHANNES "JOHN H."[5], JO HANNES[4] GERBER, NICLAUS[3], CHRIS-TIAN[2], ULRICH[1])*[29] was born December 31, 1766, in York, PA[30], and died September 05, 1836[31]. He married SUSANNA HUMBERT[31] Abt. 1790, daughter of JACOB HUMBERT. She was born 1771[31], and died 1854, in Flat Rock, Shenandoah Co., VA[31].

More about JACOB G. GARBER:
Residence: Remained in Flat Rock area, had three children and inherited the home place.

Children of JACOB GARBER and SUSANNA HUMBERT are:
[32] 3-6-1 ELIZABETH[7] GARBER, b. 1791, d. 1848.
       3-6-2 CATHERINE GARBER, b. 1796, m. ABRAHAM CRUMPACKER.
[33] 3-6-3 JACOB GARBER, JR., b. 1799, d. 1855, during yellow fever/diphtheria epidemic.
       3-6-4 JOHN GARBER, b. 1808.
       3-6-5 ? GARBER, b. Abt. 1818.
       3-6-6 ? GARBER, b. Abt. 1820.

[8] DANIEL[6] GARBER *(JOHANNES "JOHN H."[5], JO HANNES[4] GERBER, NICLAUS[3], CHRISTIAN[2], ULRICH[1])*[32] was born 1769, in Frederick Co., MD[33], and died 1849. He married (1) SUSANNA MILLER[34], daughter of JACOB MILLER. She was born Abt. 1780. He married (2) ELIZABETH SHANK[34].

Notes for DANIEL GARBER:
He left a will naming his wife Elizabeth and one son, Daniel Garber. He had land in Augusta Co. and Rockingham Co., VA. He left 58 acres of land in trust with income to be used for the poor members of the German Baptist Church (Church of the Brethren).

More about DANIEL GARBER:
Occupation: He was a Church of the Brethren minister and farmer.
Property: 1822, Donated land for the Garber's Church of the Brethren near Harrisonburg, VA. It is believed that this is land that came to Elizabeth from her uncle Daniel Miller.
Residence: They lived near Harrisonburg, VA.

Child of DANIEL GARBER and SUSANNA MILLER is:
[34] 3-7-1 DANIEL[7] GARBER, JR., b. 1804, d. 1865.

[9] CATHERINE[6] GARBER *(JOHANNES "JOHN H."[5], JO HANNES[4] GERBER, NICLAUS[3], CHRIS-TIAN[2], ULRICH[1])*[35] was born March 15, 1771, in Frederick Co., MD[36], and died September 18, 1838, in Rockingham Co., VA[36]. She married JOHN FLORY[37] April 26, 1790, son of ABRAHAM FLORY and CATHERINE BLOCKER. He was born 1766[37] and died 1845[37].

More about CATHERINE GARBER:
Burial: Early Cemetery, Pleasant Valley, Rockingham Co., VA
Residence: Lived near Cook's Creek - Garber Meeting House, Harrisonburg, VA.   Ten children

More about JOHN FLORY:
Burial: Early Cemetery, Pleasant Valley, Rockingham Co., VA
Occupation: He was a Church of the Brethren minister.
Residence: They moved from Franklin Co., PA, near Hagerstown, MD, to Pleasant Valley, VA.

Children of CATHERINE GARBER and JOHN FLORY are:
[35] 3-8-1   DANIEL[7] FLORY, b. 1791, d. 1855.
[36] 3-8-2   SUSANNA FLORY, b. 1792, d. 1871.
[37] 3-8-3   JOHN FLORY, b. 1794, d. 1853.
[38] 3-8-4   JACOB FLORY, b. 1797, d. 1842.
[39] 3-8-5   CATHERINE FLORY, b. 1799, d. 1831.
[40] 3-8-6   SAMUEL FLORY, b. 1801, d. 1869.
[41] 3-8-7   MICHAEL FLORY, b. 1803, d. 1858.
[42] 3-8-8   ELIZABETH FLORY, b. 1807, d. 1855.
[43] 3-8-9   ABRAHAM FLORY, b. 1809, d. 1880.
          3-8-10 ANNA FLORY, b. 1813, m. ABRAM EARLY.

10. JOSEPH[6] GARBER, SR. *(JOHANNES "JOHN H."[5], JO HANNES[4] GERBER, NICLAUS[3], CHRIS-TIAN[2], ULRICH[1])[38]* was born August 10, 1773, in Beaver Dam, Frederick Co., MD[39], and died October 04, 1854, in Montgomery Co., OH[39]. He married CATHERINE LEEDY[40] September 26, 1798, in Rockingham Co, VA, daughter of SAMUEL LEEDY and CATHERINE WEIDNER. She was born October 19, 1777[40], and died August 21, 1851, buried in Dunkard Cemetery in Perry Twp., Shelby County, IL[40].

Notes for JOSEPH GARBER, SR.:
Joseph lived in Randolph Twp., Montgomery Co., OH, in 1820, but was listed as living on "Ten Mile" when the Stonelick District in Clermont Co. was organized in 1802. On April 13, 1820, Joseph Garber purchased 157 acres of land in Madison Twp., Montgomery Co., OH, and built a cabin where his family lived for 12 years. Joseph was ordained an Elder and held the oversight of the Lower Stillwater Church for some years. Joseph and Catherine were parents of four children. In 1828, Joseph and Catherine sold their 157-acre farm to Felix and Elizabeth Landis for $1200, and Felix built a new home there about 1832. They were still living there in 1844, when Elder John Kline recorded spending the night with the Joseph Garbers and visiting the next day at Felix Landis'. In 1849, Felix and Elizabeth sold the farm, and with their seven youngest children and one daughter-in-law, headed west where the parents eventually landed in 1872, in Bond County, IL. Possibly about the time Felix and Elizabeth departed for the west, Elizabeth's parents, Joseph and Catherine Garber, gave up caring for them and went to Shelby County, OH, and made their home with their daughter and son-in-law, Susannah and Joseph Kessler. Catherine died on August 25, 1851, and is buried in the Dunkard Cemetery in Perry Twp., Shelby County, OH. Joseph died October 5, 1854, and is buried beside his wife in the little cemetery by the side of the road. After the parent's deaths, Joseph and Susannah Kessler moved to Bond County, IL, where he served in the ministry in the Hurricane Creek congregation.

More about JOSEPH GARBER, SR.:
Burial: Dunkard Cemetery in Perry Twp., Shelby Co., IL
Occupation: He was a Church of the Brethren minister.
Property: He purchased a farm in Madison Twp, Montgomery Co., OH. He was an Elder in the Old German Baptist Brethren Church and was in charge of the Lost Creek Church.
Residence: He was bought to Shenandoah Co., VA, when he was two years old. After his marriage, he and his brother Samuel journeyed to Johnson City, TN, on missionary work.

Children of JOSEPH GARBER and CATHERINE LEEDY are:
[44] 3-9-1   ELIZABETH[7] GARBER, b. September 04, 1799, Rockingham Co., VA,
              d. December 15, 1885, Bond Co. IL.

3-9-2   SUSANNAH GARBER, b. 1801, Rockingham Co., VA, d. 1865, Bond Co. IL; m. JOSEPH J. KESSLER; b. 1801, Wilkes Co., NC; d. 1873, Bond Co. IL.
[45]   3-9-3   CATHARINE GARBER, b. 1807, d. 1890, Bond Co., IL.
[46]   3-9-4   JOSEPH GARBER, JR., b. 1814, d. 1893.

[11] MAGADALENE[6] GARBER *(JOHANNES "JOHN H."[5], JO HANNES[4] GERBER, NICLAUS[3], CHRISTIAN[2], ULRICH[1])[41]* was born June 14, 1774, in Beaver Dam, Frederick Co., MD[42], and died July 20, 1832, in Ottobine Rock, VA[43]. She married GEORGE WINE[43] 1796, son of MICHAEL WINE and SUSANNAH MILLER. He was born 1774[43] and died 1845[43].

More about MAGADALENE GARBER:
Residence: Lived near Ottobine, Rockingham Co., VA. They had eight children.

More about GEORGE WINE:
Occupation: He was a farmer and Church of the Brethren minister.

Children of MAGADALENE GARBER and GEORGE WINE are:
[47]   3-10-1   MICHAEL[7] WINE, b. 1797, d. 1874.
[48]   3-10-2   JOHN WINE, b. 1799.
[49]   3-10-3   JACOB WINE, b. 1801, d. 1878.
[50]   3-10-4   DANIEL WINE, b. 1804.
[51]   3-10-5   BARBARA WINE, b. 1807.
[52]   3-10-6   SOLOMON WINE, b. 1812.
[53]   3-10-7   SUSANNAH WINE, b. 1813, d. 1878.
[54]   3-10-8   GEORGE WINE, b. 1817, d. 1895.

U.S. Generation No. 3

[12] MARY[7] GARBER *(JOHN H.[6], JOHANNES "JOHN H."[5], JO HANNES[4] GERBER, NICLAUS[3], CHRISTIAN[2], ULRICH[1])[44]* was born 1782 in Botetourt, VA, and died in Lexington, KY. She married PAUL CUSTER in Bertie Co., NC, son of JOHN CUSTER and ELIZABETH HOUSER. He was born 1778 and died 1864 in Dublin, IN.

Children of MARY GARBER and PAUL CUSTER are:
3-2-7-1   MARY[8] CUSTER.
3-2-7-2   JOHN CUSTER.
3-2-7-3   CHRISTOPHER CUSTER.
3-2-7-4   WILLIAM CUSTER, b. 1808, Tipton, IN.
3-2-7-5   ELIZABETH CUSTER.
3-2-7-6   JACOB CUSTER.
3-2-7-7   SOLOMON CUSTER.
3-2-7-8   PAUL CUSTER.
3-2-7-9   LEWIS CUSTER, b. 1825, d. 1855, Bloomington, IL.

[13] MAGDALENE[7] GARBER *(JOHN H.[6], JOHANNES "JOHN H."[5], JO HANNES[4] GERBER, NICLAUS[3], CHRISTIAN[2], ULRICH[1])[44]* was born 1784, in Botetourt, VA. She married (1) PETER MINNICH, SR.[44]. He was born 1783 in Lancaster, PA. She married (2) DANIEL FRANTZ. He was born 1763 in Lancaster Co., PA.

Notes for MAGDALENE GARBER:
Twelve children

Children of MAGDALENE GARBER and PETER MINNICH are:

	3-2-8-1	CATHERINE[8] MINNICH, b. 1804, Botetourt Co., VA.
	3-2-8-2	ELIZABETH MINNICH, b. 1807, VA.
	3-2-8-3	MARGARET MINNICH, b. 1808, VA.
	3-2-8-4	HANNAH MINNICH, b. 1810, Clark Co., OH.
	3-2-8-5	JOHN MINNICH, b. 1812, Clark Co., OH.
	3-2-8-6	PETER MINNICH, b. 1812, Clark Co., OH.
[55]	3-2-8-7	JACOB MINNICH, b. 1814, Clark Co., OH.

Children of MAGDALENE GARBER and DANIEL FRANTZ are:

3-2-8-8	JOEL[8] FRANTZ, m. MARY NEHER.
3-2-8-9	SALOME FRANTZ, b. 1823.
3-2-8-10	ELIZABETH FRANTZ, b. 1825.
3-2-8-11	SAMUEL FRANTZ, b. 1832.
3-2-8-12	ELIZABETH FRANTZ.

[14] JOHN[7] GARBER *(ABRAHAM[6], JOHANNES "JOHN H."[5], JO HANNES[4] GERBER, NICLAUS[3], CHRISTIAN[2], ULRICH[1])[45]* was born July 14, 1792, in New Hope, Augusta Co., VA[46], and died July 16, 1854[47]. He married CATHERINE "KITTY" MILLER[47] April 09, 1816, daughter of SAMUEL MILLER and SUSANNAH. She was born 1794[47] and died 1857[47]. They were married by Abraham Garber[47].

Notes for JOHN GARBER:
John Garber and Peter Miller were co-ministers and elders at Middle River Church from 1824-1854. Strangely they died within a month of each other at a time when their work was culminating in the opening of new churches at Pleasant Valley and Barren Ridge and just six years after the death of Abraham Garber. John died of the flux (discharge of larger quantities of fluid material). He and Catherine are buried at the Middle River Church.

More about JOHN GARBER:
Burial: Middle River Church of the Brethren in Augusta Co., VA[47]
Occupation: Farmer and minister - only son to become a minister and elder in his father's church.
Property: In 1819, John sold land along Middle River to the Huffs and Humberts. Such land was adjacent and nearby to what was later Cliff and Josie Garber's small farm.
Will: Dated 1854, John Garber's will is interesting, but not as detailed as many for that period and was prepared just nine days before his death.

More about CATHERINE "KITTY" MILLER:
Burial: Middle River Church of the Brethren in Augusta Co., VA

Children of JOHN GARBER and CATHERINE MILLER are:
    3-3-1-1   ELIZABETH[8] GARBER, b. 1818, d. 1867, m. JOHN BROWER, JR.[47], 1841.

More about ELIZABETH GARBER:
Residence: They moved to Kansas and helped establish churches there.
More about JOHN BROWER, JR.:
Occupation: Church of the Brethren minister

[56]   3-3-1-2   SAMUEL MILLER GARBER, b. 1820, d. Aft. 1860.
[57]   3-3-1-3   BENJAMIN GARBER, b. 1822, Augusta Co., VA, d. 1858.
[58]   3-3-1-4   ELI GARBER, b. 1826, d. 1884.
        3-3-1-5   JOHN H. GARBER[47], b. 1832[47], d. 1871[47]; m. BARBARA A. GROVE[47].

[15] JACOB W.[7] GARBER, SR. (*ABRAHAM[6], JOHANNES "JOHN H."[5], JO HANNES[4] GERBER, NICLAUS[3], CHRISTIAN[2], ULRICH[1]*)[48] was born October 28, 1797, in New Hope, Augusta Co., VA[49], and died September 25, 1876, in Mt. Sidney, VA, in Augusta Co.[49] He married NANCY ARNOLD[50] March 10, 1823, in Augusta Co., VA[50], and daughter of SAMUEL ARNOLD. She was born April 12, 1805, in Hampshire Co., WV[50], and died February 29, 1868, in Mt. Sidney, VA, in Augusta Co[50].
More about JACOB W. GARBER, SR.:
Burial: Middle River Church of the Brethren in Augusta County, VA
Occupation: Farmer

More about NANCY ARNOLD:
Burial: Middle River Church of the Brethren in Augusta Co., VA

Children of JACOB GARBER and NANCY ARNOLD are:
[59]   3-3-4-1   REBEKAH[8] GARBER, b. December 27, 1823, d. July 24, 1886.
[60]   3-3-4-2   ABRAHAM D. GARBER, b. December 19, 1824, d. December 01, 1911.
[61]   3-3-4-3   LEVI GARBER, b. August 21, 1828, New Hope, Augusta Co., VA,
                d. November 10, 1914, Mt. Sidney, Augusta Co., VA.
[62]   3-3-4-4   REUBEN ARNOLD GARBER, b. January 26, 1836, d. January 10, 1884.
[63]   3-3-4-5   JACOB W. GARBER, b. September 11, 1842, d. August 28, 1908.

[16] MARY[7] GARBER (*ABRAHAM[6], JOHANNES "JOHN H."[5], JO HANNES[4] GERBER, NICLAUS[3], CHRISTIAN[2], ULRICH[1]*)[50] was born 1805 in New Hope, Augusta Co, VA[51], and died 1864. She married JOHN ARION[52]. He was born 1799[53] and died Abt. 1870[53].

More about JOHN ARION:
Residence: They lived in Augusta Co., Virginia.

Children of MARY GARBER and JOHN ARION are:
    3-3-5-1   ABRAHAM[8] ARION, b. 1834.
    3-3-5-2   CORNELIUS ARION, b. 1837.
    3-3-5-3   CHARLOTTE REBECCA ARION, b. 1841.

[17] SAMUEL[7] GARBER *(ABRAHAM[6], JOHANNES "JOHN H."[5], JO HANNES[4] GERBER, NICLAUS[3], CHRISTIAN[2], ULRICH[1])*[54] was born September 22, 1806, in New Hope, Augusta Co, VA[55], and died January 18, 1892. He married on June 21, 1838, ANNA PETERS, daughter of GEORGE PETERS and REBECCA RHODES. She was born 1811 and died 1900.

More about SAMUEL GARBER:
Burial: Middle River Church of the Brethren in Augusta Co., VA[56]
Occupation: Farmer

More about ANNA PETERS:
Burial: Middle River Church of the Brethren in Augusta Co., VA

Children of SAMUEL GARBER and ANNA PETERS are:
- 3-3-6-1 ELI ABRAHAM[8] GARBER, b. 1838, d. 1908.
- 3-3-6-2 SARAH A. GARBER, b. 1840, d. 1886.
- 3-3-6-3 WILLIAM BENJAMIN GARBER, b. 1842, d. 1920.
- 3-3-6-4 JOSEPH NOAH GARBER, b. 1845, d. 1893.
- 3-3-6-5 GEORGE WASHINGTON GARBER, b. 1847, d. 1922.
- 3-3-6-6 ELIZABETH H. GARBER, b. 1848, d. 1877.
- 3-3-6-7 MARY CATHERINE GARBER, b. 1852, d. 1930.

[18] ESTHER[7] GARBER *(ABRAHAM[6], JOHANNES "JOHN H."[5], JO HANNES[4] GERBER, NICLAUS[3], CHRISTIAN[2], ULRICH[1])*[57] was born Abt. 1813 in New Hope, Augusta Co., VA[58], and died 1879. She married ABRAHAM STONER[59] May 15, 1833. She was married by Abraham Garber. He was born Abt. 1805 and died Bef. 1850.

More about ESTHER GARBER:
Residence: In 1870 she moved to Preble County, OH, with her son Levi.

Children of ESTHER GARBER and ABRAHAM STONER are:
- 3-3-7-1 LEVI GARBER[8] STONER, b. 1835, d. 1924.
- 3-3-7-2 DANIEL GARBER STONER, b. 1836, d. 1912, Eaton, OH.
- 3-3-7-3 SARAH E. STONER, b. Abt. 1842, d. 1924.

[19] ELIZABETH[7] GARBER *(MARTIN[6], JOHANNES "JOHN H."[5], JO HANNES[4] GERBER, NICLAUS[3], CHRISTIAN[2], ULRICH[1])* was born 1783 and died 1866. She married JOHN WINE, son of MICHAEL WINE and SUSANNAH MILLER. He was born 1776 and died 1844.

More about JOHN WINE:
Occupation: He was a farmer whose land adjoined his Church of the Brethren father-in-law's farm at Flat Rock, VA.

Children of ELIZABETH GARBER and JOHN WINE are:
- 3-4-1-1 REBECCA[8] WINE, b. 1804.
- 3-4-1-2 MICHAEL WINE, b. 1806.
- 3-4-1-3 SUSANNAH WINE, b. 1808.
- 3-4-1-5 JACOB WINE, b. 1811.
- 3-4-1-5 CATHERINE WINE, b. 1813.

[20] JACOB[7] GARBER *(MARTIN[6], JOHANNES "JOHN H."[5], JO HANNES[4] GERBER, NICLAUS[3], CHRISTIAN[2], ULRICH[1])* was born 1785 and died 1873. He married SALOME HOOVER, daughter of JACOB HOOVER and BARBARA MYER. She was born 1793 and died 1858.

More about JACOB GARBER:
Occupation: He was a farmer on his father's farm at Flat Rock, VA.

Children of JACOB GARBER and SALOME HOOVER are:
3-4-2-1	MARTIN[8] GARBER, b. 1814, d. 1876, m. ELIZABETH WINE.
3-4-2-2	JOHN M. GARBER, b. 1818, d. 1877, m. ANNA MYERS.
3-4-2-3	ANNA GARBER, b. 1820, d. 1877, m. MICHAEL BOWMAN.
3-4-2-4	ELIZABETH GARBER, b. 1815, m. DANIEL NEFF.
3-4-2-5	SAMUEL GARBER, b. 1822, m. HANNAH MYERS.
3-4-2-6	JOSEPH J. GARBER, b. 1823, d. 1884.
3-4-2-7	ABRAHAM GARBER, b. 1827, d. June 05, 1898, m. ANNA MILLER.

Notes for ABRAHAM GARBER:
Mr. Noah Garber's father, Abraham Garber, served as Chairman of the Board of Supervisors of Shenandoah Co. for a number of years and died on June 5, 1898. The farm, located near Flat Rock Church, where Mr. Garber was born and where he spent his entire life, was granted to his great grandfather, Elder Martin Garber, on May 19, 1788, as assignee of Jacob Baughman (Bowman) by Governor Beverly Randolph. A copy of an old deposition is available which shows at least a portion of the 620-acre plantation had formerly been granted to Mary Hill, widow, in 1757 by Thomas Lord Fairfax. This place was willed to Mr. Garber's grandfather, Jacob Garber, who passed it to his son Abraham, who willed his portion to Noah Garber and brothers.

More about ABRAHAM GARBER:
Occupation: Farmer
Residence: Owned farm near Flat Rock Church in Shenandoah Co., VA.

[21] CATHERINE[7] GARBER *(MARTIN[6], JOHANNES "JOHN H."[5], JO HANNES[4] GERBER, NICLAUS[3], CHRISTIAN[2], ULRICH[1])* Catherine married SAMUEL BOWMAN, son of JOSEPH BOWMAN and ESTHER BECHTEL. He was born 1787.

More about CATHERINE GARBER:
Religion: Church of the Brethren
Residence: They moved from PA and MD to Rockingham Co., VA, about 1784 and lived on Linville Creek somewhere around Edom, VA.

Children of CATHERINE GARBER and SAMUEL BOWMAN are:
3-4-3-1	ELIZABETH[8] BOWMAN, b. 1811, m. JACOB TROUT.
3-4-3-2	JOSEPH GARBER BOWMAN, b. 1814.
3-4-3-3	DAVID PENDELTON BOWMAN, b. 1814, d. 1858; m. DEBORAH DYERS.
3-4-3-4	JOHN J. BOWMAN, m. ABIGAIL HOMAN.
3-4-3-5	ESTHER BOWMAN, m. ELISHA JORDAN.

Notes for ESTHER BOWMAN:
Was a twin with her sister, Rebecca Bowman

3-4-3-6   REBECCA BOWMAN, m. JOHN JACOB BARGLEBAUGH.

Notes for REBECCA BOWMAN:
Was a twin with sister, Esther Bowman

3-4-3-7   JACOB C. BOWMAN.

[22] REBECCA[7] GARBER *(MARTIN[6], JOHANNES "JOHN H."[5], JO HANNES[4] GERBER, NICLAUS[3], CHRISTIAN[2], ULRICH[1])* was born 1790 and died 1866. She married JACOB BOWMAN, son of BENJAMIN BOWMAN and CATHERINE SHOEMAKER. He was born 1793 and died 1848.

More about REBECCA GARBER:
Residence: They lived in Rockingham Co., VA.

Children of REBECCA GARBER and JACOB BOWMAN are:
    3-4-4-1   CATHERINE[8] BOWMAN, b. 1817.
    3-4-4-2   ELIZABETH BOWMAN, b. 1818, d. 1889.
    3-4-4-3   REBECCA BOWMAN, b. 1820.
    3-4-4-4   BENJAMIN FRANKLIN BOWMAN, b. 1823, d. 1902.
    3-4-4-5   SAMUEL BOWMAN, b. 1825, d. 1858.
    3-4-4-6   SARAH BOWMAN, b. 1827.
    3-4-4-7   MARY BOWMAN, b. 1829.
    3-4-4-8   JACOB BOWMAN, b. 1833, m. SARAH MARGARET MALONEY.

[23] MICHAEL[7] MILLER *(ANNA[6] GARBER, JOHANNES "JOHN H."[5], JO HANNES[4] GERBER, NICLAUS[3], CHRISTIAN[2], ULRICH[1])* died 1838. He married MARY SANGER, daughter of CONRAD SANGER and ANNA BRILLINGER. She was born 1807 and died 1885.

Notes for MICHAEL MILLER:
He is reported to have burned to death in a barn fire when he attempted to get his horse out by a side door which he found locked from the outside. Mary then moved with her children to Dayton, VA, before she married Joe Matheny and moved with her children to English River, IA.

Children of MICHAEL MILLER and MARY SANGER are:
    3-5-3-1   JOHN[8] MILLER, b. 1826, d. 1907.
    3-5-3-2   ANNIE MILLER, b. 1827, d. 1915.
    3-5-3-3   NOAH MILLER, b. 1829, d. 1912.
    3-5-3-4   SUSAN MILLER, b. 1832, d. 1906.
    3-5-3-5   SARAH CATHERINE MILLER, b. 1833.
    3-5-3-6   MARY MILLER, b. 1834.
    3-5-3-7   BARBARA MILLER, b. 1835.
    3-5-3-8   LIZZIE MILLER, b. 1836, d. 1914.
    3-5-3-9   LYDIA MILLER, b. 1837.
    3-5-3-10   MICHAEL MILLER, b. 1839, d. 1922.

[24] DANIEL[7] MILLER II (*ANNA[6] GARBER, JOHANNES "JOHN H."[5], JO HANNES[4] GERBER, NICLAUS[3], CHRISTIAN[2], ULRICH[1]*) was born 1784 and died 1847. He married ANNA HOOVER, daughter of JACOB HOOVER and BARBARA MYER. She was born 1785 and died 1860.

Notes for DANIEL MILLER II:
He was an able leader in the Church of the Brethren and the Elder who presented the famous church leader Elder John Kline for the ministry. He traveled with Elder John Kline and often preached in German, which Elder Kline would follow in English. Elder John Kline gives many of the sermons of Elder Daniel Miller II in his diary. He was a farmer in the Greenmount area where they lived and are buried. Six of their sons were Church of the Brethren ministers.

Children of DANIEL MILLER and ANNA HOOVER are:

3-5-4-1	SAMUEL[8] MILLER, b. 1808, d. 1878, m. FANNIE WINE.
3-5-4-2	JOHN D. MILLER, b. 1809, d. 1878; m. ELIZABETH MOYERS, b. 1810, d. 1881.
3-5-4-3	ISAAC MILLER, b. 1810, d. 1895, m. SALLIE MOYERS.
3-5-4-4	CATHERINE MILLER, b. Abt. 1811, m. ELDER CHRISTIAN WINE, b. 1811, d. 1893.
3-5-4-5	DANIEL MILLER III, b. 1812, d. 1877, m. (1) MAGDALENA GLICK, b. 1820, d. 1851, m. (2) CATHERINE KESECKER, b. 1812, d. 1895.
3-5-4-6	JACOB MILLER, b. 1814, d. 1888, m. ELIZABETH BOWMAN, b. 1818, d. 1897.
3-5-4-7	JOSEPH MILLER, b. Abt. 1815, d. 1850, m. CATHERINE BOWMAN, b. 1816.
3-5-4-8	FREDERICK MILLER, b. 1816, d. 1899, m. MARY BOWMAN, b. 1820, d. 1864.
3-5-4-9	ABRAHAM MILLER, b. 1817, d. 1876, m. LYDIA TEETERS, b. 1820, d. 1892.
3-5-4-10	ANNIE MILLER, b. 1818, d. 1880, m. SAMUEL ZIGLER, b. 1816, d. 1901.
3-5-4-11	BARBARA MILLER, m. SAMUEL SANGER, b. 1814, d. 1879.
3-5-4-12	SALLIE MILLER, b. 1821, d. 1901, m. DANIEL BOWMAN, b. 1813, d. 1903.
3-5-4-13	MARY MILLER, b. 1822, d. 1907, m. JOHN ZIGLER, b. 1809, d. 1898.
3-5-4-14	UNNAMED CHILD.
3-5-4-15	SUSAN MILLER, m BEN WAMPLER.
3-5-4-16	ELIZABETH MILLER, b. 1826, d. 1871, m. GEORGE WASHINGTON HOGAN, b. 1820, d. 1890.
3-5-4-17	REBECCA MILLER, b. Abt. 1827, d. Abt. 1831.
3-5-4-18	BENJAMIN MILLER, b. 1829, d. 1913, m. (1) HETTIE SHOWALTER, b. 1829, d. 1898, m. (2) CATHERINE SHOWALTER FITZWATER.

[25] BARBARA ANN[7] MILLER (*ANNA[6] GARBER, JOHANNES "JOHN H."[5], JO HANNES[4] GERBER, NICLAUS[3], CHRISTIAN[2], ULRICH[1]*) was born 1785 and died 1861. She married ISSAC LONG, SR., son of JOHN LONG and FRANCES MILLER. He was born 1784 and died 1849.

Children of BARBARA MILLER and ISSAC LONG are:

3-5-5-1	JOHN S.[8] LONG, b. 1806, d. 1879, m. POLLY FIREBAUGH.
3-5-5-2	ANNIE LONG, b. 1807, d. 1881, m. DAVID WAMPLER.
3-5-5-3	DANIEL LONG, b. 1809, d. 1898, m. MARGARET RODEFFER.
3-5-5-4	SAMUEL E. LONG, b. 1812, d. 1894, m. (1) MARAGRET HEATWOLE; m. (2) BARBARA SHICKEL.
3-5-5-5	ISSAC LONG II, b. 1818, d. 1895, m. ELIZA SAUFLEY, 1841.
3-5-5-6	FRANCES LONG, m. ABRAHAM GROVE.

[26] JOSEPH[7] MILLER *(ANNA[6] GARBER, JOHANNES "JOHN H."[5], JO HANNES[4] GERBER, NICLAUS[3], CHRISTIAN[2], ULRICH[1])* was born 1787 and died 1851. He married ELIZABETH THOMAS, daughter of JOHN THOMAS and REGINA ZIEGLER. She was born 1792 and died 1849.

Children of JOSEPH MILLER and ELIZABETH THOMAS are:

  3-5-6-1   ANNIE[8] MILLER, b. 1813, d. 1897, m. JACOB SANGER.
  3-5-6-2   SUSAN MILLER, b. 1814, d. 1893, m. HENRY SANGER.
  3-5-6-3   JACOB MILLER, b. 1815, d. 1883, m. FANNIE WINE.
  3-5-6-4   ABRAHAM MILLER, b. 1817, d. 1882, m. SARAH SHICKEL.
  3-5-6-5   REGINA MILLER, b. 1818, m. JACOB SHICKEL.
  3-5-6-6   ELIZABETH MILLER, b. 1819, m. JOEL GLICK.
  3-5-6-7   BARBARA MILLER, b. 1821, d. 1902.
  3-5-6-8   JOSEPH T. MILLER, b. 1823, d. 1862, m. BARBARA GLICK.
  3-5-6-9   SARAH MILLER, b. 1824, m. SAMUEL G. GLICK.
  3-5-6-10 DANIEL MILLER, b. 1826, m. NANCY SHICKEL.
  3-5-6-11 PETER MILLER, b. 1828, d. 1904, m. (1) ELIZABETH STOUTAMYER, m. (2) MARY C. KANOST.
  3-5-6-12 INFANT - STILLBORN, b. 1830.
  3-5-6-13 JOHN J. MILLER, b. 1830, m. (1) MAGDALENE SANGER, m. (2) AMANDA L. CARICOFE.
  3-5-6-14 KATHERINE MILLER, b. 1831, d. 1832.
  3-5-6-15 LYDIA MILLER, b. 1832, d. 1910, m. DANIEL BROWER; b. 1815, d. 1893.
  3-5-6-16 HENRY MILLER, b. 1836, d. 1890, m. SARAH CATHERINE WRIGHT.

[27] JACOB[7] MILLER *(ANNA[6] GARBER, JOHANNES "JOHN H."[5], JO HANNES[4] GERBER, NICLAUS[3], CHRISTIAN[2], ULRICH[1])* was born 1789 and died 1849. He married (1) MAGDALENE SANGER. She was born 1789 and died 1849. He married (2) REGENA SHERFEY.

Children of JACOB MILLER and MAGDALENE SANGER are:

  3-5-7-1   BARBARA[8] MILLER, b. 1816, m. JAKE STOVER.
  3-5-7-2   CONRAD MILLER, b. 1821, m. MARY REAVES.
  3-5-7-3   BETTY MILLER, b. 1822, m. DAVE REEVES.
  3-5-7-4   ANNIE MILLER, b. 1824.
  3-5-7-5   SUSANNAH MILLER, b. Abt. 1824.
  3-5-7-6   MARY MILLER, b. 1825, m. SAMUEL FRANK.
  3-5-7-7   UNNAMED SON.
  3-5-7-8   JACOB MILLER, b. 1830, m. ELIZABETH PETRIE.

[28] SAMUEL[7] MILLER *(ANNA[6] GARBER, JOHANNES "JOHN H."[5], JO HANNES[4] GERBER, NICLAUS[3], CHRISTIAN[2], ULRICH[1])* was born 1793 and died 1861. He married BARBARA SANGER. She was born 1791 and died 1875.

Children of SAMUEL MILLER and BARBARA SANGER are:

  3-5-8-1   DANIEL[8] MILLER, b. 1817, m. MARY LEEDY.
  3-5-8-2   JOHN B. MILLER, b. 1818, m. (1) ELIZABETH RIGGLE; m. (2) ELIZABETH MILLER, m. (3) CHRISTINA KING, m. (4) REBECCA LEEDY.
  3-5-8-3   MARTIN MILLER, b. 1825, d. 1877, m. MARY RIGGLE.

[29] ABRAHAM⁷ MILLER *(ANNA⁶ GARBER, JOHANNES "JOHN H."⁵, JO HANNES⁴ GERBER, NICLAUS³, CHRISTIAN², ULRICH¹)* was born 1796 and died 1862. He married (1) CATHERINE LEEDY. She was born 1802 and died 1877. He married (2) SALOME FRANTZ in 1819 in Clark Co., OH, daughter of CHRISTIAN FRANTZ and MARY GARST. She was born 1794 and died 1844.

More about ABRAHAM MILLER:
Burial: Smith Cemetery in Allen Co., OH
Religion: He was a minister in the Sugar Creek Church of the Brethren.
Residence: Lived near Lima, OH

More about CATHERINE LEEDY:
Burial: Smith Cemetery in Allen Co., OH

Notes for SALOME FRANTZ:
Her family moved from Botetourt Co., VA, to Lima, OH, about 1818.

More about SALOME FRANTZ:
Burial: Smith Cemetery in Allen Co., OH

Children of ABRAHAM MILLER and SALOME FRANTZ are:

3-5-9-1 S	ARAH⁸ MILLER, b. 1820, m. DAVID EARLY.	
3-5-9-2	BARBARA MILLER, b. 1821, d. 1920, m. JOHN G. MILLER; b. 1822.	
3-5-9-3	JOSEPH MILLER, b. 1821.	
3-5-9-4	ANNA MILLER, b. 1822, m. (1) DAVID NEHER, d. 1841, m. (2) SAMUEL NEHER.	
3-5-9-5	MARY MILLER, b. 1823.	
3-5-9-6	ABRAHAM B. MILLER, b. 1825, m. DEBORAH MAXWELL.	
3-5-9-7	SALOMA MILLER, b. 1827, m. SAMUEL NEHER.	
3-5-9-8	PHOEBA MILLER, b. 1833, d. 1866, m. RIGGLE.	
3-5-9-9	DANIEL MILLER, b. 1836, d. 1917.	
3-5-9-10	SUSANNA MILLER.	
3-5-9-11	SAMUEL F. MILLER, b. 1840, d. 1912, m. MARTHA HARTER.	
3-5-9-12	MAGALENA MILLER, b. 1843, d. 1884, m. ARMENTROUT.	
3-5-9-13	ELIZABETH MILLER, b. 1845, m. SMITH.	
3-5-9-14	ALICE MILLER.	

[30] SUSANNAH⁷ MILLER *(ANNA⁶ GARBER, JOHANNES "JOHN H."⁵, JO HANNES⁴ GERBER, NICLAUS³, CHRISTIAN², ULRICH¹)* was born 1798 in VA and died 1862. She married JOHN THOMAS, son of JOHN THOMAS and REGINA ZIEGLER. He was born 1798 in Lancaster Co., PA, and died 1834.

More about SUSANNAH MILLER:
Burial: Thomas Family Cemetery on the George G. Hall farm at Dayton, VA

More about JOHN THOMAS
Burial: Thomas Family Cemetery on the George G. Hall farm at Dayton, VA
Occupation: Farmer on Crook Creek in Rockingham Co., VA

Children of SUSANNAH MILLER and JOHN THOMAS are:
    3-5-10-1   DANIEL⁸ THOMAS, b. 1822.

3-5-10-2   SARAH THOMAS.
3-5-10-3   JACOB THOMAS, b. 1823.
3-5-10-4   ANNA THOMAS, b. 1828, d. Bef. 1937.
3-5-10-5   SUSAN THOMAS, b. 1830.
3-5-10-6   ELIZABETH THOMAS, b. 1832.

[31] MARTIN[7] MILLER (*ANNA[6] GARBER, JOHANNES "JOHN H."[5], JO HANNES[4] GERBER, NICLAUS[3], CHRISTIAN[2], ULRICH[1]*) was born 1800 and died 1872. He married NANCY SANGER, daughter of CONRAD SANGER and ANNA BRILLINGER. She was born 1795 and died 1849.

More about MARTIN MILLER:
Occupation: He was a Church of the Brethren minister and farmer.
Religion: He traveled and ministered with Elder John Kline as they visited the many churches.
Residence: They lived at the Beaver Creek Church and gave the land for the church and cemetery site.

Children of MARTIN MILLER and NANCY SANGER are:
3-5-11-1   JOSEPH M.[8] MILLER, b. 1825.
3-5-11-2   ISSAC MILLER, b. 1826.
3-5-11-3   SUSAN MILLER, b. 1828.
3-5-11-4   ANNIE MILLER, b. 1832.
3-5-11-5   MARTIN MILLER, b. 1834.
3-5-11-6   ELIZABETH MILLER, b. 1835.
3-5-11-7   KATIE MILLER.
3-5-11-8   HENRY MILLER, b. 1836.
3-5-11-9   SAMUEL MILLER, b. 1839.
3-5-11-10   BARBARA MILLER, b. 1841.

[32] ELIZABETH[7] GARBER (*JACOB G.[6], JOHANNES "JOHN H."[5], JO HANNES[4] GERBER, NICLAUS[3], CHRISTIAN[2], ULRICH[1]*) was born 1791 and died 1848. She married BENJAMIN LONG, son of JOHN LONG and FRANCES MILLER. He was born 1790 and died 1848.

More about ELIZABETH GARBER:
Residence: After Benjamin's death, she moved back to Flat Rock on property her father left her.

Children of ELIZABETH GARBER and BENJAMIN LONG are:
3-6-1-1   SUSAN[8] LONG, b. 1812, m. DANIEL WAMPLER.
3-6-1-2   JOHN LONG, b. 1813, d. 1885, m. (1) ELIZABETH KIPPS,
           m. (2) REBECCA CAMPBELL.

More about JOHN LONG:
Residence: Lived at Flat Rock.

3-6-1-3   CATHERINE LONG, b. 1815, d. 1892, m. JONAS WAMPLER, b. 1814, d. 1904.

More about CATHERINE LONG:
Burial: Buried at Barren Ridge Cemetery, near Staunton, VA.

More about JONAS WAMPLER:
Burial: Buried at Barren Ridge Cemetery, near Staunton, VA.

3-6-1-4 JACOB LONG, b. 1816, d. 1855, Yellow fever, m. MARY POLLY HARPINE, b. 1815, d. 1885.

3-6-1-5 SARAH LONG, b. 1818, d. 1891, m. DANIEL STONER.

3-6-1-6 BENJAMIN LONG, b. 1820, d. 1840.

[33] JACOB[7] GARBER, JR. *(JACOB G.[6], JOHANNES "JOHN H."[5], JO HANNES[4] GERBER, NICLAUS[3], CHRISTIAN[2], ULRICH[1])* was born 1799 and died 1855 of yellow fever/diphtheria. He married LYDIA STONER, daughter of SAMUEL STONER and HANNAH STONER. She was born 1802 and died 1889.

Notes for JACOB GARBER, JR.:
Jacob, Jr., and his entire family were stricken with yellow fever. Lydia the wife, John, Daniel and Lydia the daughter were the only ones to survive. The fever was so bad that the veterinarians traveled about and carried the same medicine as medical doctors.

More about JACOB GARBER, JR.:
Burial: Garber Family Cemetery at Flat Rock, VA
Residence: They lived in Shenandoah Co. or Rockingham Co., VA.

More about LYDIA STONER:
Burial: Garber Family Cemetery at Flat Rock, VA

Children of JACOB GARBER and LYDIA STONER are:

3-6-3-1 JOHN J.[8] GARBER, b. 1829, d. 1905, m. LYDIA GETZ, b. 1832, d. 1900.

3-6-3-1 DANIEL GARBER.

3-6-3-3 SUSANNA GARBER, b. 1829, d. 1855, m. ISRAEL JONES.

More about ISRAEL JONES:
Occupation: A Confederate Army officer of the Civil War.

3-6-3-4 ELIZABETH GARBER, b. 1831, d. 1910, m. JOHN A. MILLER.

3-6-3-5 LYDIA GARBER, b. July 21, 1836, d. September 06, 1927.

More about LYDIA GARBER:
Burial: Garber Family Cemetery at Flat Rock, VA.

3-6-3-6 HANNAH GARBER, b. 1835, d. 1907, m. JOHN A. MILLER.

3-6-3-7 CATHERINE GARBER, b. 1833, d. 1855.

3-6-3-8 SALLY GARBER, b. 1835, d. 1855.

3-6-3-9 SAMUEL GARBER, b. 1838, d. 1855.

3-6-3-10 REBECCA GARBER, b. Abt. 1844, d. 1855.

3-6-3-11 JACOB GARBER, b. Abt. 1844, d. 1855.

[34] DANIEL[7] GARBER, JR. *(DANIEL[6], JOHANNES "JOHN H."[5], JO HANNES[4] GERBER,*

NICLAUS³, CHRISTIAN², ULRICH¹) was born 1804 and died 1865. He married MARY RAWLEY. She was born 1809 and died 1875.

Children of DANIEL GARBER and MARY RAWLEY are:
>   3-7-1-1   MARTIN⁸ GARBER, b. 1828, d. 1912.
>   3-7-1-2   ANNIE GARBER, b. 1837, d. 1873.
>   3-7-1-3   SUSANNA GARBER, b. 1841, d. 1927.
>   3-7-1-4   DANIEL GARBER, b. 1842, d. 1906.
>   3-7-1-5   BARBARA GARBER, b. 1848, d. 1932.
>   3-7-1-6   POLLY GARBER.
>   3-7-1-7   JOHN GARBER.

[35] DANIEL⁷ FLORY *(CATHERINE⁶ GARBER, JOHANNES "JOHN H."⁵, JO HANNES⁴ GERBER, NICLAUS³, CHRISTIAN², ULRICH¹)* was born 1791 and died 1855. He married (1) CATHERINE YOUNT, daughter of JACOB YOUNT and CATHERINE DAGEN. She died 1831. He married (2) CHRISTINA SNITEMAN. She was born 1807 and died 1871.

More about DANIEL FLORY:
Occupation: He was farmer in Augusta Co., VA, near the Barren Ridge Church of the Brethren.

Children of DANIEL FLORY and CATHERINE YOUNT are:
>   3-8-1-1   ELIZABETH⁸ FLORY, b. 1816, d. 1857.
>   3-8-1-2   JOHN FLORY, b. 1818, d. 1887.
>   3-8-1-3   BARBARA FLORY, b. 1820, d. 1891.
>   3-8-1-4   DANIEL FLORY, b. 1820.
>   3-8-1-5   CATHERINE FLORY, b. 1823, d. 1897.
>   3-8-1-6   ISSAC FLORY, b. 1825, d. 1863.
>   3-8-1-7   SAMUEL FLORY, b. 1826, d. 1914.
>   3-8-1-8   SARAH FLORY, b. 1828, d. 1871, m. DANIEL STONER.
>   3-8-1-9   ANNA FLORY, b. 1829, d. 1896.

Children of DANIEL FLORY and CHRISTINA SNITEMAN are:
>   3-8-1-10   MARY⁸ FLORY, b. 1836, d. 1898.
>   3-8-1-11   SUSAN FLORY, b. 1837, d. 1868.
>   3-8-1-12   JACOB FLORY, b. 1839.
>   3-8-1-13   ABRAHAM FLORY, b. 1841, d. 1861.
>   3-8-1-14   JOSEPH FLORY, b. 1844, d. 1923.
>   3-8-1-15   HENRY FLORY, b. 1848, d. 1904, m. ELIZABETH TAUVER.

[36] SUSANNA⁷ FLORY *(CATHERINE⁶ GARBER, JOHANNES "JOHN H."⁵, JO HANNES⁴ GERBER, NICLAUS³, CHRISTIAN², ULRICH¹)* was born 1792 and died 1871. She married CHRISTIAN MILLER, son of ABRAHAM MILLER and CATHERINE BYERLY. He was born 1784 and died 1852.

Children of SUSANNA FLORY and CHRISTIAN MILLER are:
>   3-8-2-1   SARAH⁸ MILLER, b. 1818, d. 1876, m. JOHN CLICK IV.
>   3-8-2-2   SUSAN MILLER, b. 1822, d. 1913, m. ABRAM CLICK, b. 1818, d. 1892.
>   3-8-2-3   ELIZABETH MILLER, b. 1824, d. 1850, m. ISSAC CLICK.
>   3-8-2-4   JOHN C. MILLER, b. 1826, d. 1890, m. (1) REBECCA LONG, m. (2) MARY SNELL.

3-8-2-5   SAMUEL F. MILLER, b. 1833, d. 1917, m. ELIZABETH V. NEFF, b. 1833, d. 1917.
3-8-2-6   REBECCA MILLER, b. 1821, d. 1854, m. DAVID GARBER.
3-8-2-7   CATHERINE MILLER, b. 1827, d. 1898, m. DAVID MILLER.
3-8-2-8   ANNA MILLER, b. 1828, d. 1911, m. JOSEPH M. MILLER.

[37] JOHN[7] FLORY (*CATHERINE[6] GARBER, JOHANNES "JOHN H."[5], JO HANNES[4] GERBER, NICLAUS[3], CHRISTIAN[2], ULRICH[1]*) was born 1794 and died 1853. He married ELIZABETH WHITMORE. She was born in Montgomery Co., OH.

Notes for JOHN FLORY:
He was in the War of 1812.

More about JOHN FLORY:
Burial: VA

Children of JOHN FLORY and ELIZABETH WHITMORE are:
3-8-3-1   JONATHAN[8] FLORY.
3-8-3-2   JOEL FLORY.
3-8-3-3   JOHN FLORY.

More about JOHN FLORY:
Residence: Went west and died in IA.

3-8-3-4   ABRAHAM FLORY.

More about ABRAHAM FLORY:
Residence: Went west and died in Johnson Co., MO.

3-8-3-5   DAVID FLORY, b. 1831, d. 1908.

More about DAVID FLORY:
Residence: Went to MI.

3-8-3-5   POLLY FLORY, m. ANDERSON JONES.

[38] JACOB[7] FLORY (*CATHERINE[6] GARBER, JOHANNES "JOHN H."[5], JO HANNES[4] GERBER, NICLAUS[3], CHRISTIAN[2], ULRICH[1]*) was born 1797 and died 1842. He married CATHERINE STONER. She was born 1803 and died 1873.

Children of JACOB FLORY and CATHERINE STONER are:
3-8-4-1   SOLOMON[8] FLORY, b. 1826.
3-8-4-2   JOEL FLORY, b. 1827, d. 1907.

More about JOEL FLORY:
Residence: Moved to South English, IA.

3-8-4-3   JOHN FLORY, m. SARA GARBER.

More about JOHN FLORY:
Residence: Lived in Gratis, OH.

     3-8-4-4   SAMUEL N. FLORY, b. 1833, d. 1917.

     3-8-4-5   MICHAEL FLORY, m. MOLLIE KEPLAR.

More about MICHAEL FLORY:
Residence: Lived in Dayton, OH.

     3-8-4-6   DAVID S. FLORY, b. 1840, d. 1924, m. SARAH STONER.
     3-8-4-7   ANN HANNAH FLORY.
     3-8-4-8   SARAH CATHERINE FLORY, b. 1831, d. 1891, m. LEVI STONER.
     3-8-4-9   LYDIA FLORY.
     3-8-4-10   MARY FLORY, b. Abt. 1840.
     3-8-4-11   ELIZABETH FLORY, b. 1842, d. 1925, m. ROBERT HOLT.

More about ELIZABETH FLORY:
Residence: They lived in Kansas.

[39] CATHERINE[7] FLORY (*CATHERINE[6] GARBER, JOHANNES "JOHN H."[5], JO HANNES[4] GERBER, NICLAUS[3], CHRISTIAN[2], ULRICH[1]*) was born 1799 and died 1831. She married CONRAD SANGER II, son of CONRAD SANGER and ANN BRILLINGER. He was born 1799 and died 1872.

More about CONRAD SANGER II:
Occupation: He was a farmer and, along with the Daniel Bowman family, operated a mill at Silver Lake, Dayton, VA.

Children of CATHERINE FLORY and CONRAD SANGER are:
     3-8-5-1   JOHN[8] SANGER, b. 1822.
     3-8-5-2   JACOB SANGER, b. 1824.
     3-8-5-3   CONRAD SANGER III, b. 1826.
     3-8-5-4   SAMUEL SANGER.

[40] SAMUEL[7] FLORY (*CATHERINE[6] GARBER, JOHANNES "JOHN H."[5], JO HANNES[4] GERBER, NICLAUS[3], CHRISTIAN[2], ULRICH[1]*) was born 1801 and died 1869. He married ELIZABETH YOUNG, daughter of FREDERICK YOUNG and NANCY MILLER. She was born 1805.

More about SAMUEL FLORY:
Residence: He moved to VA from PA and settled near Pleasant Valley, VA.

Children of SAMUEL FLORY and ELIZABETH YOUNG are:
     3-8-6-1   NANCY[8] FLORY, b. Abt. 1825.
     3-8-6-2   CATHERINE FLORY, b. Abt. 1827.
     3-8-6-3   MARY FLORY, b. Abt. 1827.
     3-8-6-4   ABRAHAM FLORY, b. Abt. 1829.
     3-8-6-5   DANIEL FLORY, b. 1833; d. 1901.
     3-8-6-6   ELIZABETH FLORY, b. Abt. 1834.

3-8-6-7 HANNAH FLORY, b. Abt. 1835.
3-8-6-8 NOAH FLORY, b. 1836, d. 1883.

[41] MICHAEL[7] FLORY (*CATHERINE[6] GARBER, JOHANNES "JOHN H."[5], JO HANNES[4] GERBER, NICLAUS[3], CHRISTIAN[2], ULRICH[1]*) was born 1803 and died 1858. He married SARAH HEDRICH. She was born 1806 and died 1868.

Children of MICHAEL FLORY and SARAH HEDRICH are:
3-8-7-1 BARBARA[8] FLORY, b. 1826, d. 1849, m. GEORGE HOLLAR.
3-8-7-2 CATHERINE FLORY, b. 1828, m. JOSEPH HARSHBARGER, b. 1827.
3-8-7-3 REBECCA FLORY, b. 1830, m. ? KISER.
3-8-7-4 JOHN MICHAEL FLORY, b. 1832, d. 1891.
3-8-7-5 ANNA FLORY, b. 1834, d. 1834.
3-8-7-6 SUSANNAH FLORY, m. ABRAHAM KOONTZ.
3-8-7-7 ELIZABETH FLORY, b. 1837, d. 1846.
3-8-7-8 SARAH FLORY, b. 1839, d. 1923, m. JOSEPH BOWMAN.
3-8-7-9 HANNAH FLORY, b. 1842, d. 1845.
3-8-7-10 MICHAEL FLORY, b. 1844, d. 1844.
3-8-7-11 MICHAEL FLORY, JR., b. 1848, d. 1931.

[42] ELIZABETH[7] FLORY (*CATHERINE[6] GARBER, JOHANNES "JOHN H."[5], JO HANNES[4] GERBER, NICLAUS[3], CHRISTIAN[2], ULRICH[1]*) was born 1807 and died 1855. She married JOHN SANGER, son of CONRAD SANGER and ANNA BRILLINGER. He was born 1801 and died 1883.

More about JOHN SANGER:
Naturalization: He was a farmer at Pleasant Valley. Sometime after 1855, he moved to Augusta Co. and, with his brother Jacob, started the hamlet of Sangersville. The hamlet had a post office, a flour mill and later a paper mill.

Children of ELIZABETH FLORY and JOHN SANGER are:
3-8-8-1 CATHERINE[8] SANGER, b. 1826.
3-8-8-2 SUSAN SANGER, b. 1827.
3-8-8-3 ANNA SANGER, b. 1829.
3-8-8-4 ELIZABETH SANGER, b. 1831.
3-8-8-5 SAMUEL SANGER, b. 1835, d. 1835.
3-8-8-6 LYDIA SANGER, b. 1836.
3-8-8-7 SON B & D SAME DAY SANGER.****
3-8-8-8 SALLIE SANGER, b. 1840.
3-8-8-9 DAVID I. SANGER, b. 1842.
3-8-8-10 REBECCA SANGER, b. 1845.
3-8-8-11 JOHN E. SANGER, b. 1847.
3-8-8-12 SAMUEL F. SANGER, b. 1849.

[43] ABRAHAM[7] FLORY (*CATHERINE[6] GARBER, JOHANNES "JOHN H."[5], JO HANNES[4] GERBER, NICLAUS[3], CHRISTIAN[2], ULRICH[1]*) was born 1809 and died 1880. He married SUSAN STONER, daughter of ABRAHAM STONER and SALLY. She was born 1809 and died 1873.

More about ABRAHAM FLORY:
Residence: They moved from Augusta Co., VA, to South English, IA, after 1860.

Children of ABRAHAM FLORY and SUSAN STONER are:
      3-8-9-1   BENJAMIN FRANKLIN[8] FLORY, b. 1832, d. Abt. 1895.
      3-8-9-2   MANASSES MONROE FLORY, b. 1834, d. 1907.
[64] 3-8-9-3   JACOB STONER FLORY, b. 1836, d. 1911.
      3-8-9-4   SARAH E. FLORY, b. Abt. 1838, m. LOLLER.
      3-8-9-5   JOHN G. FLORY, b. 1841, d. 1925, m. REBECCA FRIEND.
      3-8-9-6   ABRAHAM O. FLORY, b. Abt. 1844.

[44] ELIZABETH[7] GARBER (*JOSEPH*[6], *JOHANNES "JOHN H."*[5], *JO HANNES*[4] *GERBER*, *NICLAUS*[3], *CHRISTIAN*[2], *ULRICH*[1]) was born September 04, 1799, in Rockingham Co., VA, and died December 15, 1885, in Bond Co., IL. She married FELIX LANDIS 1818 in Rockingham Co., VA, son of JACOB LANDES and FANNY. He was born November 09, 1797, in Lancaster Co., PA, and died October 26, 1875, in Bond Co., IL.

More about ELIZABETH GARBER:
Burial: Stillwater Cemetery or Dunkard Church Cemetery, Randolph Twp., Montgomery Co., OH

More about FELIX LANDIS:
Burial: Maxie Cemetery Pleasant Mond Twp., Bond Co., IL

Children of ELIZABETH GARBER and FELIX LANDIS are:
      3-9-1-1   SAMUEL[8] LANDIS, b. March 03, 1820, Montgomery Co., OH.
      3-9-1-2   JOHN LANDIS, b. 1824, m. MATIDA LANKIN, October 24, 1849,
                Montgomery Co., OH, b. Abt. 1828.
      3-9-1-3   CATHERINE LANDIS, b. Abt. 1825, Montgomery Co., OH, m. JOSEPH WEAVER,
                September 06, 1848, Montgomery Co., OH, b. Abt. 1821.
      3-9-1-4   JACOB LANDIS, b. January 22, 1826, Montgomery Co., OH, d. March 25, 1893,
                m. SARAH ARRINGTON, November 24, 1849, Montgomery Co., OH, b. Abt. 1832.

More about JACOB LANDIS:
Burial: Dunkard Church, Randolph Twp., Montgomery Co., OH

Notes for SARAH ARRINGTON:
She went west to IL with her parents in 1849.

      3-9-1-5   JOSEPH LANDIS, b. 1830, Montgomery Co., OH, d. 1875.
      3-9-1-6   ELIZABETH LANDIS, b. Abt. 1832, Montgomery Co., OH, d. May 28, 1878, Bond
                Co., IL, m. MARTIN WHITENECK, November 04, 1852, Wabash Co., IL,
                b. Abt. 1828.
      3-9-1-7   SUSANNAH LANDIS, b. Abt. 1834, Montgomery Co., OH, d. 1884, m. MARTIN
                COBLE, JR., October 14, 1852, Wabash Co., IL, b. Abt. 1830.
      3-9-1-8   ISAAC LANDIS, b. Abt. 1836, Montgomery Co., OH, d. 1886, Dayton,
                Montgomery Co., OH.
      3-9-1-9   DANIEL LANDIS, b. Abt. 1839, Montgomery Co., OH, d. 1885.
    3-9-1-10 DAVID LANDIS, b. Abt. 1843, Montgomery Co., OH, d. 1885.

Notes for DAVID LANDIS:
He went west to IL with his parents in 1849.

[45] CATHARINE[7] GARBER *(JOSEPH[6], JOHANNES "JOHN H."[5], JO HANNES[4] GERBER,*
NICLAUS[3], CHRISTIAN[2], ULRICH[1]) was born 1807 and died 1890 in Bond Co., IL. She married
JONATHAN KESSLER, son of JOSEPH KESSLER and MARY STEELE. He was born 1809 and died
1893 in MD.

Children of CATHARINE GARBER and JONATHAN KESSLER are:
    3-9-3-1   JEREMIAH[8] KESSLER.
    3-9-3-2   PHILIP KESSLER.
    3-9-3-3   CORNELIA KESSLER.
    3-9-3-4   JOSHUA KESSLER.
    3-9-3-5   CATHERINE KESSLER, m. JOHN EMERY GROVER.
    3-9-3-6   RACHEL KESSLER, m. DANIEL COBLE.

[46] JOSEPH[7] GARBER, JR. *(JOSEPH[6], JOHANNES "JOHN H."[5], JO HANNES[4] GERBER,*
NICLAUS[3], CHRISTIAN[2], ULRICH[1]) was born 1814 and died 1893. He married MARY ANN
WAMPLER, daughter of DAVID WAMPLER. She was born 1816 and died 1897.

More about JOSEPH GARBER, JR.:
Occupation: He was an Old German Baptist Brethren Elder, and they lived in Montgomery Co., OH.

Children of JOSEPH GARBER and MARY WAMPLER are:
    3-9-4-1   CATHARINE[8] GARBER, b. 1836, d. May 24, 1838.
    3-9-4-2   SARAH GARBER, b. 1838, d. March 10, 1872, m. ABRAHAM DENLINGER,
                   March 26, 1857, b. February 25, 1836, d. December 31, 1897.
    3-9-4-3   LUCINDA GARBER, b. 1842, d. November 22, 1858.
    3-9-4-4   ELIZABETH GARBER, b. 1840, d. 1880, m. ELI FIFER, January 11, 1866,
                   b. September 04, 1844, d. September 03, 1870.
    3-9-4-5   MARY ANN GARBER, b. May 26, 1844, d. January 03, 1930, m. ISRAEL
                   DENLINGER, November 28, 1861, b. June 27, 1840, d. February 1917.
    3-9-4-6   WILLIAM GARBER, b. 1846, d. 1872, He died in a barn raising accident.,
                   m. MARY A. TOBIAS.
    3-9-4-7   ANNIE GARBER, b. May 09, 1848.
    3-9-4-8   JOSEPH L. GARBER, b. July 12, 1852, d. 1934, m. LAURA DINKENS,
                   b. 1853, d. November 21, 1917.
    3-9-4-9   MARTHA GARBER, b. 1855, d. April 01, 1855.
    3-9-4-10   PHILLIP W. GARBER, b. July 15, 1856, d. 1918, m. EMMA HUFFMAN, 1877,
                   b. February 17, 1859.
    3-9-4-11   JESSE W. GARBER, b. April 26, 1859, d. July 10, 1943, m. FLORA APPLEGATE,
                   1884, b. December 19, 1859, d. 1897.

[47] MICHAEL[7] WINE *(MAGADALENE[6] GARBER, JOHANNES "JOHN H."[5], JO HANNES[4]*
GERBER, NICLAUS[3], CHRISTIAN[2], ULRICH[1]) was born 1797 and died 1874. He married
CATHERINE ARNOLD, daughter of DANIEL ARNOLD and ELIZABETH THOMAS. She was born
1803 and died 1881.

More about MICHAEL WINE:
Occupation: He was a farmer and lived near Ottobine, VA.
Religion: Church of the Brethren

Children of MICHAEL WINE and CATHERINE ARNOLD are:
　　　3-10-1-1　ELIZABETH[8] WINE, b. 1826.
　　　3-10-1-2　MAGDALENE WINE, b. 1827.
　　　3-10-1-3　ANNIE WINE, b. 1839.
　　　3-10-1-4　DANIEL A. WINE, b. 1831.
　　　3-10-1-5　JOHN WINE, b. 1836, d. 1841.
　　　3-10-1-6　SAMUEL N. WINE, b. 1838.
　　　3-10-1-7　SOLOMON WINE, b. 1840.
　　　3-10-1-8　CATHERINE WINE, b. 1842.
　　　3-10-1-9　BARBARA WINE, b. 1847, d. 1848.
[65]　3-10-1-10　REBECCA WINE, b. June 17, 1834, d. December 13, 1915.

[48] JOHN[7] WINE (*MAGADALENE[6] GARBER, JOHANNES "JOHN H."[5], JO HANNES[4] GERBER, NICLAUS[3], CHRISTIAN[2], ULRICH[1]*) was born 1799. He married ANNIE BURNER, daughter of ISAAC BURNER and BARBARA SCHRUM. She was born 1799.

More about JOHN WINE:
Occupation: He was a farmer near Ottobine and a Church of the Brethren minister who did missionary work in WV.

Children of JOHN WINE and ANNIE BURNER are:
　　　3-10-2-1　BARBARA[8] WINE, b. 1828.
　　　3-10-2-2　CATHERINE WINE, b. 1830, d. 1837.
　　　3-10-2-3　SUSANNAH WINE, b. 1831.
　　　3-10-2-4　GEORGE W. WINE, b. 1834.
　　　3-10-2-5　LYDIA E. WINE, b. 1835.
　　　3-10-2-6　MARY WINE, b. 1836.
　　　3-10-2-7　ELIZABETH WINE, b. 1839.
　　　3-10-2-8　ANNIE BURNER WINE, b. 1840.
　　　3-10-2-9　JOHN WINE, b. 1842, d. 1845.

[49] JACOB[7] WINE (*MAGADALENE[6] GARBER, JOHANNES "JOHN H."[5], JO HANNES[4] GERBER, NICLAUS[3], CHRISTIAN[2], ULRICH[1]*) was born 1801 and died 1878. He married ELIZABETH GARBER, daughter of CHRISTIAN GARBER and MARY MORNINGSTAR. She was born 1806 and died 1874.

More about JACOB WINE:
Occupation: He was a farmer, and they lived near Mr. Solon, VA.

Children of JACOB WINE and ELIZABETH GARBER are:
　　　3-10-3-1　SOLOMON[8] WINE, b. 1827.
　　　3-10-3-2　CHRISTIAN WINE, b. 1829.
　　　3-10-3-3　MARY WINE, b. 1831.

3-10-3-4   CHRISTINA WINE, b. 1835.
3-10-3-5   SAMUEL WINE, b. 1837.
3-10-3-6   DAVID D. WINE, b. 1839.
3-10-3-7   ANNA WINE, b. 1842.
3-10-3-8   GEORGE WINE, b. 1845.

[50] DANIEL[7] WINE (*MAGADALENE[6] GARBER, JOHANNES "JOHN H."[5], JO HANNES[4] GERBER, NICLAUS[3], CHRISTIAN[2], ULRICH[1]*) was born 1804. He married LYDIA SULLENBERGER. She was born 1806 and died 1874.

More about DANIEL WINE:
Occupation: He was a farmer and carpenter, and they lived in Jasper, MO.

Children of DANIEL WINE and LYDIA SULLENBERGER are:
3-10-4-1   NOAH M[8] WINE, b. 1830.
3-10-4-2   MARY WINE, b. 1831.
3-10-4-3   HANNAH WINE, b. 1833.
3-10-4-4   ELIZABETH WINE, b. 1835.
3-10-4-5   GEORGE W. WINE, b. 1836.
3-10-4-6   LYDIA WINE, b. 1838.
3-10-4-7   LEAH WINE, b. 1842.
3-10-4-8   ISAAC WINE, b. 1844.

[51] BARBARA[7] WINE (*MAGADALENE[6] GARBER, JOHANNES "JOHN H."[5], JO HANNES[4] GERBER, NICLAUS[3], CHRISTIAN[2], ULRICH[1]*) was born 1807. She married SOLOMON GARBER, son of CHRISTIAN GARBER and MARY MORNINGSTAR. He was born 1808 and died 1892.

Notes for SOLOMON GARBER:
He descended from immigrant, Niclous Garber. He was a distinguished Church of the Brethren minister and member of the Virginia Normal School, later named to Bridgewater College, Board of Trustees. He was a missionary who regularly traveled and preached with Elder John Kline. They lived near Bridgewater, VA.

Children of BARBARA WINE and SOLOMON GARBER are:
3-10-5-1   CHRISTIAN[8] GARBER, b. 1836.
3-10-5-2   SUSANNAH GARBER, b. 1839.

[52] SOLOMON[7] WINE (*MAGADALENE[6] GARBER, JOHANNES "JOHN H."[5], JO HANNES[4] GERBER, NICLAUS[3], CHRISTIAN[2], ULRICH[1]*) was born 1812. He married (1) KATIE SHRUM. She died 1837. He married (2) SARAH GOCHENOUR.   He married (3) CATHERINE MYERS COFFMAN MATHENY.

More about SOLOMON WINE:
Residence: They lived in Lima, OH, and South English, IA.

Children of SOLOMON WINE and KATIE SHRUM are:

    3-10-6-1   SARAH^8 WINE, b. 1835.

    3-10-6-2   CATHERINE WINE, b. 1837.

Children of SOLOMON WINE and SARAH GOCHENOUR are:

    3-10-6-3   GEORGE S.^{8} WINE, b. 1841.

    3-10-6-4   MARGARET WINE, b. 1844.

    3-10-6-5   LINDA E. WINE, b. 1847.

    3-10-6-6   BENJAMIN WINE, b. 1860.

[53] SUSANNAH^7 WINE (*MAGADALENE^6 GARBER, JOHANNES "JOHN H."^{5}, JO HANNES^4 GERBER, NICLAUS^3, CHRISTIAN^2, ULRICH^1*) was born 1813 and died 1878. She married CHRISTIAN SNELL. He was born 1813 and died 1866.

More about CHRISTIAN SNELL:
Occupation: He was a farmer.

Children of SUSANNAH WINE and CHRISTIAN SNELL are:

    3-10-7-1   BARBARA^8 SNELL, b. 1835.

    3-10-7-2   GEORGE W. SNELL, b. 1837.

    3-10-7-3   ANNA SNELL, b. 1840, d. 1863.

    3-10-7-4   MARY SNELL, b. 1842.

    3-10-7-5   SOLOMON SNELL, b. 1845.

[54] GEORGE^7 WINE (*MAGADALENE^6 GARBER, JOHANNES "JOHN H."^{5}, JO HANNES^4 GERBER, NICLAUS^3, CHRISTIAN^2, ULRICH^1*) was born 1817 and died 1895. He married MARY ANN CALWELL. She was born 1820 and died 1896.

More about GEORGE WINE:
Residence: They lived at Doe Hill and Spring Creek, VA. He was a farmer and a Church of the Brethren minister and the Elder at Beaver Creek Church in VA.

Children of GEORGE WINE and MARY CALWELL are:

    3-10-8-1   CATHERINE^8 WINE, b. 1841.

    3-10-8-2   PETER WINE, b. 1843.

    3-10-8-3   BENJAMIN WINE, b. 1845, d. 1846.

    3-10-8-4   HANNAH WINE, b. 1847, d. 1862.

    3-10-8-5   BARBARA WINE, b. 1849, d. 1862.

    3-10-8-6   SOLOMON WINE, b. 1851, d. 1862.

    3-10-8-7   JOHN WINE, b. 1853, d. 1862.

    3-10-8-8   MARY MAGDALEN WINE, b. 1855.

    3-10-8-9   GEORGE WILLIAM WINE, b. 1857, d. 1862.

    3-10-8-10 JOSEPH MARTIN WINE, b. 1860, d. 1862.

U.S. Generation No. 4

[55] JACOB[8] MINNICH *(MAGDALENE[7] GARBER, JOHN H.[6], JOHANNES "JOHN H."[5], JO HANNES[4] GERBER, NICLAUS[3], CHRISTIAN[2], ULRICH[1])* was born 1814 in Clark Co., OH. He married CHRISTINA EBERSOLE. She was born 1815 in Clark Co., OH.

Children of JACOB MINNICH and CHRISTINA EBERSOLE are:
- 3-2-10-7-1 JOHN B.[9] MINNICH, b. 1837, m. MARY MAGDALENE HUFFMAN, OH.
- 3-2-10-7-2 PHOEBE MINNICH, b. 1838, m. PETER WRIGHT, b. 1828, OH.
- 3-2-10-7-3 SARAH MINNICH, b. 1840, m. GEORGE E. HARROLD, b. 1837, NC.
- 3-2-10-7-4 MARY M. MINNICH, b. 1842, m. WILLIAM MATTHEW IRVIN, b. 1838, Preble Co., OH.
- 3-2-10-7-5 PETER M. MINNICH, b. 1845, Wells, IN, m. MARTHA JANE CLAMPITT, b. 1847, Stokes, NC.
- 3-2-10-7-6 MICHAEL MINNICH, b. 1847, IN, m. (1) MARGARET SUSAN BLACK, b. 1849, m. (2) HANNAH SPAULDING, b. 1843, IN.
- 3-2-10-7-7 MARGARET S. MINNICH, b. 1849, Wells, IN.

[56] SAMUEL MILLER[8] GARBER *(JOHN[7], ABRAHAM[6], JOHANNES "JOHN H."[5], JO HANNES[4] GERBER, NICLAUS[3], CHRISTIAN[2], ULRICH[1])* was born 1820 and died Abt. 1860. He married (1) FRANCES S. HUMBERT. She was born 1825 and died 1857. He married (2) SARAH JANE HUFF[59] in 1858, in Middle River Church of the Brethren[59], daughter of JACOB HUFF and MARGARET FELLERS. She was born Abt. 1839[59] and died 1895[59].

Notes for SAMUEL MILLER GARBER:
Samuel's lengthy will (Will Book 39-105, Will signed April 3, 1863, Probated April 27, 1863, Executors: Eli Garber and David Myers) bequeathed to Daniel A. certain items at age 21 and to his wife numerous items including the roan mare and black stud. The will also provided, "It is my wish that land I own on the other side of the river (note - meaning east or New Hope side of the Middle River) known as the Ellerson land and my interest in the Round Hill land (note - meaning a hill next to New Hope) be sold as soon as possible after my death as convenient." Clifton, Enos and Sally were not mentioned, probably because they were very small children.

The land "on the other side of the river" contained approximately 110 acres and a large brick house. The remaining land on the west side contained approximately 40 acres and a smaller wooden house. It was here that Sarah Jane raised her four children. The 1860 census shows the real estate value of Samuel M. Garber as $6,805. The 1870 census shows the real estate value of Sarah H. Garber (head of household) as $656. Allowing for post war depreciation, the drastic drop in land value indicates that Sarah Jane sold the property and that supports the family story that it was sold for confederate money since the value of her personal property in 1870 was a mere $400. (Maybe she thought the south would win or rise again.) Incidentally, the 1870 census shows in her household four children, Clifton, Enos, Sarah C. and James F. and, in addition, two younger brothers, Levi Huff, 28, farmer, and Gideon Huff, 22, farm laborer. That is the "Uncle Gid" who committed suicide in 1925.

More about SAMUEL MILLER GARBER:
Burial: Abt. 1860, the cause and date of death is unknown. He was buried in a small private cemetery

approximately one quarter mile south of the back fence of the Middle River Church Cemetery. The cemetery has been lost to neglect and expanding farm land.

Occupation: He was farmer, and they lived near Round Hill at New Hope, VA.

Notes for SARAH JANE HUFF:

Sarah Jane Huff was Samuel's second wife and an older sister of Elizabeth Frances Huff. Jacob consented to the marriage since Sarah Jane was less than 21 years of age. Elder Brower of the Middle River Church conducted the ceremony, appropriate since Samuel's father, grandfather and great grandfather had been elders.

Sarah Jane moved into Harrison Ross' log house (later replaced) about 100 yards up the hill on SR 927 from the bridge that spans Middle River on SR 616 between Ft. Defiance and New Hope. At this time Cliff was given approximately nine acres along the river and Enos was given the house and remaining land.

More about SARAH JANE HUFF:

Burial: Middle River Church of the Brethren in Augusta Co., VA[59]

Children of SAMUEL GARBER and FRANCES HUMBERT are:

[66]   3-3-1-2-1   DANIEL ALEXANDER[9] GARBER, b. 1846, d. 1908, Middle River Cemetery.
       3-3-1-2-2   INFANT SON GARBER.

Children of SAMUEL GARBER and SARAH HUFF are:

[67]   3-3-1-2-3   CLIFTON BENJAMIN[9] GARBER, b. 1859, Augusta Co., VA, d. 1931, Augusta Co., VA.
       3-3-1-2-4   SARAH "SALLY" C. GARBER[59], b. 1861[59], d. 1877[59].

Notes for SARAH "SALLY" C. GARBER:

Sarah C. Garber was always Sally to her family, probably because she had the same Christian name as her mother. Precious little is known about Sally. She is rumored to have died of "consumption" - better known currently as tuberculosis. Burial site is unknown but most likely in the private "lost" cemetery where her father is buried.

[68]   3-3-1-2-5   AMES FRANKLIN GARBER, b. 1869, d. 1939.
       3-3-1-2-6   ENOS F. GARBER, b. January 12, 1860, Augusta Co., VA, d. September 20, 1934, Augusta Co., VA[60]; m. (1) VIRGINIA "GINNY" G.[61]; b. 1856[61], d. 1919[61], m. (2) ANNA REBECCA GARBER[62], November 25, 1920[62], b. June 09, 1861, Mt. Sidney, Augusta Co., VA[62], d. August 24, 1940, Augusta Co., VA[62].

Notes for ENOS F. GARBER:

Enos had no children by either wife; he left the propagation to his three prolific brothers, Daniel Alex, Cliff and James F. Leta B. Garber (1888-1965), a relative and a good friend of Carson from early years, was in need of a home at an early age. Thus she lived with Enos and Ginny and later Becky. After Becky's death, she had a room in the home of Will, Betty and Jane, unmarried children of Daniel Alex. All four are buried at the Middle River Church.

More about ENOS F. GARBER:

Burial: Middle River Church of the Brethren in Augusta Co., VA[63]

Occupation: Farmer
Religion: Deacon at Middle River Church

[57] BENJAMIN[8] GARBER *(JOHN[7], ABRAHAM[6], JOHANNES "JOHN H."[5], JO HANNES[4] GERBER, NICLAUS[3], CHRISTIAN[2], ULRICH[1])* was born 1822 in Augusta Co., VA, and died 1858[63]. He married ELIZABETH CRUMPACKER 1846, daughter of ABRAHAM CRUMPACKER and CATHERINE. She was born 1823 in Augusta Co., VA, and died 1890.

More about BENJAMIN GARBER:
Burial: Middle River Church of the Brethren in Augusta Co., VA

More about ELIZABETH CRUMPACKER:
Burial: Middle River Church of the Brethren in Augusta Co., VA

Children of BENJAMIN GARBER and ELIZABETH CRUMPACKER are:

	3-3-1-3-1	SAMUEL PRESTON[9] GARBER, b. 1847.
	3-3-1-3-2	JOHN DANIEL GARBER, b. 1850.
	3-3-1-3-3	CATHERINE REBECCA GARBER, b. 1852, d. 1852.
[69]	3-3-1-3-4	BENJAMIN FRANKLIN GARBER, b. 1855.
	3-3-1-3-5	ABI ELIZABETH GARBER, b. 1858, d. 1878.

[58] ELI[8] GARBER *(JOHN[7], ABRAHAM[6], JOHANNES "JOHN H."[5], JO HANNES[4] GERBER, NICLAUS[3], CHRISTIAN[2], ULRICH[1])* was born 1826 and died 1884[63]. He married (1) SUSANNAH COFFMAN[63], daughter of CHRISTIAN JR. and ANNA GARBER. She was born 1824[63] and died 1863[63]. He married (2) ELIZABETH YOUNT[63], daughter of MARTIN YOUNT and NANCY MYERS. She was born 1841[63] and died 1903[63].

Notes for ELIZABETH YOUNT:
The seven children were of the second marriage.

Children of ELI GARBER and ELIZABETH YOUNT are:

3-3-1-4-1   CORA ALICE[9] GARBER[63], b. 1865[63], d. 1957, m. JAMES HENRY BORDEN[63].

Notes for CORA ALICE GARBER:
Had six children

3-3-1-4-2   MARTIN LUTHER GARBER[63], m. SALLIE WRIGHT.

Notes for MARTIN LUTHER GARBER:
Had two children

3-3-1-4-3   SAMUEL BELL GARBER[63], b. 1869[63], d. 1909[63], m. MAGGIE PENCE[63].

Notes for SAMUEL BELL GARBER:
Had seven children

3-3-1-4-4   BENJAMIN BOWMAN GARBER[63], m. MARY E. SNELL[63], b. 1876[63], d. 1946[63].
3-3-1-4-5   FLORENCE ELLA GARBER[63], b. 1874[63], d. 1878[63].
3-3-1-4-6   LIDA REBECCA GARBER[63], b. 1876[63], d. 1955[63].

Notes for LIDA REBECCA GARBER:
Single

3-3-1-4-7   MARY BLANCHE GARBER[63], b. 1879[63], d. 1961[63], m. JOSEPH E. BROWER[63], b. 1872[63], d. 1943[63].

Notes for MARY BLANCHE GARBER:
Had three children

[59] REBEKAH[8] GARBER *(JACOB W.[7], ABRAHAM[6], JOHANNES "JOHN H."[5], JO HANNES[4] GERBER, NICLAUS[3], CHRISTIAN[2], ULRICH[1])*[64] was born December 27, 1823[65], and died July 24, 1886[65]. She married DANIEL MILLER[65] September 21, 1846, son of PETER MILLER and BARBARA MILLER. He was born April 19, 1816[65], and died January 23, 1901[65].

More about DANIEL MILLER:
Burial: Pleasant Valley Church of the Brethren in Augusta Co., VA
Occupation: Farmer
Religion: Deacon in Church of the Brethren
Residence: Their farm was one mile east of Mt. Sidney, VA.

Children of REBEKAH GARBER and DANIEL MILLER are:
[70]   3-3-4-1-1   NANCY[9] MILLER, b. July 21, 1847, d. January 28, 1930.
[71]   3-3-4-1-2   BARBARA MILLER, b. January 03, 1849, d. March 04, 1933.

[60] ABRAHAM D.[8] GARBER *(JACOB W.[7], ABRAHAM[6], JOHANNES "JOHN H."[5], JO HANNES[4] GERBER, NICLAUS[3], CHRISTIAN[2], ULRICH[1])*[66] was born December 19, 1824, and died December 01, 1911. He married (1) MAGDALENE WINE May 09, 1848, daughter of MICHAEL WINE and CATHERINE ARNOLD. She was born October 17, 1827, and died May 09, 1868. He married (2) SOPHIA BYRD HAYES October 05, 1869, daughter of WILLIAM BYRD and HANNAH SHOWALTER. She was born July 30, 1833, and died March 03, 1905.

Notes for ABRAHAM D. GARBER:
He united with the church in 1847 and was chosen to the ministry on March 31, 1855. He was devoted to his ministerial duties, residing and laboring within the bounds of the Pleasant Valley Congregation. He also did a great amount of mission work in other districts. He was one of the horseback riders in his work and made many trips across the mountains east of the Blue Ridge. At the time of his death, he was the oldest minister in the Second District of Virginia and possibly the oldest in the state. He served in the ministry 56 years. During the Civil War, when various diseases were raging, he was called to preach many funerals. He lived 63 years at the same home where all ten of his children were born and where he and both of his wives died. The Abraham D. Garber old brick house burned February 13, 1899, and the present house was built in the summer of 1899. The farm is now owned by his great-grandson, Lowell Garber.

More about ABRAHAM D. GARBER:
Occupation: Church of the Brethren minister for over 56 years.
Residence: Lived near Mt. Sidney, VA

Children of ABRAHAM GARBER and MAGDALENE WINE are:
[72] 3-3-4-2-1 SOLOMON W.[9] GARBER, b. April 25, 1849, d. January 26, 1934.
[73] 3-3-4-2-1 NANCY CATHERINE GARBER, b. December 30, 1850, d. March 04, 1918.
[74] 3-3-4-2-3 DANIEL ARNOLD GARBER, b. November 23, 1852, d. December 27, 1931.
[75] 3-3-4-2-4 MELISSA MARGARET GARBER, b. June 07, 1856, d. August 09, 1921.
[76] 3-3-4-2-5 PRISCILLA ELIZABETH GARBER, b. May 01, 1858, d. September 04, 1928.
      3-3-4-2-6 ACOB MICHAEL GARBER.
[77] 3-3-4-2-7 SAMUEL ABRAHAM GARBER, b. July 01, 1863, d. January 27, 1933.
[78] 3-3-4-2-8 SOPHIA MAGDALENE BYRD GARBER, b. March 30, 1871, d. July 10, 1958.

[61] LEVI[8] GARBER *(JACOB W.[7], ABRAHAM[6], JOHANNES "JOHN H."[5], JO HANNES[4] GERBER, NICLAUS[3], CHRISTIAN[2], ULRICH[1])[66]* was born August 21, 1828, in New Hope, Augusta County, VA[67], and died November 10, 1914, in Mt. Sidney, Augusta Co., VA[67]. He married BARBARA MILLER[67] February 21, 1850, in Mt. Sidney, Augusta Co., Virginia[67], daughter of PETER MILLER and BARBARA LAIRD. She was born February 25, 1825, in Augusta Co., VA[67], and died February 29, 1868, in Augusta Co., VA[67].

More about LEVI GARBER:
Burial: Middle River Church of the Brethren, Augusta Co., VA
Occupation: Farmer
Religion: Church of the Brethren

More about BARBARA MILLER:
Burial: Middle River Church of the Brethren, Augusta Co., VA

Children of LEVI GARBER and BARBARA MILLER are:
[79] 3-3-4-3-1 PETER[9] GARBER, b. December 09, 1850, Mt. Sidney, in Augusta Co., VA, d. May 08, 1932.
[80] 3-3-4-3-2 ACOB A. GARBER, b. October 08, 1853, Augusta Co., VA, d. October 11, 1915, Rockingham Co., VA.
[81] 3-3-4-3-3 DANIEL SAMUEL GARBER, b. August 22, 1855, Levi Garber house near Mt. Sidney, Augusta Co., VA, d. December 30, 1923, House near Mt. Sidney, Augusta Co., VA.
[82] 3-3-4-3-4 LYDIA CATHERINE GARBER, b. June 23, 1857, Mt. Sidney, Augusta Co., VA, d. July 27, 1936.
      3-3-4-3-5 NANCY JANE GARBER[67], b. April 30, 1859[67], d. July 09, 1890[67].
      3-3-4-3-6 ANNA REBECCA GARBER[67], b. June 09, 1861, Mt Sidney, Augusta Co., VA[67], d. August 24, 1940, Augusta Co., VA[67], m. ENOS F. GARBER, November 25, 1920[67], b. January 12, 1860, Augusta Co., VA, d. September 20, 1934, Augusta Co., VA[67].

More about ANNA REBECCA GARBER:
Burial: Middle River Church of the Brethren in Augusta Co., VA[68]
Residence: Becky lived with her father, Levi, and then her sister, Barbara Norford, until marrying in the very early 1920s. Becky's grandfather was Jacob, brother of John, Enos' grandfather.

[83] 3-3-4-3-7 BARBARA ELIZABETH GARBER, b. November 16, 1863, in Mt. Sidney, Augusta Co., VA, d. May 05, 1949.

[84] 3-3-4-3-8 FRANCES "FANNIE" V. GARBER, b. March 15, 1866, Mt. Sidney, Augusta Co., VA, d. August 14, 1925.

[62] REUBEN ARNOLD[8] GARBER *(JACOB W.[7], ABRAHAM[6], JOHANNES "JOHN H."[5], JO HANNES[4] GERBER, NICLAUS[3], CHRISTIAN[2], ULRICH[1])[69]* was born January 26, 1836[70], and died January 10, 1884[70]. He married MARY FLORY[70] March 19, 1857[70], daughter of DANIEL FLORY and CHRISTINE S. She was born January 05, 1836[70], and died July 24, 1898[70].

Children of REUBEN GARBER and MARY FLORY are:
      3-3-4-4-1 CHRISTINA SUSAN[9] GARBER[70], b. July 29, 1858, d. September 04, 1938.
      3-3-4-4-2 NANCY REBECCA GARBER[70], b. November 05, 1859, d. June 23, 1894.
      3-3-4-4-3 SARAH CATHERINE GARBER[70], b. January 28, 1862, d. June 28, 1931.
      3-3-4-4-4 LEVI JOSEPH GARBER[70], b. January 06, 1864, d. November 06, 1864.
      3-3-4-4-5 HENRY JACOB GARBER[70], b. July 09, 1866, d. November 01, 1872.
[85] 3-3-4-4-6 JOHN REUBEN GARBER, b. January 12, 1869, d. May 30, 1938.
[86] 3-3-4-4-7 MARY ANNE GARBER, b. May 18, 1871, d. November 21, 1950.

[63] JACOB W.[8] GARBER *(JACOB W.[7], ABRAHAM[6], JOHANNES "JOHN H."[5], JO HANNES[4] GERBER, NICLAUS[3], CHRISTIAN[2], ULRICH[1])[71]* was born September 11, 1842[72], and died August 28, 1908[72]. He married SUSAN A. HAM[72] May 18, 1865, in New Hope, Augusta Co., VA[72], daughter of ROBERT HAM and MARY DOUGLAS. She was born February 02, 1848[72], and died November 11, 1934[72].

More about JACOB W. GARBER:
Residence: Their home was made at the Jacob Garber homestead.[73,73]

Children of JACOB GARBER and SUSAN HAM are:
[87] 3-3-4-5-1 ROBERT ISSAC[9] GARBER, b. April 09, 1866, d. December 06, 1952.
[88] 3-3-4-5-2 BENJAMIN JACOB GARBER, b. January 06, 1868, d. November 05, 1924.
      3-3-4-5-3 IRA LEVI GARBER[74], b. August 21, 1869, d. May 27, 1941, m. CORA V. BYRD, December 21, 1893, M.E. Parsonage, Harrisonburg, VA.

Notes for IRA LEVI GARBER:
No children

[89] 3-3-4-5-4 MARY ADA GARBER, b. January 19, 1873, d. June 28, 1955.
      3-3-4-5-5 WILLIAM ALLEN GARBER[74], b. April 09, 1874, d. January 07, 1914.

More about WILLIAM ALLEN GARBER:
Occupation: As a lawyer he was brilliant and tactful in his profession and later successful as an evangelist in the Church of the Brethren.

      4-4-4-5-6 IDA NANCY JANE GARBER[74], b. 1876, d. 1955, m. E. DAVID KINDIG, d. 1935.

More about IDA NANCY JANE GARBER:
Occupation: Trained nurse
Residence: Dayton, VA, with her mother

3-3-4-5-7   AINSLIE R. L. GARBER[74], b. October 03, 1882[75], d. March 22, 1884[75].

3-3-4-5-8   OSCAR J.R. GARBER[76], b. October 03, 1882[77], d. March 22, 1884[77].

[90]   3-3-4-5-9   JOHN ADAM GARBER, b. May 01, 1884, d. November 28, 1975, Decatur, GA.

3-3-4-5-10 ARTHUR DANIEL GARBER[78], b. January 06, 1886[79], d. 1976[79].

More about ARTHUR DANIEL GARBER:
Property: Church of the Brethren
Residence: Dayton, VA

[64] JACOB STONER[8] FLORY (*ABRAHAM[7], CATHERINE[6] GARBER, JOHANNES "JOHN H."[5], JO HANNES[4] GERBER, NICLAUS[3], CHRISTIAN[2], ULRICH[1]*) was born 1836 and died 1911. He married (1) ELIZABETH SANGER. She was born 1834 and died 1907. He married (2) ANNA WEAVER.

Notes for JACOB STONER FLORY:
He was a Church of the Brethren Elder at 32 years of age, in Fayette Co., VA, and moved to CO after the war. There he sold Buffalo Robes and patent medicine and published several periodicals, "The Home Mirror" and "Our Flag." He also authored "Echoes," "Wild Frontier," "Mind Mysteries" and some smaller works. He organized the St. Vrian (Hygiene) congregation in 1877, the first in CO. He was the postmaster at Buffalo, 85 miles east of Greeley in 1875, and then moved to Greeley for better schooling for his children. There he built a three-story building called his "Hygienic Sanitarium" in 1882. This was torn down in 1926. In 1888, they went to Southern CA and lived there for 15 years.

More about JACOB STONER FLORY:
Occupation: Church of the Brethren minister.

Children of JACOB FLORY and ELIZABETH SANGER are:
3-8-9-3-1   WILLIAM HOWARD[9] FLORY, b. 1858, m. FANNIE HAMLIN.
3-8-9-3-2   EMMA VIRGINIA FLORY, b. 1859, d. 1942, m. MADISON BASHOR.
3-8-9-3-3   MARY ANN FLORY, b. Abt. 1863.
3-8-9-3-4   MAGGIE SUSAN FLORY, b. 1863, m. JAMES BOOTS.
3-8-9-3-5   SARAH JANE FLORY, b. 1865, m. JOHN O. TALLY.
3-8-9-3-6   ELIZABETH HULDA FLORY, m. CALVERT.
3-8-9-3-7   DAVID PLANE FLORY, b. 1869, d. 1952, m. (1) FLELTA TROBAUGH, m. (2) HILDA STOBBE.
3-8-9-3-8   CHARLES ABRAHAM FLORY, b. 1871, d. 1969, m. MARY STANCIFF, b. 1875, d. 1966.
3-8-9-3-9   CHARLOTTE E. FLORY, b. 1876, d. 1969, m. WILLIAM H. NEHER.

[65] REBECCA[8] WINE (*MICHAEL[7], MAGADALENE[6] GARBER, JOHANNES "JOHN H."[5], JO HANNES[4] GERBER, NICLAUS[3], CHRISTIAN[2], ULRICH[1]*) was born June 17, 1834[80], and died December 13, 1915[80]. She married SAMUEL T. GLICK[80] October 05, 1856[80], son of DANIEL GLICK and MARY WAMPLER. He was born April 27, 1824, and died April 18, 1904[80].

Children of REBECCA WINE and SAMUEL GLICK are:
3-10-1-10-1   DANIEL MICHAEL[9] GLICK, b. July 16, 1857, Weyers Cave, VA[80]; d. July 04, 1938, Trevilian, VA[80].

More about DANIEL MICHAEL GLICK:
Burial: Valley Church Cemetery
Education: Augusta County schools and the Shenandoah Institute, Dayton, VA, and at Bethany Biblical Seminary
Occupation: Farmer and 35 years as a professional music teacher specializing in vocal music and leadership in sacred and congregational singing
Residence: Lived at Trevilian, VA

        3-10-1-10-2   CATHERINE ANN GLICK[80], b. October 28, 1858[80], d. September 08, 1863[80].
[91]   3-10-1-10-3   ELIZABETH MARGARET GLICK, b. August 26, 1860, Weyers Cave, Rockingham Co., VA, d. March 08, 1949, at Daniel S. Garber house near Mt. Sidney, Augusta Co., VA.
[92]   3-10-1-10-4   BENJ. FRANKLIN GLICK, b. September 07, 1862, d. August 03, 1928.
[93]   3-10-1-10-5   MARY MAGDALENE GLICK, b. February 11, 1865, d. October 15, 1932.
[94]   3-10-1-10-6   JOHN WILLIAM GLICK, b. May 28, 1867, d. August 18, 1911.
[95]   3-10-1-10-7   MARTHA JANE GLICK, b. May 03, 1869, d. April 12, 1950.
[96]   3-10-1-10-8   SARAH FRANCES GLICK, b. September 27, 1870, d. July 20, 1943.

Middle River Cemetery

U.S. Generation No. 5

[66] DANIEL ALEXANDER[9] GARBER (*SAMUEL MILLER*[8], *JOHN*[7], *ABRAHAM*[6], *JOHANNES "JOHN H."*[5], *JO HANNES*[4] *GERBER, NICLAUS*[3], *CHRISTIAN*[2], *ULRICH*[1]) was born 1846 and died 1908 in Middle River Cemetery. He married ELIZABETH FRANCES HUFF. She was born 1850 and died 1921.

More about ELIZABETH FRANCES HUFF:
Burial: Middle River Cemetery

Children of DANIEL GARBER and ELIZABETH HUFF are:
[97]   3-3-1-2-1-1   NATHANIEL BELL[10] GARBER, b. September 09, 1873, d. 1941.
        3-3-1-2-1-2   MAGGIE GARBER, b. May 17, 1876, d. February 15, 1902.

More about MAGGIE GARBER:
Burial: Middle River Cemetery

        3-3-1-2-1-3   JAMES WILLIAM GARBER, b. 1878, d. 1959.

More about JAMES WILLIAM GARBER:
Burial: Middle River Cemetery

[98]   3-3-1-2-1-4   HOMER F. GARBER, b. April 12, 1882, d. August 10, 1948.
[99]   3-3-1-2-1-5   BERTIE GARBER, b. June 10, 1891.

[67] CLIFTON BENJAMIN[9] GARBER *(SAMUEL MILLER[8], JOHN[7], ABRAHAM[6], JOHANNES "JOHN H."[5], JO HANNES[4] GERBER, NICLAUS[3], CHRISTIAN[2], ULRICH[1])[81]* was born 1859 in Augusta Co., VA, and died 1931 in Augusta Co., VA. He married JOSIE BELL MOORE[81] 1883, Knightly, Augusta, Co., VA[81], daughter of PAGE MOORE and CATHERINE BEARD. She was born 1866 in Augusta Co., VA[81], and died 1944 in Augusta Co., VA[81].

Notes for CLIFTON BENJAMIN GARBER:
Brothers Daniel Alex's children and Cliff's children had a double cousin relationship; (1) they had the same grandfather, Samuel M. and (2) Daniel Alex children's mother, Elizabeth Frances Huff, was a younger sister of Cliff's children's grandmother, Sarah Jane Huff.

Around the time of Sarah Jane's remarriage in 1884, she let Cliff and Josie have approximately nine acres along the west side of Middle River; the land begins about 200 yards upstream from the dam where SR 616 spans the river on the Ft. Defiance - New Hope road. Their home was built in three stages - facing the front, the left section in late 1885 or early 1886, the center section in probably 1898 and the right section in the summer of 1913. Each section had one room down, one up, but often temporary partitions were needed. Nine of the ten children were born in the house; Viola was born at the Huff's home about 50 yards up the hill from the site of the to-be-house.

Cliff was a farmer but could not support his family on such small acreage and thus also worked for other farmers. Cliff and Josie lived their entire lives on the farm except for a short period around 1913, when Andy Garber vacated his farm and they lived in Andy's house while farming for him. But they retained their farm on the river.

Incredibly, the birth years of Cliff and Josie on their tombstone at the Middle River Church are in error. Birth records and other evidence clearly establish that Cliff was born in 1859, not 1858, and Josie in 1866, not 1867. Family members sometimes confused his birth year with his parent's marriage year. No explanation for the error on Josie's birth year or why it was just recently noticed.

More about CLIFTON BENJAMIN GARBER:
Burial: Middle River Church of the Brethren in Augusta Co., VA[81]
Occupation: Farmer

Notes for JOSIE BELL MOORE:
Page Moore, a miller, and his family lived near Sarah Jane Huff Garber at the time of her daughter Sally's death in 1877. In order to have some help in the house and companionship, and just possibly to display some local talent for her bachelor sons, Sarah Jane often invited Josie Moore to her home, sometimes for extended periods. In any event, Cliff found his bride. Clifton B. Garber (1859-1931), fifth generation American, married Josie Bell Moore (1866-1944), third generation American, at her parent's home in 1883, several days before her seventeenth birthday.

More about JOSIE BELL MOORE:
Burial: Middle River Church of the Brethren in Augusta Co., VA[81]
Residence: Her parents lived in Knightly on what is currently SR 778. The house, now destroyed, was at the foot of the far side of the hill where the bridge spans Middle River - about two miles from the Middle River Church.

Children of CLIFTON GARBER and JOSIE MOORE are:
[100]   3-3-1-2-3-1   MAUDY VIOLA[10] GARBER, b. 1885, d. 1977.
        3-3-1-2-3-2   STUART GUY GARBER[81], b. 1886[81], d. 1976, FL[81], m. DELLA M. LISKEY[81], 1916[81], b. 1892[81], d. 1954.

More about STUART GUY GARBER:
Burial: South Annville Church of the Brethren near Annville, PA[81]
Occupation: Stuart was a farmer. Della taught school periodically.
Residence: Lived briefly in IL and Ft. Defiance, VA, but spent most of their lives in the Lebanon-Annville, PA, area.

More about DELLA M. LISKEY:
Burial: South Annville Church of the Brethren near Annville, PA[81]

        3-3-1-2-3-3   CARSON GROVER GARBER[81], b. 1889[81], d. 1953[81], m. ADDIE M. WALTER[81], b. 1890[81], d. 1976[81].

More about CARSON GROVER GARBER:
Burial: Middle River Church of the Brethren in Augusta Co., VA[81]
Occupation: Farmer and flour miller
Residence: Lived in the New Hope - Ft. Defiance area

More about ADDIE M. WALTER:
Burial: Middle River Church of the Brethren in Augusta Co., VA[81]
Occupation: The Walter families lived several miles north of Waynesboro and were farmers, blacksmiths and plant employees.

        3-3-1-2-3-4   BEULAH LYDA GARBER[81], b. 1891, d. 1977, m. EMERY SIMMONS.
        3-3-1-2-3-5   LUCY IVY GARBER, b. 1896, d. 1987, m. HERBERT ROACH.

More about LUCY IVY GARBER:
Burial: Middle River Church of the Brethren in Augusta Co., VA

        3-3-1-2-3-6   SADIE IVY GARBER, b. 1896, m. JAMES H. LANDIS.
        3-3-1-2-3-7   JOHN EVERETT GARBER, b. 1898; d. 1966, m. CLARA BELL FIX.
        3-3-1-2-3-8   BERTHA LURTY GARBER, b. 1900, d. 1901.
        3-3-1-2-3-9   HAZEL MARGERY GARBER, b. 1904.
        3-3-1-2-3-10   VADA LAVELLE GARBER, b. 1906, d. 1991, m. WALTER HAYS.

[68] JAMES FRANKLIN[9] GARBER (*SAMUEL MILLER*[8], *JOHN*[7], *ABRAHAM*[6], *JOHANNES "JOHN H."*[5], *JO HANNES*[4] *GERBER, NICLAUS*[3], *CHRISTIAN*[2], *ULRICH*[1])[81] was born 1869[81] and died 1939[81]. He married SARAH CLAUDIA YARBROUGH[81] 1889[81], daughter of R. H. YARBROUGH. She was born 1871[81] and died 1963[81].

Notes for JAMES FRANKLIN GARBER:

Jim's mother, Sarah Jane Huff Garber, had remarried in 1884, and he later told his TX family that he could not "get along with his stepfather." No doubt true, but his stepfather had at home two daughters and a son, who could have also caused Jim some grief. In addition, at the time of her remarriage, Sarah Jane divided her farm between sons Cliff and Enos. The Shenandoah Valley was not recovering quickly from the Civil War and prospects were bleak for an ambitious young man.

TX looked promising, so Jim arrived in Whitney in 1888. He was a merchant (gifted salesman), raised cattle, a politician at times, an accomplished singer, music teacher and choir director in several Baptist churches. He lived in numerous TX towns and was always prosperous until forced into bankruptcy during the Great Depression. At his death in 1939, from complications of a fall and broken hip, he was Treasurer of Crosby Co., some 30 miles east of Lubbock and 110 miles south of Amarillo in west TX.

Jim never forgot his native VA. He returned in 1907 to visit with Cliff and niece Viola, to see Jamestown and its tri-centennial celebration. He sent daughters Ruby and Pansy to summer courses at Harrisonburg State Teachers College (now James Madison University) and visited, along with his wife Claudia, around 1920 when driving to Baltimore to make purchases for his chain of dry goods and grocery stores.

More about JAMES FRANKLIN GARBER:
Burial: Bethlehem Cemetery two to three miles outside Whitney, TX

More about SARAH CLAUDIA YARBROUGH:
Burial: Bethlehem Cemetery two to three miles outside Whitney, TX

Children of JAMES GARBER and SARAH YARBROUGH are:
[101]   3-3-1-2-5-1   GRACE MYRTLE[10] GARBER.
[102]   3-3-1-2-5-2   PANSY GARBER.
[103]   3-3-1-2-5-3   ROBERT ESTES GARBER.
        3-3-1-2-5-4   JAMES FRANKLIN GARBER, JR.[81], d. at age 21, unmarried, of pneumonia.
[104]   3-3-1-2-5-5   RUBY GARBER.
[105]   3-3-1-2-5-6   BLANCHE LERA GARBER, b. 1901.
[106]   3-3-1-2-5-7   SARAH ELIZABETH GARBER, b. 1914.

[69] BENJAMIN FRANKLIN[9] GARBER (*BENJAMIN[8], JOHN[7], ABRAHAM[6], JOHANNES "JOHN H."[5], JO HANNES[4] GERBER, NICLAUS[3], CHRISTIAN[2], ULRICH[1]*) was born 1855. He married MARY E. GROVE, daughter of MARTIN GROVE and BARBARA WENGER. She was born 1861 and died 1924.

More about BENJAMIN FRANKLIN GARBER:
Burial: Middle River Church of the Brethren in Augusta Co., VA
Residence: They lived at New Hope, VA.

More about MARY E. GROVE:
Burial: Middle River Church of the Brethren in Augusta Co., VA

Children of BENJAMIN GARBER and MARY GROVE are:
[107]   3-3-1-3-4-1   ANDREW MARTIN[10] GARBER, b. 1883, d. 1972.
        3-3-1-3-4-2   MINO FRANKLIN GARBER, b. 1885, d. 1887.
        3-3-1-3-4-3   EFFIE BELLE GARBER, b. 1887, d. 1970, m. JOHN GOCHENOUR.

[70] NANCY[9] MILLER *(REBEKAH[8] GARBER, JACOB W.[7], ABRAHAM[6], JOHANNES "JOHN H."[5], JO HANNES[4] GERBER, NICLAUS[3], CHRISTIAN[2], ULRICH[1])*[82] was born July 21, 1847[82], and died January 28, 1930[82]. She married FREDERICK KLINE[82] August 07, 1864[82], son of CHRISTIAN KLINE and REBECCA MYERS. He was born June 16, 1839[82], and died March 09, 1915[82].

Notes for FREDERICK KLINE:
A number of years after the Civil War, Frederick purchased a farm about two miles north of New Hope quite near the Middle River Church. On this farm was the principal scene of the Battle of Piedmont, which took place on Sunday, June 5, 1864.

Children of NANCY MILLER and FREDERICK KLINE are:

3-3-4-1-1-1   DANIEL CHRISTIAN[10] CLINE, b. August 29, 1865, d. 1933, m. IDA FRANCES LONG, December 24, 1893, b. October 02, 1870, d. December 24, 1959.
3-3-4-1-1-2   SALOMA REBECCA CLINE, b. March 10, 1867, d. January 13, 1950[83], m. JOHN BURKHOLDER[83], March 09, 1941[83].
3-3-4-1-1-3   IDA BARBARA CLINE, b. May 30, 1869[83], d. August 31, 1927[83].
3-3-4-1-1-4   MARTHA ANN CLINE, b. January 28, 1873[83], d. December 23, 1937[83].
3-3-4-1-1-5   VIRTIE NANCY JANE CLINE, b. September 08, 1877[83], d. October 06, 1934[83], m. T. KENNIE KOONTZ[83], December 24, 1911.
3-3-4-1-1-6   LOTTIE VIOLA CLINE, b. March 09, 1883[83], d. October 26, 1916[83].

[71] BARBARA[9] MILLER *(REBEKAH[8] GARBER, JACOB W.[7], ABRAHAM[6], JOHANNES "JOHN H."[5], JO HANNES[4] GERBER, NICLAUS[3], CHRISTIAN[2], ULRICH[1])*[84] was born January 03, 1849[84], and died March 04, 1933[84]. She married MILTON H. SHAVER[84] October 26, 1871[84], son of CORNELIUS SHAVER and CATHERINE HOCKMAN. He was born August 25, 1847, in New Hope, VA[84], and died September 08, 1928[84].

Children of BARBARA MILLER and MILTON SHAVER are:

3-3-4-1-2-1   LAURA REBECCA[10] SHAVER[85], b. November 02, 1872, d. January 29, 1946.
[108] 3-3-4-1-2-2   NANNIE CATHERINE SHAVER, b. July 12, 1874, d. August 04, 1938.
3-3-4-1-2-3   RUTH EMMAN SHAVER[85], b. September 25, 1882[85], d. November 05, 1954[85].
3-3-4-1-2-4   MINOR MONROE SHAVER[85], b. August 03, 1885[85], d. September 23, 1885[85].

[72] SOLOMON W.[9] GARBER *(ABRAHAM D.[8], JACOB W.[7], ABRAHAM[6], JOHANNES "JOHN H."[5], JO HANNES[4] GERBER, NICLAUS[3], CHRISTIAN[2], ULRICH[1])* was born April 25, 1849, and died January 26, 1934. He married CATHERINE SUSAN HARNSBERGER September 21, 1876[85], daughter of GEORGE HARNSBERGER and REBECCA. She was born December 10, 1849, and died December 24, 1916.

More about SOLOMON W. GARBER:
Occupation: Minister in the Church of the Brethren

Children of SOLOMON GARBER and CATHERINE HARNSBERGER are:

3-3-4-2-1-1   HOWARD MILLER[10] GARBER[85], b. August 21, 1877, d. August 28, 1962.
3-3-4-2-1-2   NINA REBECCA GARBER, b. November 11, 1878, d. 1956.
3-3-4-2-1-3   WILLIAM ARNOLD GARBER[85], b. September 05, 1881[85], d. December 09, 1917, Dudley, MO[85].
3-3-4-2-1-4   GEORGE ABRAHAM GARBER[85], b. November 14, 1887[85], m. IDA WAGNER[85], June 20, 1912[85].

[73] NANCY CATHERINE[9] GARBER *(ABRAHAM D.[8], JACOB W.[7], ABRAHAM[6], JOHANNES "JOHN H."[5], JO HANNES[4] GERBER, NICLAUS[3], CHRISTIAN[2], ULRICH[1])[85]* was born December 30, 1850[85], and died March 04, 1918[85]. She married ANANIAS JOCEPHUS MOOMAW[85] February 15, 1876[85].

Children of NANCY GARBER and ANANIAS MOOMAW are:
- 3-3-4-2-2-1 EDWARD OCTOR[10] MOOMAW[85], b. July 11, 1878, d. August 18, 1884.
- 3-3-4-2-2-2 SOPHIA MAGDALENE CATHERINE MOOMAW[85], b. December 15, 1879.
- 3-3-4-2-2-3 CHARLES RICE MOOMAW[85], b. March 22, 1881.
- 3-3-4-2-2-4 OSINA WILLIAM MOOMAW[85], b. September 27, 1882.
- 3-3-4-2-2-5 OMEGA FRANKLIN MOOMAW[85], b. September 27, 1882, d. April 15, 1946.
- 3-3-4-2-2-6 DAVID BOWMAN MOOMAW[85], b. June 29, 1885, d. May 20, 1946.
- 3-3-4-2-2-7 DANIEL YOUNT MOOMAW, b. June 29, 1885.
- 3-3-4-2-2-8 JOHN CALVIN MOOMAW[85], b. May 24, 1892, d. December 1986, LaVerne, CA.

[74] DANIEL ARNOLD[9] GARBER *(ABRAHAM D.[8], JACOB W.[7], ABRAHAM[6], JOHANNES "JOHN H."[5], JO HANNES[4] GERBER, NICLAUS[3], CHRISTIAN[2], ULRICH[1])[85]* was born November 23, 1852, and died December 27, 1931. He married WILMA A. HUTCHENS[85] September 01, 1883[85].

More about DANIEL ARNOLD GARBER:
Occupation: Real estate business
Residence: Lived in Roanoke, VA, for more than 35 years

Children of DANIEL GARBER and WILMA HUTCHENS are:
- 3-3-4-2-3-1 ANNE IONA[10] GARBER, b. August 01, 1884.
- 3-3-4-2-3-2 STANLEY MORRISON GARBER[85], b. September 29, 1887, d. January 1980, Camden, SC.

[75] MELISSA MARGARET[9] GARBER *(ABRAHAM D.[8], JACOB W.[7], ABRAHAM[6], JOHANNES "JOHN H."[5], JO HANNES[4] GERBER, NICLAUS[3], CHRISTIAN[2], ULRICH[1])[85]* was born June 07, 1856, and died August 09, 1921. She married JOHN NEWTON HALE[85] October 16, 1879[85].

Children of MELISSA GARBER and JOHN HALE are:
- 3-3-4-2-4-1 CHARLES ARNOLD[10] HALE[85], b. March 15, 1882, d. August 26, 1929.
- 3-3-4-2-4-2 DELFIE SUSAN HALE[85], b. May 13, 1886, d. October 1966, Annville, PA.
- 3-3-4-2-4-3 EFFIE SOPHIA HALE[85], b. May 13, 1886, d. September 1969, Belle Glade, FL.
- 3-3-4-2-4-4 WILBER GARBER HALE[85], b. November 16, 1889, d. January 1969, Arlington, VA.

[76] PRISCILLA ELIZABETH[9] GARBER *(ABRAHAM D.[8], JACOB W.[7], ABRAHAM[6], JOHANNES "JOHN H."[5], JO HANNES[4] GERBER, NICLAUS[3], CHRISTIAN[2], ULRICH[1])[85]* was born May 01, 1858, and died September 04, 1928. She married CHARLES LUTHER SHUMAKE[85] September 04, 1890[85].

Children of PRISCILLA GARBER and CHARLES SHUMAKE are:
- 3-3-4-2-5-1 LAWRENCE ARNOLD[10] SHUMAKE[85], b. June 02, 1891, d. August 13, 1990.
- 3-3-4-2-5-2 MERLE REBECCA SHUMAKE[85], b. March 19, 1894, d. September 11, 1987.
- 3-3-4-2-5-3 CHARLES MILLER SHUMAKE[85], b. December 27, 1897, d. July 27, 1965.
- 3-3-4-2-5-4 AUSTIN WINE SHUMAKE[85], b. January 22, 1900, d. January 1986, Orange, VA.

[77] SAMUEL ABRAHAM⁹ GARBER *(ABRAHAM D.⁸, JACOB W.⁷, ABRAHAM⁶, JOHANNES "JOHN H."⁵, JO HANNES⁴ GERBER, NICLAUS³, CHRISTIAN², ULRICH¹)*⁸⁵ was born July 01, 1863, and died January 27, 1933. He married HETTIE ELLEN SHOWALTER⁸⁵ November 08, 1905⁸⁵, daughter of HENRY SHOWALTER and BETTY. She was born Abt. 1874 and died 1957.

Notes for SAMUEL ABRAHAM GARBER:
Samuel Garber was a well-known farmer, highly respected for his patience, kindness and strength of character. Their son Vernon followed his father's footsteps, remaining at home and farming until a short time prior to his death in January 1997. Today the home place is known as Garber Farms, Inc., and has been in the family for over 150 years. The animal and crop farming is operated by Vernon's son Lowell and his two sons Wayne and Brian.

Children of SAMUEL GARBER and HETTIE SHOWALTER are:
    3-3-4-2-7-1   ELIZABETH REBECCA¹⁰ GARBER⁸⁵, b. October 16, 1906, d. June 13, 1996, m. RAY RENALDS, 1928.

More about ELIZABETH REBECCA GARBER:
Occupation: 1926, Taught at Rocky Bar School in Rockingham Co.

    3-3-4-2-7-2   WELTY ABRAHAM GARBER⁸⁵, b. February 05, 1908, d. June 15, 1984.
    3-3-4-2-7-3   HUBERT MICHAEL GARBER⁸⁵, b. October 29, 1909, d. May 10, 2004, Woodruff, SC, m. DORTHY MAE BAILEY⁸⁵, February 11, 1979⁸⁵.
    3-3-4-2-7-4   ESTON LEVI GARBER, b. June 06, 1912, d. July 25, 2000.

More about ESTON LEVI GARBER:
Burial: Pleasant Valley Church of the Brethren

    3-3-4-2-7-5   VERNON LONG GARBER⁸⁵, b. June 26, 1914, Augusta Co., VA, d. January 12, 1997, Mt. Sidney, VA., in Augusta Co.

[78] SOPHIA MAGDALENE BYRD⁹ GARBER *(ABRAHAM D.⁸, JACOB W.⁷, ABRAHAM⁶, JOHANNES "JOHN H."⁵, JO HANNES⁴ GERBER, NICLAUS³, CHRISTIAN², ULRICH¹)* was born March 30, 1871, and died July 10, 1958. She married (1) FRANK ROUDABUSH. She married (2) JAMES ROBERT MANUEL February 13, 1895.

Children of SOPHIA GARBER and JAMES MANUEL are:
    3-3-4-2-8-1   WHITSON GARBER¹⁰ MANUEL⁸⁵, b. April 20, 1897, d. April 07, 1898.
    3-3-4-2-8-2   SOPHIA BYRD MANUEL⁸⁵, b. December 10, 1900, d. April 21, 1996.
    3-3-4-2-8-3   REBECCA ELIZABETH MANUEL⁸⁵, b. May 12, 1908.
    3-3-4-2-8-4   JAMES ARNOLD MANUEL⁸⁵, b. January 22, 1915, d. October 02, 1980, College Park, MD⁸⁵.

[79] PETER⁹ GARBER *(LEVI⁸, JACOB W.⁷, ABRAHAM⁶, JOHANNES "JOHN H."⁵, JO HANNES⁴ GERBER, NICLAUS³, CHRISTIAN², ULRICH¹)*⁸⁶ was born December 09, 1850, in Mt. Sidney, in Augusta Co., VA⁸⁶, and died May 08, 1932⁸⁶. He married EMMA CATHERINE CLINE⁸⁶ October 29, 1876⁸⁶. She was born October 29, 1852⁸⁶, and died January 01, 1915⁸⁶.

Notes for PETER GARBER:
Peter Garber united with the church in his sixteenth year. He was elected to the deacon office August 1877. He was chosen to the ministry August 1881 and ordained to the Eldership August 1897. His home is within the bounds of the Pleasant Valley congregation. He was Senior Elder of the Pleasant Valley and Summit congregations.

Children of PETER GARBER and EMMA CLINE are:
[109]   3-3-4-3-1-1   MARY ELIZABETH^{10} GARBER, b. September 28, 1878, d. December 18, 1973.
[110]   3-3-4-3-1-2   JOHN CLINE GARBER, b. August 07, 1883, d. January 22, 1963.
[111]   3-3-4-3-1-3   BENJAMIN FREDERICK GARBER, b. January 02, 1885, d. March 05, 1971.
[112]   3-3-4-3-1-4   FRANKLIN LEVI GARBER, b. August 10, 1889.

[80] JACOB A.^{9} GARBER (*LEVI^8, JACOB W.^{7}, ABRAHAM^6, JOHANNES "JOHN H."^{5}, JO HANNES^4 GERBER, NICLAUS^3, CHRISTIAN^2, ULRICH^1)*[86] was born October 08, 1853, in Augusta Co., VA[86], and died October 11, 1915, in Rockingham Co., VA[86]. He married MARY ELIZABETH "LIZZIE" MYERS[86] November 20, 1873[86], daughter of SAMUEL MYERS and ELIZABETH HAGERDON. She was born April 16, 1853[86], and died February 28, 1928[86].

Notes for JACOB A. GARBER:
Their home was made at the Myers homestead in Rockingham Co., VA, at the Big Spring fountain source of Linville Creek. This being in the bounds of the Green Mount congregation, and quite near the church, he became active in the affairs of the church. He was elected to the deacon office March 1874, to the ministry in 1877 and ordained to the Eldership in 1902. He served the Green Mount church until the time of his death. He also did a great amount of mission work in the mountainous sections of WV. This territory at one time had been worked jointly by the Linville Creek and Green Mount churches, later organized into two congregations, known as North Mill Creek and South Fork congregations with Jacob A. Garber Elder in charge. He made many extensive trips through these mountainous sections, and from his general mode of travel he was known as the horseback evangelist. He preached 760 funerals, officiated at 160 marriages and held a good many series of meetings.

More about JACOB A. GARBER:
Burial: October 13, 1915, Rockingham Co., VA[86]

Children of JACOB GARBER and MARY MYERS are:
[113]   3-3-4-3-2-1   SAMUEL LEVI^{10} GARBER, b. November 16, 1875, d. November 02, 1945.
[114]   3-3-4-3-2-2   PETER ISAAC GARBER, b. August 06, 1877, d. October 15, 1949.
[115]   3-3-4-3-2-3   DANIEL BENJAMIN GARBER, b. March 02, 1879, d. July 15, 1957.
[116]   3-3-4-3-2-4   JOHN DAVID GARBER, b. April 15, 1881, d. July 19, 1935.
[117]   3-3-4-3-2-5   WILLIAM FRANKLIN GARBER, b. February 14, 1883, d. September 20, 1949.

[81] DANIEL SAMUEL^9 GARBER (*LEVI^8, JACOB W.^{7}, ABRAHAM^6, JOHANNES "JOHN H."^{5}, JO HANNES^4 GERBER, NICLAUS^3, CHRISTIAN^2, ULRICH^1)*[86] was born August 22, 1855, in Levi Garber house near Mt. Sidney, Augusta Co., VA[86], and died December 30, 1923, in his house near Mt. Sidney, Augusta Co., VA[87]. He married ELIZABETH MARGARET GLICK[88] March 09, 1879, in Middle River Church, Augusta Co., VA[88], daughter of SAMUEL GLICK and REBECCA WINE. She was born August 26, 1860, in Weyers Cave, Rockingham Co., VA[88], and died March 08, 1949, Daniel S. Garber house near Mt. Sidney, Augusta Co., VA[88].

More about DANIEL SAMUEL GARBER:
Baptism: 1870
Burial: January 01, 1924, Middle River Church of the Brethren in Augusta Co., VA[89]
Religion: 1880, Elected deacon
Residence: The family resided on the Levi Garber homestead, one and three-fourths miles east of Mt. Sidney.

Notes for ELIZABETH MARGARET GLICK:
Elizabeth was first cousin to Ida Stover, mother of Dwight D. Eisenhower, who visited Mt. Sidney and Ft. Defiance area, his home place.

More about ELIZABETH MARGARET GLICK:
Burial: Middle River Church of the Brethren, Augusta Co., VA[90]

Children of DANIEL GARBER and ELIZABETH GLICK are:
[118] 3-3-4-3-3-1   ANTHONY A.[10] GARBER, b. May 20, 1880, Levi Garber house near Mt. Sidney in Augusta Co., VA, d. November 18, 1951, Washington, DC, Area.

      3-3-4-3-3-2   ADA R. GARBER[91], b. October 29, 1881, Augusta Co., VA[91], d. December 22, 1962, Augusta Co., VA[91]; m. DAVID REED[91], October 05, 1902[91], b. December 24, 1877[91], d. February 10, 1903, Augusta Co., VA[91].

More about ADA R. GARBER:
Burial: 1962, Middle River Church of the Brethren in Augusta Co., VA[91]

      3-3-4-3-3-3   REGINA GARBER, b. September 07, 1884, d. September 07, 1884.
[119] 3-3-4-3-3-4   HOMER FRANKLIN GARBER, b. August 12, 1886, Levi Garber House near Mt. Sidney, Augusta Co., VA, d. October 14, 1973, Staunton Manor Nursing Home, Staunton, VA.
      3-3-4-3-3-5   MARTHA D. GARBER[91], b. August 30, 1888[91], d. September 25, 1914[91], m. ROY W. SLONAKER[91], December 17, 1913[91], b. Abt. 1888[91].

Notes for MARTHA D. GARBER:
Letter From: Franklin Grove, IL
            Sept. 25, 1914
To: D. S. Garber
         Ft. Defiance, VA
Martha and our baby died tonight. I will bring her home as soon as I can. We did all we could to save her, but all in vain. I will leave here with her for Virginia Sunday morning; expect to arrive at Ft. Defiance Monday noon at 12:27.
R. W. Slonaker

More about MARTHA D. GARBER:
Residence: Franklin Grove, IL

[120] 3-3-4-3-3-6   MINOR WILLIAM GARBER, b. March 24, 1891, Mt. Sidney, Augusta Co.,
      3-3-4-3-3-7   CORA V. GARBER[91], b. November 14, 1899, Augusta Co., VA[91], d. 1985, Rockingham Co., VA[91].

More about CORA V. GARBER:
Burial: May 1985, Middle River Church of the Brethren, Augusta Co., VA[92]
Residence: Bet. 1899 - 1970, Lived on father's farm at Knightly, VA, with her sister, Ada

[82] LYDIA CATHERINE[9] GARBER *(LEVI[8], JACOB W.[7], ABRAHAM[6], JOHANNES "JOHN H."[5], JO HANNES[4] GERBER, NICLAUS[3], CHRISTIAN[2], ULRICH[1])[93]* was born June 23, 1857, in Mt. Sidney, Augusta Co., VA[93], and died July 27, 1936[93]. She married JACOB H. FLORY[93] May 13, 1880[93]. He was born January 15, 1853[93], and died October 17, 1927[93].

Children of LYDIA GARBER and JACOB FLORY are:

	3-3-4-3-4-1	ERNEST GARBER[10] FLORY[93], b. June 19, 1884, d. October 26, 1943.
	3-3-4-3-4-2	IDA ELIZABETH FLORY[93], b. December 07, 1885, d. January 06, 1997.
[121]	3-3-4-3-4-3	LUELLA VIRGINIA FLORY, b. August 14, 1888, d. April 20, 1968.
[122]	3-3-4-3-4-4	WILLIAM FRANKLIN FLORY, b. June 05, 1891, d. December 30, 1973, Harrisonburg, VA.
	3-3-4-3-4-5	WALTER EARL FLORY[93], b. December 02, 1893, d. July 12, 1964.
	3-3-4-3-4-6	OLIVE MAE FLORY[93], b. August 03, 1895, d. January 11, 1984, Bridgewater, VA.

[83] BARBARA ELIZABETH[9] GARBER *(LEVI[8], JACOB W.[7], ABRAHAM[6], JOHANNES "JOHN H."[5], JO HANNES[4] GERBER, NICLAUS[3], CHRISTIAN[2], ULRICH[1])[93]* was born November 16, 1863, in Mt. Sidney, Augusta Co., VA[93], and died May 05, 1949[93]. She married JOSEPH SAMUEL NORFORD October 17, 1889[93]. He was born October 12, 1870, and died February 03, 1940[93].

Children of BARBARA GARBER and JOSEPH NORFORD are:

	3-3-4-3-7-1	INFANT[10] NORFORD[94], b. September 26, 1890, d. September 26, 1890.
[123]	3-3-4-3-7-2	EARL RAYMOND NORFORD, b. September 07, 1894, d. April 10, 1991.
	3-3-4-3-7-3	INFANT NORFORD[94], b. July 30, 1900, d. July 30, 1900.

[84] FRANCES "FANNIE" V.[9] GARBER *(LEVI[8], JACOB W.[7], ABRAHAM[6], JOHANNES "JOHN H."[5], JO HANNES[4] GERBER, NICLAUS[3], CHRISTIAN[2], ULRICH[1])[95]* was born March 15, 1866, in Mt. Sidney, Augusta Co., VA[95], and died August 14, 1925[95]. She married JACOB L. HUFFMAN March 15, 1900[95]. He was born August 14, 1862, and died September 22, 1950[95].

Children of FRANCES GARBER and JACOB HUFFMAN are:

	3-3-4-3-8-1	OSCAR[10] HUFFMAN[96], b. January 25, 1902, d. January 25, 1902.
	3-3-4-3-8-2	LESTER W. HUFFMAN[96], b. November 23, 1903, d. June 25, 1994, Dorris, CA; m. BERNICE A. POTTER, May 18, 1945.
[124]	3-3-4-3-8-3	ETHEL V. HUFFMAN, b. March 26, 1905.
	3-3-4-3-8-4	FLORENCE R. HUFFMAN[96], b. July 18, 1907, d. February 1920.

[85] JOHN REUBEN[9] GARBER *(REUBEN ARNOLD[8], JACOB W.[7], ABRAHAM[6], JOHANNES "JOHN H."[5], JO HANNES[4] GERBER, NICLAUS[3], CHRISTIAN[2], ULRICH[1])[97]* was born January 12, 1869, and died May 30, 1938. He married MATTIE LENORA NORFORD[98] November 12, 1891, daughter of JAMES NORFORD and JULIA.

Children of JOHN GARBER and MATTIE NORFORD are:

	3-3-4-4-6-1	EVIE BEULAH[10] GARBER[98], b. August 27, 1892.
	3-3-4-4-6-2	OLA BELLE GARBER[98], b. July 10, 1894, d. May 13, 1984.

3-3-4-4-6-3   MARY JULIA GARBER[98], b. February 14, 1896, d. September 30, 1988, Mt. Sidney, Augusta Co., VA.

3-3-4-4-6-4   DEWEY MCKINLEY GARBER[98], b. March 12, 1898, d. August 13, 1963[98].

3-3-4-4-6-5   ROY QUINTER GARBER[98], b. January 26, 1900, d. September 22, 1986.

3-3-4-4-6-6   JOHN LAWRENCE GARBER[98], b. April 17, 1908, d. August 11, 1979.

3-3-4-4-6-7   RUBY LEAH MARGARET GARBER[98], b. January 16, 1910.

[86] MARY ANNE[9] GARBER (*REUBEN ARNOLD[8], JACOB W.[7], ABRAHAM[6], JOHANNES "JOHN H."[5], JO HANNES[4] GERBER, NICLAUS[3], CHRISTIAN[2], ULRICH[1]*)[99] was born May 18, 1871, and died November 21, 1950. She married ISAAC ALEXANDER REED[100] April 30, 1893[100].

Children of MARY GARBER and ISAAC REED are:
3-3-4-4-7-1   INFANT[10] REED[100], b. October 24, 1902.
3-3-4-4-7-2   MAE VIRGINIA REED[100], b. January 01, 1904.
3-3-4-4-7-3   LLOYD ALEXANDER REED[100], b. June 23, 1905, d. February 15, 1993, Mt. Sidney, Augusta Co., VA[100].

[87] ROBERT ISSAC[9] GARBER (*JACOB W.[8], JACOB W.[7], ABRAHAM[6], JOHANNES "JOHN H."[5], JO HANNES[4] GERBER, NICLAUS[3], CHRISTIAN[2], ULRICH[1]*)[101] was born April 09, 1866, and died December 06, 1952. He married DAISY L. PFOUTZ February 15, 1900, in Washington, DC, daughter of JOHN PFOUTZ and ELIZA MYERS.

Children of ROBERT GARBER and DAISY PFOUTZ are:
3-3-4-5-1-1   ROBERT PARSONS[10] GARBER[102], b. April 23, 1903, d. March 06, 1988, FL.
3-3-4-5-1-2   MILDRED JANE GARBER[102], b. September 24, 1910, d. August 04, 1987.
3-3-4-5-1-3   SUSAN ANITA GARBER[102], b. March 17, 1914, m. HANS SCHMIDT UN-KNOWN[102].
3-3-4-5-1-4   JOHN WILLIAM GARBER[102], b. September 02, 1915.

[88] BENJAMIN JACOB[9] GARBER (*JACOB W.[8], JACOB W.[7], ABRAHAM[6], JOHANNES "JOHN H."[5], JO HANNES[4] GERBER, NICLAUS[3], CHRISTIAN[2], ULRICH[1]*)[103] was born January 06, 1868, and died November 05, 1924. He married NETTIE CRAIGGE CURD[104] March 19, 1902, in Fishersville, VA, daughter of ALBERT CURD and MARY PATTERSON.

Children of BENJAMIN GARBER and NETTIE CURD are:
3-3-4-5-2-1   CORNELIA CURD[10] GARBER[104], b. February 03, 1903, d. February 11, 1903.
3-3-4-5-2-2   WILLIAM ALBERT GARBER[104], b. February 10, 1904, d. January 22, 1990.
3-3-4-5-2-3   MARY MARGARET GARBER[104], b. October 08, 1908.

[89] MARY ADA[9] GARBER (*JACOB W.[8], JACOB W.[7], ABRAHAM[6], JOHANNES "JOHN H."[5], JO HANNES[4] GERBER, NICLAUS[3], CHRISTIAN[2], ULRICH[1]*)[105] was born January 19, 1873, and died June 28, 1955. She married (1) CHARLES E. BYRD[106] March 01, 1894, in M.E. Church, New Hope, VA, son of LEWIS BYRD and MARGARET AREY. She married (2) WILLIAM ELLIOT[106] April 30, 1939.

Children of MARY GARBER and CHARLES BYRD are:
3-3-4-5-4-1   PAULINE MAY[10] BYRD[106], b. May 29, 1895, Dayton. VA, d. August 28, 1954, Emporia, KS.

3-3-4-5-4-2   WINIFRED GRACE BYRD[106], b. September 22, 1899, Ottawa, IL.
3-3-4-5-4-3   MARSHALL ROYCE BYRD[106], b. December 13, 1905, d. November 04, 1991.

[90] JOHN ADAM[9] GARBER *(JACOB W.[8], JACOB W.[7], ABRAHAM[6], JOHANNES "JOHN H."[5], JO HANNES[4] GERBER, NICLAUS[3], CHRISTIAN[2], ULRICH[1])[107]* was born May 01, 1884[108], and died November 28, 1975, in Decatur, GA[108]. He married (1) IVA LESLIE[108] September 02, 1909 in Ashland, OH, daughter of GUILFORD LESLIE and SARAH EARLY. He married (2) JEAN BOON BATCHELOR[108] February 18, 1958.

Child of JOHN GARBER and IVA LESLIE is:
3-3-4-5-9-1   PAUL LESLIE[10] GARBER, SR.[108], b. April 27, 1911, Johnstown, PA, d. April 20, 1996, Hospice Atlanta, GA.

[91] ELIZABETH MARGARET[9] GLICK *(REBECCA[8] WINE, MICHAEL[7], MAGADALENE[6] GARBER, JOHANNES "JOHN H."[5], JO HANNES[4] GERBER, NICLAUS[3], CHRISTIAN[2], ULRICH[1])[109]* was born August 26, 1860, in Weyers Cave, Rockingham Co., VA[109], and died March 08, 1949, in Daniel S. Garber house near Mt. Sidney, Augusta Co., VA[109]. She married DANIEL SAMUEL GARBER[109] March 09, 1879, in Middle River Church, Augusta Co., VA[109], son of LEVI GARBER and BARBARA MILLER. He was born August 22, 1855, in Levi Garber house near Mt. Sidney, Augusta Co., VA[109], and died December 30, 1923 in his house near Mt. Sidney, Augusta Co., VA[110].

Notes for ELIZABETH MARGARET GLICK:
Elizabeth was first cousin to Ida Stover, mother of Dwight D. Eisenhower, who visited Mt. Sidney and Ft. Defiance area, his home place.

More about ELIZABETH MARGARET GLICK:
Burial: Middle River Church of the Brethren, Augusta Co., VA[111]

More about DANIEL SAMUEL GARBER:
Baptism: 1870
Burial: January 01, 1924, Middle River Church of the Brethren in Augusta Co., VA[112]
Religion: 1880, Elected deacon
Residence: The family resided on the Levi Garber homestead, one and three-fourths miles east of Mt. Sidney.

Children are listed above under (81) Daniel Samuel Garber.

[92] BENJ. FRANKLIN[9] GLICK *(REBECCA[8] WINE, MICHAEL[7], MAGADALENE[6] GARBER, JOHANNES "JOHN H."[5], JO HANNES[4] GERBER, NICLAUS[3], CHRISTIAN[2], ULRICH[1])[112]* was born September 07, 1862, and died August 03, 1928[112]. He married EMMA WHISLER[112] March 1900[112].

Children of BENJ. GLICK and EMMA WHISLER are:
3-10-1-10-4-1 REBECCA[10] GLICK.
[125] 3-10-1-10-4-2 LAURENCE GLICK.
3-10-1-10-4-3 CHARLES GLICK[113], m. VIOLA WITT[113], August 22, 1944[113].

[93] MARY MAGDALENE[9] GLICK *(REBECCA[8] WINE, MICHAEL[7], MAGADALENE[6] GARBER, JOHANNES "JOHN H."[5], JO HANNES[4] GERBER, NICLAUS[3], CHRISTIAN[2], ULRICH[1])* was born February 11, 1865[114], and died October 15, 1932[114]. She married J. HARMAN STOVER September 1888[114]. He died April 27, 1922[114].

Children of MARY GLICK and J. STOVER are:
[126]   3-10-1-10-5-1   HARRY[10] STOVER, d. 1951.
      3-10-1-10-5-2   ARTHUR STOVER[115], m. RUTH.

Notes for ARTHUR STOVER:
No children

      3-10-1-10-5-3   JOHN STOVER[115], m. PAT.

Notes for JOHN STOVER:
No children

[127]   3-10-1-10-5-4   DORA STOVER.

[94] JOHN WILLIAM[9] GLICK *(REBECCA[8] WINE, MICHAEL[7], MAGADALENE[6] GARBER, JOHANNES "JOHN H."[5], JO HANNES[4] GERBER, NICLAUS[3], CHRISTIAN[2], ULRICH[1])* was born May 28, 1867[116], and died August 18, 1911[116]. He married MAUDE CRAUN[116] 1895[116]. She died July 09, 1903[116].

Children of JOHN GLICK and MAUDE CRAUN are:
[128]   3-10-1-10-6-1   CARL[10] GLICK.
[129]   3-10-1-10-6-2   FRANK GLICK.

[95] MARTHA JANE[9] GLICK *(REBECCA[8] WINE, MICHAEL[7], MAGADALENE[6] GARBER, JOHANNES "JOHN H."[5], JO HANNES[4] GERBER, NICLAUS[3], CHRISTIAN[2], ULRICH[1])* was born May 03, 1869[116], and died April 12, 1950[116]. She married D. B. SENGER June 11, 1900[116]. He died January 02, 1908[116].

Children of MARTHA GLICK and D. SENGER are:
[130]   3-10-1-10-7-1   RUTH[10] SENGER.
[131]   3-10-1-10-7-2   MERLE SENGER.

[96] SARAH FRANCES[9] GLICK *(REBECCA[8] WINE, MICHAEL[7], MAGADALENE[6] GARBER, JOHANNES "JOHN H."[5], JO HANNES[4] GERBER, NICLAUS[3], CHRISTIAN[2], ULRICH[1])* was born September 27, 1870[116], and died July 20, 1943[116]. She married J. G. MILLER February 22, 1893[116].

Children of SARAH GLICK and J. MILLER are:
[132]   3-10-1-10-8-1   BEUFORD[10] MILLER, b. 1895.
[133]   3-10-1-10-8-2   ETHEL MILLER, b. 1899.
[134]   3-10-1-10-8-3   RAY MILLER, b. 1897.
[135]   3-10-1-10-8-4   WALTER MILLER, b. 1901.

3-10-1-10-8-5 C.D. MILLER[117], m. ELLA[117].
3-10-1-10-8-6 EDITH MILLER[117], b. 1907[117].
[136] 3-10-1-10-8-7 ESTHER MILLER.

U.S. Generation No. 6

[97] NATHANIEL BELL[10] GARBER *(DANIEL ALEXANDER[9], SAMUEL MILLER[8], JOHN[7], ABRAHAM[6], JOHANNES "JOHN H."[5], JO HANNES[4] GERBER, NICLAUS[3], CHRISTIAN[2], ULRICH[1])* was born September 09, 1873, and died 1941. He married MARY C. FIX[118] November 18, 1894. She was born March 1881[118].

More about NATHANIEL BELL GARBER:
Burial: Middle River Cemetery

More about MARY C. FIX:
Burial: Middle River Church of the Brethren in Augusta Co., VA

Children of NATHANIEL GARBER and MARY FIX are:
  3-3-1-2-1-1-1 NELLIE[11] GARBER.
  3-3-1-2-1-1-2 ANNIE GARBER.
  3-3-1-2-1-1-3 RUTH GARBER.
  3-3-1-2-1-1-4 CECIL GARBER.

[98] HOMER F.[10] GARBER *(DANIEL ALEXANDER[9], SAMUEL MILLER[8], JOHN[7], ABRAHAM[6], JOHANNES "JOHN H."[5], JO HANNES[4] GERBER, NICLAUS[3], CHRISTIAN[2], ULRICH[1])* was born April 12, 1882, and died August 10, 1948. He married EDITH STOVER, daughter of JOHN STOVER and BARBARA GARBER.

More about HOMER F. GARBER:
Burial: Barren Ridge Church Cemetery

Children of HOMER GARBER and EDITH STOVER are:
  3-3-1-2-1-4-1 CLYDE[11] GARBER.
  3-3-1-2-1-4-2 LOUISE GARBER.
  3-3-1-2-1-4-3 BARBARA GARBER.
  3-3-1-2-1-4-4 FRANCES GARBER.
  3-3-1-2-1-4-5 AGNES GARBER.
  3-3-1-2-1-4-5 CORA LEE GARBER.
  3-3-1-2-1-4-7 HOMER GARBER, JR.

[99] BERTIE[10] GARBER *(DANIEL ALEXANDER[9], SAMUEL MILLER[8], JOHN[7], ABRAHAM[6], JOHANNES "JOHN H."[5], JO HANNES[4] GERBER, NICLAUS[3], CHRISTIAN[2], ULRICH[1])* was born June 10, 1891. She married J. SAMUEL FOLEY. He died August 09, 1962.

Children of BERTIE GARBER and J. FOLEY are:
  3-3-1-2-1-5-1 CALEB[11] FOLEY.
  3-3-1-2-1-5-2 ELBERT FOLEY.

[100] MAUDY VIOLA[10] GARBER *(CLIFTON BENJAMIN[9], SAMUEL MILLER[8], JOHN[7], ABRAHAM[6], JOHANNES "JOHN H."[5], JO HANNES[4] GERBER, NICLAUS[3], CHRISTIAN[2], ULRICH[1])[118]* was born 1885[118] and died 1977. She married HEDRICK C. GORDON[118] 1914. He was born 1884[118] and died 1968[118].

More about MAUDY VIOLA GARBER:
Burial: Middle River Church of the Brethren in Augusta Co., VA[118]
Residence: Newport (Moffetts Creek), address Middlebrook, area of Augusta Co., VA

More about HEDRICK C. GORDON:
Burial: Middle River Church of the Brethren in Augusta Co., VA[118]
Occupation: Farmer and trapper

Children of MAUDY GARBER and HEDRICK GORDON are:
    3-3-1-2-3-1   MARY LEE[11] GORDON, b. 1916, m. BURMAN W. CASH.
    3-3-1-2-3-2   JUANITA GARBER GORDON, b. 1917, m. THOMAS W. CASH, Leeburg.
    3-3-1-2-3-4   LENNA BELL GORDON, b. 1921, m. WILLIAM CALVIN REID, b. 1923.
    3-3-1-2-3-5   CLYDE WILSON GORDON, b. 1923, m. LILLIAN L. LUCAS.

[101] GRACE MYRTLE[10] GARBER *(JAMES FRANKLIN[9], SAMUEL MILLER[8], JOHN[7], ABRAHAM[6], JOHANNES "JOHN H."[5], JO HANNES[4] GERBER, NICLAUS[3], CHRISTIAN[2], ULRICH[1])[118]*. She married J.M. "BOSS" WHITE[118].

Notes for GRACE MYRTLE GARBER:
All of the immediate family deceased. Boss and Grace were in Midland, TX, after the Depression and became very prosperous in land leasing. They contributed generously to Baylor University in Waco.

Children of GRACE GARBER and J.M. WHITE are:
    3-3-1-2-5-1-1   JAMES GARBER[11] WHITE[118].
    3-3-1-2-5-1-2   ROBERT KEITH WHITE[118].
    3-3-1-2-5-1-3   J.M. WHITE, JR.[118].

[102] PANSY[10] GARBER *(JAMES FRANKLIN[9], SAMUEL MILLER[8], JOHN[7], ABRAHAM[6], JOHANNES "JOHN H."[5], JO HANNES[4] GERBER, NICLAUS[3], CHRISTIAN[2], ULRICH[1])[118]*. She married FRANK PUGH[118].

Children of PANSY GARBER and FRANK PUGH are:
    3-3-1-2-5-1-1   JAMES FRANKLIN[11] PUGH[118].
    3-3-1-2-5-1-2   BETTY GRACE PUGH[118].

[103] ROBERT ESTES[10] GARBER *(JAMES FRANKLIN[9], SAMUEL MILLER[8], JOHN[7], ABRAHAM[6], JOHANNES "JOHN H."[5], JO HANNES[4] GERBER, NICLAUS[3], CHRISTIAN[2], ULRICH[1])[118]*. He married ZUELENA JOHNSON[118].

Notes for ROBERT ESTES GARBER:
No sons by the latter two (Robert E. Garber, Jr., and James F. Garber III), thus no descendants of the TX family branch bearing a Garber surname.

Children of ROBERT GARBER and ZUELENA JOHNSON are:
>   3-3-1-2-5-3-1   ROBERT E.[11] GARBER, JR.[118].
>   3-3-1-2-5-3-2   JAMES F. GARBER III[118].

[104] RUBY[10] GARBER *(JAMES FRANKLIN[9], SAMUEL MILLER[8], JOHN[7], ABRAHAM[6], JOHANNES "JOHN H."[5], JO HANNES[4] GERBER, NICLAUS[3], CHRISTIAN[2], ULRICH[1])[118]*. She married JAMES M. HERRINGTON[118].

Children of RUBY GARBER and JAMES HERRINGTON are:
>   3-3-1-2-5-5-1   JACK DONALD[11] HERRINGTON[118].
>   3-3-1-2-5-5-2   DORIS HERRINGTON WESTBROOK[118].

[105] BLANCHE LERA[10] GARBER *(JAMES FRANKLIN[9], SAMUEL MILLER[8], JOHN[7], ABRAHAM[6], JOHANNES "JOHN H."[5], JO HANNES[4] GERBER, NICLAUS[3], CHRISTIAN[2], ULRICH[1])[118]* was born 1901. She married BYRON DREW HAMPTON[118].

Notes for BLANCHE LERA GARBER:
Blanche was in a nursing home in Dallas for six to eight years.

Child of BLANCHE GARBER and BYRON HAMPTON is:
>   3-3-1-2-5-6-1   BRYON D.[11] HAMPTON, JR.[118].

[106] SARAH ELIZABETH[10] GARBER *(JAMES FRANKLIN[9], SAMUEL MILLER[8], JOHN[7], ABRAHAM[6], JOHANNES "JOHN H."[5], JO HANNES[4] GERBER, NICLAUS[3], CHRISTIAN[2], ULRICH[1])[118]* was born 1914. She married F. T. ALEXANDER[118].

Child of SARAH GARBER and F.T. ALEXANDER is:
>   3-3-1-2-5-7-1   SARA BETH[11] ALEXANDER[118], m. DICK (T.D.) SELLS, JR..

Notes for SARA BETH ALEXANDER:
Lived in Houston, TX, and had one daughter Sara Beth married to Dick (T .D.) Sells, Jr. They had three sons and one daughter.

[107] ANDREW MARTIN[10] GARBER *(BENJAMIN FRANKLIN[9], BENJAMIN[8], JOHN[7], ABRAHAM[6], JOHANNES "JOHN H."[5], JO HANNES[4] GERBER, NICLAUS[3], CHRISTIAN[2], ULRICH[1])* was born 1883 and died 1972. He married GRACE A. SAUFLEY. She was born 1890 and died 1977.

Children of ANDREW GARBER and GRACE SAUFLEY are:
>   3-3-1-3-4-1-1   THELMA MAE[11] GARBER, d. 1970, m. BERNARD H. ROLLER.
>   3-3-1-3-4-1-2   NELSON ANDREW GARBER.
>   3-3-1-3-4-1-3   MABEL LOUISE GARBER, b. 1915, m. WILLIAM DURWOOD YOUNG.
>   3-3-1-3-4-1-4   MARY LILLIAN GARBER, b. 1917, m. CALLIE JOHN DIEHL.
>   3-3-1-3-4-1-5   DONALD FRANKLIN GARBER, d. 1930.
>   3-3-1-3-4-1-6   GENE SAUFLEY GARBER, b. 1932, m. BETTY JO GROVE.

[108] NANNIE CATHERINE[10] SHAVER *(BARBARA[9] MILLER, REBEKAH[8] GARBER, JACOB W.[7], ABRAHAM[6], JOHANNES "JOHN H."[5], JO HANNES[4] GERBER, NICLAUS[3], CHRISTIAN[2], ULRICH[1])[119]* was born July 12, 1874[119], and died August 04, 1938[119]. She married JOHN DAVID WESTERN[119]. He was born August 28, 1865, and died July 31, 1935.

Child of NANNIE SHAVER and JOHN WESTERN is:
[137]   3-3-4-1-2-2-1   RENA BARBARA[11] WESTERN, b. December 15, 1892, New Hope, VA,
                  d. May 16, 1982, Harrisonburg, VA.

[109] MARY ELIZABETH[10] GARBER *(PETER[9], LEVI[8], JACOB W.[7], ABRAHAM[6], JOHANNES "JOHN H."[5], JO HANNES[4] GERBER, NICLAUS[3], CHRISTIAN[2], ULRICH[1])[120]* was born September 28, 1878, and died December 18, 1973. She married LUTHER DAVID WAMPLER[121] November 24, 1905.

Children of MARY GARBER and LUTHER WAMPLER are:
            3-3-4-3-1-1-1   RUTH EMMA[11] WAMPLER[121], b. August 14, 1907, d. July 24, 1954.
            3-3-4-3-1-1-2   PETER FRANKLIN WAMPLER[121], b. May 27, 1909, d. September 30, 1911.
            3-3-4-3-1-1-3   CARL MICHAEL WAMPLER[121], b. April 16, 1911, d. June 07, 1938.
[138]   3-3-4-3-1-1-4   MAE ELIZABETH WAMPLER, b. September 13, 1915.
[139]   3-3-4-3-1-1-5   EVA REBECCA WAMPLER, b. September 26, 1917.
[140]   3-3-4-3-1-1-6   FREDERICK CLINE WAMPLER, b. November 20, 1920.

[110] JOHN CLINE[10] GARBER *(PETER[9], LEVI[8], JACOB W.[7], ABRAHAM[6], JOHANNES "JOHN H."[5], JO HANNES[4] GERBER, NICLAUS[3], CHRISTIAN[2], ULRICH[1])[122]* was born August 07, 1883, and died January 22, 1963. He married SADA ESTELLA HOUFF July 23, 1907. She was born February 04, 1886.

More about JOHN CLINE GARBER:
Occupation: Pastor of the Staunton Church of the Brethren for 29 years

Children of JOHN GARBER and SADA HOUFF are:
[141]   3-3-4-3-1-2-1   CASPER WHITMORE[11] GARBER, b. August 02, 1908, d. August 08, 1991.
[142]   3-3-4-3-1-2-2   MERLIN ESTES GARBER, b. March 26, 1912.
[143]   3-3-4-3-1-2-3   ELVA OTELIA GARBER, b. January 28, 1916, Buena Vista, VA.
[144]   3-3-4-3-1-2-4   MAYNARD AUBRY GARBER, b. February 23, 1920, Staunton, VA.

[111] BENJAMIN FREDERICK[10] GARBER *(PETER[9], LEVI[8], JACOB W.[7], ABRAHAM[6], JOHANNES "JOHN H."[5], JO HANNES[4] GERBER, NICLAUS[3], CHRISTIAN[2], ULRICH[1])[122]* was born January 02, 1885, and died March 05, 1971. He married FLORENCE CLINE WAMPLER May 10, 1910.

Children of BENJAMIN GARBER and FLORENCE WAMPLER are:
            3-3-4-3-1-3-1   VERMA ELIZA[11] GARBER, b. March 23, 1913.
[145]   3-3-4-3-1-3-2   CALVIN WILLIAM GARBER, b. May 22, 1916.
[146]   3-3-4-3-1-3-3   ALDA ETHEL GARBER, b. July 27, 1918.

[112] FRANKLIN LEVI[10] GARBER *(PETER[9], LEVI[8], JACOB W.[7], ABRAHAM[6], JOHANNES "JOHN H."[5], JO HANNES[4] GERBER, NICLAUS[3], CHRISTIAN[2], ULRICH[1])[122]* was born August 10, 1889. He married (1) MAE ANNA EARLY[123] June 08, 1916. He married (2) ETHEL MAY CLINE April 24, 1953.

Children of FRANKLIN GARBER and MAE EARLY are:

[147] 3-3-4-3-1-4-1   ESTHER FRANCES[11] GARBER, b. August 25, 1917.

          3-3-4-3-1-4-2   HELEN REBECCA GARBER[123], b. April 22, 1919, d. September 08, 1920.

[148] 3-3-4-3-1-4-3   ETHEL MAE GARBER, b. April 18, 1921.

[149] 3-3-4-3-1-4-4   IRENE EDITH GARBER, b. June 28, 1923.

          3-3-4-3-1-4-5   MELVIN WELTY GARBER[123], b. September 29, 1927.

[150] 3-3-4-3-1-4-6   GERALDINE EARLY GARBER, b. August 05, 1929.

[113] SAMUEL LEVI[10] GARBER *(JACOB A.[9], LEVI[8], JACOB W.[7], ABRAHAM[6], JOHANNES "JOHN H."[5], JO HANNES[4] GERBER, NICLAUS[3], CHRISTIAN[2], ULRICH[1])[123]* was born November 16, 1875, and died November 02, 1945. He married MAGDALENE ALICE WAMPLER[123] December 23, 1897[123], daughter of FREDERICK WAMPLER.

Children of SAMUEL GARBER and MAGDALENE WAMPLER are:

[151] 3-3-4-3-2-1-1   MARY ELIZABETH[11] GARBER, b. April 21, 1900, d. December 20, 1976, Gordonsville, VA.

[152] 3-3-4-3-2-1-2   ANNA REBECCA GARBER, b. August 09, 1903, d. August 25, 1962.

[153] 3-3-4-3-2-1-3   CARL LEVI GARBER, b. July 30, 1905, d. December 08, 1982.

[154] 3-3-4-3-2-1-4   FRANCES WILLARD GARBER, b. September 07, 1908, d. June 24, 1973.

          3-3-4-3-2-1-5   INFANT SON GARBER[123], b. September 07, 1908.

[155] 3-3-4-3-2-1-6   LILLIAN MAY GARBER, b. May 13, 1911.

[156] 3-3-4-3-2-1-7   REINETTE MAGDALENA GARBER, b. September 23, 1917, d. August 21, 1978.

[114] PETER ISAAC[10] GARBER *(JACOB A.[9], LEVI[8], JACOB W.[7], ABRAHAM[6], JOHANNES "JOHN H."[5], JO HANNES[4] GERBER, NICLAUS[3], CHRISTIAN[2], ULRICH[1])[123]* was born August 06, 1877, and died October 15, 1949. He married LILLIAN FRANCES CLINE[123] December 14, 1899, daughter of MARTIN CLINE and SUSANNA.

Children of PETER GARBER and LILLIAN CLINE are:

[157] 3-3-4-3-2-2-1   JACOB MARTIN[11] GARBER, b. August 29, 1901, d. February 10, 1993, McLean, VA.

[158] 3-3-4-3-2-2-2   EDWARD FRANKLIN GARBER, b. September 21, 1903, d. March 10, 1990, Elkton, Rockingham Co., VA.

[159] 3-3-4-3-2-2-3   FANNIE VIRGINIA GARBER, b. March 19, 1905, d. January 15, 1955.

[160] 3-3-4-3-2-2-4   CLARENCE BENJAMIN GARBER, b. October 11, 1906.

[161] 3-3-4-3-2-2-5   ERNEST CLINE GARBER, b. August 27, 1909.

[162] 3-3-4-3-2-2-6   ELIZABETH SUSAN GARBER, b. June 02, 1914.

[115] DANIEL BENJAMIN[10] GARBER *(JACOB A.[9], LEVI[8], JACOB W.[7], ABRAHAM[6], JOHANNES "JOHN H."[5], JO HANNES[4] GERBER, NICLAUS[3], CHRISTIAN[2], ULRICH[1])[123]* was born March 02, 1879, and died July 15, 1957. He married (1) NORA B. CRICKENBERGER. He married (2) ANNIE CATHERINE WAMPLER[123] December 22, 1902.

Children of DANIEL GARBER and ANNIE WAMPLER are:

          3-3-4-3-2-3-1   INFANT SON[11] GARBER[123], b. March 07, 1904.

[163] 3-3-4-3-2-3-2   ISAAC JONATHAN GARBER, b. January 05, 1906.

[164]	3-3-4-3-2-3-3	WILLIAM JACOB GARBER, b. January 17, 1909.
[165]	3-3-4-3-2-3-4	JOSEPH DANIEL GARBER, b. April 12, 1912, d. January 29, 1995, Washington, VA.
[166]	3-3-4-3-2-3-5	ANNA ELIZABETH GARBER, b. February 20, 1918.
[167]	3-3-4-3-2-3-6	MARY VIRGINIA GARBER, b. July 15, 1922, Waynesboro, VA.

[116] JOHN DAVID[10] GARBER *(JACOB A.[9], LEVI[8], JACOB W.[7], ABRAHAM[6], JOHANNES "JOHN H."[5], JO HANNES[4] GERBER, NICLAUS[3], CHRISTIAN[2], ULRICH[1])[123]* was born April 15, 1881, and died July 19, 1935. He married NINA E. THOMAS April 25, 1904.

Children of JOHN GARBER and NINA THOMAS are:

3-3-4-3-2-4-1	ALDA E.[11] GARBER[123], b. April 09, 1905; d. October 08, 1989.
3-3-4-3-2-4-2	FREDERICK THOMAS GARBER[123], B. August 17, 1906, D. February 06, 1987.
3-3-4-3-2-4-3	MARGUERITE REBECCA GARBER[123], b. July 28, 1909, d. Bef. 1988, Dayton, VA.
3-3-4-3-2-4-4	ROBERT FRANKLIN GARBER[123], b. May 02, 1911, d. February 22, 1981, Dayton, VA.
3-3-4-3-2-4-5	JAMES DINKLE GARBER[123], b. December 06, 1912, d. October 02, 1929.
3-3-4-3-2-4-6	ELLIS JACOB GARBER[123], b. October 12, 1914, d. January 03, 1982.
3-3-4-3-2-4-8	JOHN WILLIAM GARBER[123], b. August 23, 1920.

[117] WILLIAM FRANKLIN[10] GARBER *(JACOB A.[9], LEVI[8], JACOB W.[7], ABRAHAM[6], JOHANNES "JOHN H."[5], JO HANNES[4] GERBER, NICLAUS[3], CHRISTIAN[2], ULRICH[1])[123]* was born February 14, 1883, and died September 20, 1949. He married ISA D. MILLER[123] May 11, 1905.

Children of WILLIAM GARBER and ISA MILLER are:

3-3-4-3-2-5-1	RAYMOND S.[11] GARBER[123], b. April 20, 1906.
3-3-4-3-2-5-2	EDNA V. GARBER[123], b. February 05, 1909, d. December 24, 1977.
3-3-4-3-2-5-3	REBECCA E. GARBER[123], b. February 12, 1914.
3-3-4-3-2-5-4	RALPH W. GARBER[123], b. March 19, 1918, d. August 24, 1991, m. MILDRED R. LIGHT, March 27, 1937.
3-3-4-3-2-5-5	RUTH MAE GARBER[123], b. May 14, 1923.

[118] ANTHONY A.[10] GARBER *(DANIEL SAMUEL[9], LEVI[8], JACOB W.[7], ABRAHAM[6], JOHANNES "JOHN H."[5], JO HANNES[4] GERBER, NICLAUS[3], CHRISTIAN[2], ULRICH[1])[124]* was born May 20, 1880, in Levi Garber house near Mt. Sidney in Augusta Co., VA[124], and died November 18, 1951, in Washington, DC, area[124]. He married ADA EARLY[124] February 17, 1904[124], daughter of J. EARLY and ALICE. She was born February 22, 1885[124].

Children of ANTHONY GARBER and ADA EARLY are:

3-3-4-3-3-1-1	NOAH L.[11] GARBER[124], b. May 01, 1906, Levi Garber House near Mt. Sidney, Augusta Co., VA[124]; d. July 25, 1980, m. CATHERINE EAKLE[124], December 24, 1930[124]; b. February 22, 1910[124].
3-3-4-3-3-1-2	JAMES GARBER[124], b. 1907, Levi Garber House near Mt. Sidney, Augusta Co., VA[124]; d. 1907[124].

[168] 3-3-4-3-3-1-3   CLARENCE A. GARBER, b. September 03, 1908, Levi Garber house near Mt. Sidney, Augusta Co., VA, d. May 01, 1998, Huntington, MD.

[169] 3-3-4-3-3-1-4   RUTH ELIZABETH GARBER, b. November 17, 1909, Levi Garber house near Mt. Sidney, Augusta Co., VA.

[170] 3-3-4-3-3-1-5   PAULINE A. GARBER, b. January 29, 1911.

[119] HOMER FRANKLIN[10] GARBER *(DANIEL SAMUEL*[9]*, LEVI*[8]*, JACOB W.*[7]*, ABRAHAM*[6]*, JOHANNES "JOHN H."*[5]*, JO HANNES*[4] *GERBER, NICLAUS*[3]*, CHRISTIAN*[2]*, ULRICH*[1]*)*[125] was born August 12, 1886, in Levi Garber House near Mt. Sidney, Augusta Co., VA[126], and died October 14, 1973, in Staunton Manor Nursing Home, Staunton, VA[127]. He married SALLIE BELLE REED[128] October 25, 1909, in Hagerstown, MD[128], daughter of JOHN REED and AMANDA SHIFLET. She was born September 23, 1887, in Laurel Hill, Augusta Co., VA[128], and died April 13, 1989, in Bridgewater Retirement Community, Bridgewater, VA[129].

More about HOMER FRANKLIN GARBER:
Burial: Middle River Church of the Brethren, Augusta Co., VA[130]
Cause of Death: Old age

More about SALLIE BELLE REED:
Burial: Middle River Church of the Brethren, Augusta Co., VA
Religion: Middle River Church of the Brethren in Augusta Co., VA
Residence: Bet. 1910 - 1928, Farm at Mt. Sidney, VA

Children of HOMER GARBER and SALLIE REED are:

[171] 3-3-4-3-3-4-1   CLEATIS FRANKLIN[11] GARBER, b. April 19, 1911, Levi Garber House near Mt. Sidney in Augusta Co., VA.

[172] 3-3-4-3-3-4-2   HAROLD LAVERN GARBER, b. March 10, 1912, Levi Garber House near Mt. Sidney, Augusta Co., VA; d. March 04, 2002, Summit Square, 501 Oak Ave., Waynesboro, VA.

[173] 3-3-4-3-3-4-3   PAUL WILSON GARBER, b. December 31, 1913, Levi Garber House near Mt. Sidney, Augusta Co., VA; d. July 16, 2001, Died at his residence at 100 Berkeley Drive, Waynesboro, VA, where he lived from 1989 until 2001.

[174] 3-3-4-3-3-4-4   MARGARET ELIZABETH GARBER, b. November 04, 1915, Augusta Co., VA, d. April 1981, Myrtle Beach, SC.

[175] 3-3-4-3-3-4-5   ANNA LEE "DOLLY" VIRGINIA GARBER, b. March 24, 1928, Levi Garber house near Mt. Sidney, Augusta Co., VA.

[120] MINOR WILLIAM[10] GARBER *(DANIEL SAMUEL*[9]*, LEVI*[8]*, JACOB W.*[7]*, ABRAHAM*[6]*, JOHANNES "JOHN H."*[5]*, JO HANNES*[4] *GERBER, NICLAUS*[3]*, CHRISTIAN*[2]*, ULRICH*[1]*)*[131] was born March 24, 1891, in Mt. Sidney, Augusta Co., VA[131], and died April 24, 1966, in Harrisonburg, VA. He married RENA BARBARA WESTERN[131] May 29, 1912[131], daughter of JOHN WESTERN and NANNIE SHAVER. She was born December 15, 1892, in New Hope, VA[131], and died May 16, 1982, in Harrisonburg, VA.

Notes for MINOR WILLIAM GARBER:
Per John W. Wayland in "Men of Mark and Representative Citizens of Harrisonburg and Rockingham County Virginia," Minor Garber grew up and worked on his father's farm, attending local schools. In

1910, after completing his course in Bridgewater College, he entered into the flour-milling business in the Cline Mills at Knightly, his father having a half interest in these mills. Further of his work, he says: "In 1912, I purchased a one-third interest in this mill. In 1913, our firm purchased another mill, known as the Ft. Defiance Mill. In 1914, I persuaded our firm to enter into the electric light and power business by purchasing the necessary machinery and using the available water power. The necessary franchises were secured to extend lines in the greater portion of Middle River District in Augusta County. This was the beginning of rural electrification in this state. The electrical business developed to the point that by 1927, the milling end was discontinued. In 1929, we sold this business to the Virginia Public Service Company. I was transferred to Staunton as rural engineer following this sale and had charge of the rural development in Staunton and Waynesboro in addition to supervising all construction in these areas. In 1935, I was transferred to Harrisonburg in a similar capacity and in June 1936, was made Division Manager of the Valley Division of the Company, which is my present position."

Mr. Garber is a member and past president of the Harrisonburg Rotary Club and director of the Chamber of Commerce. He, like many of his family have been, is a member of the Church of the Brethren. He gives golf, bowling and fishing as his favorite recreations.

More about MINOR WILLIAM GARBER:
Burial: Middle River Church of the Brethren, Augusta Co., VA
Education: 1910, Bridgewater College
Occupation: Miller of flour and Division Manager of the Valley Division of Virginia Public Service Company (Virginia Power)
Residence: Franklin Street, Harrisonburg, VA

More about RENA BARBARA WESTERN:
Burial: Middle River Church of the Brethren, Augusta Co., VA

Child of MINOR GARBER and RENA WESTERN is:
[176] 3-3-4-3-3-6-1   CATHERINE LOUISE[11] GARBER, b. March 11, 1913, Augusta County, VA, d. October 23, 2005, Harrisonburg, Rockingham Co., VA.

[121] LUELLA VIRGINIA[10] FLORY (*LYDIA CATHERINE[9] GARBER, LEVI[8], JACOB W.[7], ABRAHAM[6], JOHANNES "JOHN H."[5], JO HANNES[4] GERBER, NICLAUS[3], CHRISTIAN[2], ULRICH[1]*)[131] was born August 14, 1888, and died April 20, 1968. She married THURSTON J. MILLER January 15, 1913. He died February 09, 1957.

Child of LUELLA FLORY and THURSTON MILLER is:
    3-3-4-3-4-3-1   MILDRED VIRGINIA[11] MILLER, b. September 26, 1915.

[122] WILLIAM FRANKLIN[10] FLORY (*LYDIA CATHERINE[9] GARBER, LEVI[8], JACOB W.[7], ABRAHAM[6], JOHANNES "JOHN H."[5], JO HANNES[4] GERBER, NICLAUS[3], CHRISTIAN[2], ULRICH[1]*)[131] was born June 05, 1891, and died December 30, 1973, in Harrisonburg, VA. He married LINNIE ROSAMOND DRIVER June 01, 1916.

Children of WILLIAM FLORY and LINNIE DRIVER are:
    3-3-4-3-4-4-1   VERNON DRIVER[11] FLORY, b. December 29, 1919.
    3-3-4-3-4-4-2   MARVIN WILLIAM FLORY, b. April 17, 1923.
    3-3-4-3-4-4-3   CARL EDWARD FLORY, b. April 10, 1928.

[123] EARL RAYMOND[10] NORFORD (*BARBARA ELIZABETH[9] GARBER, LEVI[8], JACOB W.[7], ABRAHAM[6], JOHANNES "JOHN H."[5], JO HANNES[4] GERBER, NICLAUS[3], CHRISTIAN[2], ULRICH[1]*)[132] was born September 07, 1894, and died April 10, 1991. He married LENA BORDEN[132] September 22, 1920.

Children of EARL NORFORD and LENA BORDEN are:
[177] 3-3-4-3-7-2-1   NELSON KEITH[11] NORFORD, b. February 09, 1925.
       3-3-4-3-7-2-2   ANN REBECCA NORFORD[132], b. November 26, 1929, d. February 02, 1935.
[178] 3-3-4-3-7-2-3   RICHARD FRANCES NORFORD, b. May 03, 1931.
[179] 3-3-4-3-7-2-4   JEAN GARBER NORFORD, b. July 29, 1933.

[124] ETHEL V.[10] HUFFMAN (*FRANCES "FANNIE" V.[9] GARBER, LEVI[8], JACOB W.[7], ABRAHAM[6], JOHANNES "JOHN H."[5], JO HANNES[4] GERBER, NICLAUS[3], CHRISTIAN[2], ULRICH[1]*)[132] was born March 26, 1905. She married ROLLA E. SHOEMAKER[132] June 08, 1927.

Child of ETHEL HUFFMAN and ROLLA SHOEMAKER is:
[180] 3-3-4-3-8-3-1   LOIS[11] SHOEMAKER, b. September 09, 1928.

[125] LAURENCE[10] GLICK (*BENJ. FRANKLIN[9], REBECCA[8] WINE, MICHAEL[7], MAGADALENE[6] GARBER, JOHANNES "JOHN H."[5], JO HANNES[4] GERBER, NICLAUS[3], CHRISTIAN[2], ULRICH[1]*)[133]. He married PATRICIA ARMENTROUT[133] August 19, 1938.

Children of LAURENCE GLICK and PATRICIA ARMENTROUT are:
       3-10-1-10-4-2-1   PATRICIA[11] GLICK[133].
       3-10-1-10-4-2-2   DAVID GLICK[133].
       3-10-1-10-4-2-3   BETTY LOU GLICK[133].

[126] HARRY[10] STOVER (*MARY MAGDALENE[9] GLICK, REBECCA[8] WINE, MICHAEL[7], MAGADALENE[6] GARBER, JOHANNES "JOHN H."[5], JO HANNES[4] GERBER, NICLAUS[3], CHRISTIAN[2], ULRICH[1]*)[133] died 1951[133]. He married WINNIE[133].

Children of HARRY STOVER and WINNIE are:
       3-10-1-10-5-1-1   BILL[11] STOVER[133].
       3-10-1-10-5-1-2   BEVERLYN STOVER[133].
       3-10-1-10-5-1-3   BETTIE STOVER[133].
       3-10-1-10-5-1-4   BOBBY STOVER[133].

[127] DORA[10] STOVER (*MARY MAGDALENE[9] GLICK, REBECCA[8] WINE, MICHAEL[7], MAGADALENE[6] GARBER, JOHANNES "JOHN H."[5], JO HANNES[4] GERBER, NICLAUS[3], CHRISTIAN[2], ULRICH[1]*)[133]. She married ? MCKINNEY.

Children of DORA STOVER and MCKINNEY are:
       3-10-1-10-5-4-1   JIM[11] MCKINNEY.
       3-10-1-10-5-4-2   HAROLD MCKINNEY.

[128] CARL[10] GLICK (*JOHN WILLIAM*[9], *REBECCA*[8] *WINE, MICHAEL*[7], *MAGADALENE*[6] *GARBER, JOHANNES "JOHN H."*[5], *JO HANNES*[4] *GERBER, NICLAUS*[3], *CHRISTIAN*[2], *ULRICH*[1])[133]. He married ANNA BRITTON[133].

Children of CARL GLICK and ANNA BRITTON are:
[181] 3-10-1-10-6-1-1   MARTHA[11] GLICK.
        3-10-1-10-6-1-2   LAURA GLICK[133].
[182] 3-10-1-10-6-1-3   J. RUTH GLICK.

[129] FRANK[10] GLICK (*JOHN WILLIAM*[9], *REBECCA*[8] *WINE, MICHAEL*[7], *MAGADALENE*[6] *GARBER, JOHANNES "JOHN H."*[5], *JO HANNES*[4] *GERBER, NICLAUS*[3], *CHRISTIAN*[2], *ULRICH*[1]) He married MARY GINGRY[133].

Children of FRANK GLICK and MARY GINGRY are:
        3-10-1-10-6-2-1   PEARL[11] GLICK[133].
        3-10-1-10-6-2-2   THEODORE GLICK[133].
        3-10-1-10-6-2-3   DAVID GLICK[133].

[130\ RUTH[10] SENGER (*MARTHA JANE*[9] *GLICK, REBECCA*[8] *WINE, MICHAEL*[7], *MAGADALENE*[6] *GARBER, JOHANNES "JOHN H."*[5], *JO HANNES*[4] *GERBER, NICLAUS*[3], *CHRISTIAN*[2], *ULRICH*[1])[133]. She married CLYDE MATTEWS[133].

Children of RUTH SENGER and CLYDE MATTEWS are:
[183] 3-10-1-10-7-1-1   JEAN[11] MATTEWS, b. 1923.
[184] 3-10-1-10-7-1-2   BILL MATTEWS, b. 1934.

[131] MERLE[10] SENGER (*MARTHA JANE*[9] *GLICK, REBECCA*[8] *WINE, MICHAEL*[7], *MAGADALENE*[6] *GARBER, JOHANNES "JOHN H."*[5], *JO HANNES*[4] *GERBER, NICLAUS*[3], *CHRISTIAN*[2], *ULRICH*[1])[133]. She married HARRY BICKERS.

Children of MERLE SENGER and HARRY BICKERS are:
        3-10-1-10-7-2-1   BETTIE[11] BICKERS.
        3-10-1-10-7-2-2   HARRIET BICKERS.

[132] BEUFORD[10] MILLER (*SARAH FRANCES*[9] *GLICK, REBECCA*[8] *WINE, MICHAEL*[7], *MAGADALENE*[6] *GARBER, JOHANNES "JOHN H."*[5], *JO HANNES*[4] *GERBER, NICLAUS*[3], *CHRISTIAN*[2], *ULRICH*[1])[133] was born 1895[133]. He married CALLIE[133]. She was born 1898[133].

Children of BEUFORD MILLER and CALLIE are:
        3-10-1-10-8-1-1   DWAIN[11] MILLER[133], b. 1921[133].
        3-10-1-10-8-1-2   MERLIN MILLER[133], b. 1927[133].
        3-10-1-10-8-1-3   RICHARD MILLER[133], b. 1935[133].
        3-10-1-10-8-1-4   PAUL MILLER[133], b. 1938[133].
        3-10-1-10-8-1-5   MARGARET MILLER[133].

[133] ETHEL[10] MILLER *(SARAH FRANCES[9] GLICK, REBECCA[8] WINE, MICHAEL[7], MAGADALENE[6] GARBER, JOHANNES "JOHN H."[5], JO HANNES[4] GERBER, NICLAUS[3], CHRISTIAN[2], ULRICH[1])[133]* was born 1899. She married CLIFFTON JOHNSON. He was born 1899.

Children of ETHEL MILLER and CLIFFTON JOHNSON are:
  3-10-1-10-8-2-1 ROBERT[11] JOHNSON[133], b. 1924[133].
  3-10-1-10-8-2-2 RUTH JOHNSON[133], b. 1928[133].
 [185] 3-10-1-10-8-2-3 ROY JOHNSON, b. 1933.

[134] RAY[10] MILLER *(SARAH FRANCES[9] GLICK, REBECCA[8] WINE, MICHAEL[7], MAGADALENE[6] GARBER, JOHANNES "JOHN H."[5], JO HANNES[4] GERBER, NICLAUS[3], CHRISTIAN[2], ULRICH[1])[133]* was born 1897. He married OLIVE[133]. She was born 1903[133].

Children of RAY MILLER and OLIVE are:
  3-10-1-10-8-3-1 MARILYN[11] MILLER[133], b. 1932.
  3-10-1-10-8-3-2 MARGARET MILLER[133], b. 1935.
  3-10-1-10-8-3-3 KAREN MILLER[133], b. 1944[133].

[135] WALTER[10] MILLER *(SARAH FRANCES[9] GLICK, REBECCA[8] WINE, MICHAEL[7], MAGADALENE[6] GARBER, JOHANNES "JOHN H."[5], JO HANNES[4] GERBER, NICLAUS[3], CHRISTIAN[2], ULRICH[1])[133]* was born 1901[133]. He married MARIE[133]. She was born 1901[133].

Children of WALTER MILLER and MARIE are:
  3-10-1-10-8-4-1 WANDA[11] MILLER[133], b. 1936[133].
  3-10-1-10-8-4-2 CAROL MILLER[133], b. 1939[133].

[136] ESTHER[10] MILLER *(SARAH FRANCES[9] GLICK, REBECCA[8] WINE, MICHAEL[7], MAGADALENE[6] GARBER, JOHANNES "JOHN H."[5], JO HANNES[4] GERBER, NICLAUS[3], CHRISTIAN[2], ULRICH[1])[133].* She married WILLIAM LENARD OWEN[133].

Children of ESTHER MILLER and WILLIAM OWEN are:
  3 -10-1-10-8-7-1 PENOLOPE[11] OWEN[133], b. 1936[133].
  3-10-1-10-8-7-2 DAN DARBY OWEN[133], b. 1941[133].
  3-10-1-10-8-7-3 WESLEY OWEN[133], b. 1945[133].

U.S. Generation No. 7

[137] RENA BARBARA[11] WESTERN *(NANNIE CATHERINE[10] SHAVER, BARBARA[9] MILLER, REBEKAH[8] GARBER, JACOB W.[7], ABRAHAM[6], JOHANNES "JOHN H."[5], JO HANNES[4] GERBER, NICLAUS[3], CHRISTIAN[2], ULRICH[1])[134]* was born December 15, 1892, in New Hope, VA[134], and died May 16, 1982, in Harrisonburg, VA. She married MINOR WILLIAM GARBER[134] May 29, 1912[134], son of DANIEL GARBER and ELIZABETH GLICK. He was born March 24, 1891, in Mt. Sidney, Augusta Co., VA[134], and died April 24, 1966, in Harrisonburg, VA.

More about RENA BARBARA WESTERN:
Burial: Middle River Church of the Brethren, Augusta Co., VA

Child is listed above under (120) Minor William Garber.

[138] MAE ELIZABETH[11] WAMPLER *(MARY ELIZABETH[10] GARBER, PETER[9], LEVI[8], JACOB W.[7], ABRAHAM[6], JOHANNES "JOHN H."[5], JO HANNES[4] GERBER, NICLAUS[3], CHRISTIAN[2], ULRICH[1])*[135] was born September 13, 1915. She married WELDON B. HUFFMAN[135] August 13, 1938.

    Children of MAE WAMPLER and WELDON HUFFMAN are:
    3-3-4-3-1-1-4-1   KENNETH WELDON[12] HUFFMAN[135], b. May 13, 1940.
    3-3-4-3-1-1-4-2   GARY WAMPLER HUFFMAN[135], b. February 14, 1945.
    3-3-4-3-1-1-4-3   SAMUEL FREDERICK HUFFMAN[135], b. July 19, 1946.

[139] EVA REBECCA[11] WAMPLER *(MARY ELIZABETH[10] GARBER, PETER[9], LEVI[8], JACOB W.[7], ABRAHAM[6], JOHANNES "JOHN H."[5], JO HANNES[4] GERBER, NICLAUS[3], CHRISTIAN[2], ULRICH[1])*[135] was born September 26, 1917. She married JACOB RUDOLPH CLINE[135] June 13, 1948.

Children of EVA WAMPLER and JACOB CLINE are:
    3-3-4-3-1-1-5-1   JAMES EDWARD[12] CLINE[135], b. December 01, 1950.
    3-3-4-3-1-1-5-2   MARY BETH CLINE[135], b. August 02, 1952.
    3-3-4-3-1-1-5-3   CYNTHIA HOPE CLINE[135], b. December 16, 1955.

[140] FREDERICK CLINE[11] WAMPLER *(MARY ELIZABETH[10] GARBER, PETER[9], LEVI[8], JACOB W.[7], ABRAHAM[6], JOHANNES "JOHN H."[5], JO HANNES[4] GERBER, NICLAUS[3], CHRISTIAN[2], ULRICH[1])*[135] was born November 20, 1920. He married NANCY FRANCES BRUBAKER[135] June 06, 1946.

Children of FREDERICK WAMPLER and NANCY BRUBAKER are:
    3-3-4-3-1-1-6-1   DAVID CLINE[12] WAMPLER[135], b. April 18, 1947.
    3-3-4-3-1-1-6-2   WAYNE BRUBAKER WAMPLER[135], b. January 30, 1949.
    3-3-4-3-1-1-6-3   WANDA RUTH WAMPLER[135], b. April 19, 1951.
    3-3-4-3-1-1-6-4   JOHN FREDERICK WAMPLER[135], b. January 21, 1953.
    3-3-4-3-1-1-6-5   RICHARD THOMAS WAMPLER[135], b. December 04, 1955.
    3-3-4-3-1-1-6-6   SUSAN LANE WAMPLER[135], b. December 17, 1957.
    3-3-4-3-1-1-6-7   NANCY JUNE WAMPLER[135], b. August 06, 1959.

[141] CASPER WHITMORE[11] GARBER *(JOHN CLINE[10], PETER[9], LEVI[8], JACOB W.[7], ABRAHAM[6], JOHANNES "JOHN H."[5], JO HANNES[4] GERBER, NICLAUS[3], CHRISTIAN[2], ULRICH[1])*[135] was born August 02, 1908, and died August 08, 1991. He married HELEN KATHERINE CLEMMER[135] July 05, 1930.

Children of CASPER GARBER and HELEN CLEMMER are:
    3-3-4-3-1-2-1-1   PATRICIA ANN[12] GARBER[135], b. February 08, 1933.
    3-3-4-3-1-2-1-2   BARBARA JOYCE GARBER[135], b. July 29, 1937.

[142] MERLIN ESTES[11] GARBER *(JOHN CLINE[10], PETER[9], LEVI[8], JACOB W.[7], ABRAHAM[6], JOHANNES "JOHN H."[5], JO HANNES[4] GERBER, NICLAUS[3], CHRISTIAN[2], ULRICH[1])[135]* was born March 26, 1912. He married DOROTHY FAW[135] June 03, 1934.

Children of MERLIN GARBER and DOROTHY FAW are:
    3-3-4-3-1-2-2-1   LELAND FAW[12] GARBER[135], b. August 04, 1937.
    3-3-4-3-1-2-2-2   ELAINE ESTELLA GARBER[135], b. March 09, 1940.

[143] ELVA OTELIA[11] GARBER *(JOHN CLINE[10], PETER[9], LEVI[8], JACOB W.[7], ABRAHAM[6], JOHANNES "JOHN H."[5], JO HANNES[4] GERBER, NICLAUS[3], CHRISTIAN[2], ULRICH[1])[135]* was born January 28, 1916, in Buena Vista, VA. She married WARREN JUSTUS HUFFMAN[135] August 20, 1938.

Children of ELVA GARBER and WARREN HUFFMAN are:
    3-3-4-3-1-2-3-1   JAMES WARREN[12] HUFFMAN[135], b. October 28, 1940, Champaign, IL.
    3-3-4-3-1-2-3-2   LARRY RICHARD HUFFMAN[135], b. November 14, 1942, Champaign, IL.
    3-3-4-3-1-2-3-3   ROGER ALLEN HUFFMAN[135], b. May 05, 1951, Champaign, IL.
    3-3-4-3-1-2-3-4   BRUCE EDWARD HUFFMAN[135], b. November 14, 1952, Champaign, IL.
    3-3-4-3-1-2-3-5   DAVID CHARLES HUFFMAN[135], b. November 07, 1954, Champaign, IL.

[144] MAYNARD AUBRY[11] GARBER *(JOHN CLINE[10], PETER[9], LEVI[8], JACOB W.[7], ABRAHAM[6], JOHANNES "JOHN H."[5], JO HANNES[4] GERBER, NICLAUS[3], CHRISTIAN[2], ULRICH[1])[135]* was born February 23, 1920, in Staunton, VA. He married VIOLET ASHBY[135] October 08, 1949.

Child of MAYNARD GARBER and VIOLET ASHBY is:
    3-3-4-3-1-2-4-1   DEBORAH KAY[12] GARBER[135], b. July 08, 1954.

[145] CALVIN WILLIAM[11] GARBER *(BENJAMIN FREDERICK[10], PETER[9], LEVI[8], JACOB W.[7], ABRAHAM[6], JOHANNES "JOHN H."[5], JO HANNES[4] GERBER, NICLAUS[3], CHRISTIAN[2], ULRICH[1])* was born May 22, 1916. He married EDITH MAGDALENE CLINE[135] June 07, 1942.

Children of CALVIN GARBER and EDITH CLINE are:
    3-3-4-3-1-3-2-1   FREDERICK CLINE[12] GARBER[135], b. June 16, 1944.
    3-3-4-3-1-3-2-2   DONALD JOSEPH GARBER[135], b. December 16, 1945.
    3-3-4-3-1-3-2-3   GERALD WILLIAM GARBER[135], b. October 25, 1950.

[146] ALDA ETHEL[11] GARBER *(BENJAMIN FREDERICK[10], PETER[9], LEVI[8], JACOB W.[7], ABRAHAM[6], JOHANNES "JOHN H."[5], JO HANNES[4] GERBER, NICLAUS[3], CHRISTIAN[2], ULRICH[1])* was born July 27, 1918. She married JESSE AUTEN HEDDINGS[135] September 09, 1943. He was born October 19, 1920.

Children of ALDA GARBER and JESSE HEDDINGS are:
    3-3-4-3-1-3-3-1   GALEN ROBERT[12] HEDDINGS[135], b. August 29, 1946, d. November 07, 1965.

3-3-4-3-1-3-3-2   MARILYN LOIS HEDDINGS[135], b. January 26, 1949.
3-3-4-3-1-3-3-3   HAZEL JEANETTE HEDDINGS[135], b. May 19, 1951.
3-3-4-3-1-3-3-4   JOHN WAYNE HEDDINGS[135], b. April 20, 1956.

[147] ESTHER FRANCES[11] GARBER *(FRANKLIN LEVI*[10], *PETER*[9], *LEVI*[8], *JACOB W.*[7], *ABRAHAM*[6], *JOHANNES "JOHN H."*[5], *JO HANNES*[4] *GERBER, NICLAUS*[3], *CHRISTIAN*[2], *ULRICH*[1]*)*[135] was born August 25, 1917. She married ORVIN CLINE[135] October 14, 1938.

Children of ESTHER GARBER and ORVIN CLINE are:
     3-3-4-3-1-4-1-1   FRANKLIN HUBERT[12] CLINE[135], b. January 18, 1940.
     3-3-4-3-1-4-1-2   LEROY RUSSEL CLINE[135], b. June 30, 1949.
     3-3-4-3-1-4-1-3   LEWIS ELSON CLINE[135], b. October 27, 1953.

[148] ETHEL MAE[11] GARBER *(FRANKLIN LEVI*[10], *PETER*[9], *LEVI*[8], *JACOB W.*[7], *ABRAHAM*[6], *JOHANNES "JOHN H."*[5], *JO HANNES*[4] *GERBER, NICLAUS*[3], *CHRISTIAN*[2], *ULRICH*[1]*)*[135] was born April 18, 1921. She married OLIVER WENDELL CLINE[135] April 21, 1945.

Child of ETHEL GARBER and OLIVER CLINE is:
     3-3-4-3-1-4-3-1   CAROL ANNE[12] CLINE[135], b. January 03, 1947.

[149] IRENE EDITH[11] GARBER *(FRANKLIN LEVI*[10], *PETER*[9], *LEVI*[8], *JACOB W.*[7], *ABRAHAM*[6], *JOHANNES "JOHN H."*[5], *JO HANNES*[4] *GERBER, NICLAUS*[3], *CHRISTIAN*[2], *ULRICH*[1]*)*[135] was born June 28, 1923. She married BERMAN WALTON WEEKS[135] March 19, 1949.

Children of IRENE GARBER and BERMAN WEEKS are:
     3-3-4-3-1-4-4-1   WAYNE HARLEY[12] WEEKS[135], b. June 21, 1951.
     3-3-4-3-1-4-4-2   GLENN FRANKLIN WEEKS[135], b. June 14, 1953.
     3-3-4-3-1-4-4-3   SANDRA MAE WEEKS[135], b. December 18, 1956.

[150] GERALDINE EARLY[11] GARBER *(FRANKLIN LEVI*[10], *PETER*[9], *LEVI*[8], *JACOB W.*[7], *ABRAHAM*[6], *JOHANNES "JOHN H."*[5], *JO HANNES*[4] *GERBER, NICLAUS*[3], *CHRISTIAN*[2], *ULRICH*[1]*)*[135] was born August 05, 1929. She married CARROLL EDWARD CONNER[135] August 14, 1951.

Children of GERALDINE GARBER and CARROLL CONNER are:
     3-3-4-3-1-4-6-1   JEAN CAROL[12] CONNER[135], b. February 16, 1956.
     3-3-4-3-1-4-6-2   JOYCE ANN CONNER[135], b. February 16, 1956.

[151] MARY ELIZABETH[11] GARBER *(SAMUEL LEVI*[10], *JACOB A.*[9], *LEVI*[8], *JACOB W.*[7], *ABRAHAM*[6], *JOHANNES "JOHN H."*[5], *JO HANNES*[4] *GERBER, NICLAUS*[3], *CHRISTIAN*[2], *ULRICH*[1]*)*[135] was born April 21, 1900, and died December 20, 1976, in Gordonsville, VA. She married OZIAS TIFFANY FUNKHOUSER[135] August 30, 1923.

Children of MARY GARBER and OZIAS FUNKHOUSER are:
     3-3-4-3-2-1-1-1   JOYCE VIRGINIA[12] FUNKHOUSER[135], b. July 29, 1924.
     3-3-4-3-2-1-1-2   SAMUEL FRANCIS FUNKHOUSER[135], b. August 31, 1925.

[152] ANNA REBECCA[11] GARBER *(SAMUEL LEVI[10], JACOB A.[9], LEVI[8], JACOB W.[7], ABRAHAM[6], JOHANNES "JOHN H."[5], JO HANNES[4] GERBER, NICLAUS[3], CHRISTIAN[2], ULRICH[1])*[135] was born August 09, 1903, and died August 25, 1962. She married LURTY ANG SHIFFLETT March 01, 1930[135].

Children of ANNA GARBER and LURTY SHIFFLETT are:

3-3-4-3-2-1-2-1	REBECCA FRANCES[12] SHIFFLETT[135], b. May 25, 1932.
3-3-4-3-2-1-2-2	ELIZABETH JEAN SHIFFLETT[135], b. January 29, 1934, m. (1) ROBERT LEE HARTMAN[135], February 14, 1959; m. (2) LEON WATSON MOYERS[135], September 09, 1967.
3-3-4-3-2-1-2-3	PATRICIA ANN SHIFFLETT[135], b. November 03, 1938.
3-3-4-3-2-1-2-4	JAMES EDWARD SHIFFLETT[135], b. May 13, 1941.
3-3-4-3-2-1-2-5	DONNIE LEE SHIFFLETT[135], b. November 13, 1943.
3-3-4-3-2-1-2-6	SAMUEL CARROLL SHIFFLETT[135], b. December 14, 1948, m. TERRY SWISHER WHEELBARGER[135].

[153] CARL LEVI[11] GARBER *(SAMUEL LEVI[10], JACOB A.[9], LEVI[8], JACOB W.[7], ABRAHAM[6], JOHANNES "JOHN H."[5], JO HANNES[4] GERBER, NICLAUS[3], CHRISTIAN[2], ULRICH[1])*[135] was born July 30, 1905, and died December 08, 1982. He married FRANCES EVELYN LAYMAN[135] August 28, 1940.

Children of CARL GARBER and FRANCES LAYMAN are:

3-3-4-3-2-1-3-1	SARA ALYCE[12] GARBER[135], b. August 05, 1944.
3-3-4-3-2-1-3-2	CARLENE EVELYN GARBER[135], b. October 11, 1945.
3-3-4-3-2-1-3-3	THERESA GAYLE GARBER[135], b. November 17, 1946.
3-3-4-3-2-1-3-4	DORIS ELAINE GARBER[135], b. April 29, 1948.
3-3-4-3-2-1-3-5	BENJAMIN LEVI GARBER[135], b. January 27, 1952, d. November 01, 1971.
3-3-4-3-2-1-3-6	VALDA ANN GARBER[135], b. April 06, 1953, m. RICHARD BRUCE WEIDER[135], October 09, 1982.

[154] FRANCES WILLARD[11] GARBER *(SAMUEL LEVI[10], JACOB A.[9], LEVI[8], JACOB W.[7], ABRAHAM[6], JOHANNES "JOHN H."[5], JO HANNES[4] GERBER, NICLAUS[3], CHRISTIAN[2], ULRICH[1])*[135] was born September 07, 1908, and died June 24, 1973. She married GEORGE THOMPSON[135] June 12, 1946.

Child of FRANCES GARBER and GEORGE THOMPSON is:

3-3-4-3-2-1-4-1	ROYCE ERROL[12] THOMPSON[135], b. November 20, 1949, m. DIANNE AREY[135], June 23, 1972.

[155] LILLIAN MAY[11] GARBER *(SAMUEL LEVI[10], JACOB A.[9], LEVI[8], JACOB W.[7], ABRAHAM[6], JOHANNES "JOHN H."[5], JO HANNES[4] GERBER, NICLAUS[3], CHRISTIAN[2], ULRICH[1])*[135] was born May 13, 1911. She married (1) LEONARD NELSON LAM, SR.[135]. She married (2) LESTER EUGENE MYERS[135] October 04, 1930. She married (3) GEORGE MONTGOMERY KENNEDY[135] March 10, 1967.

Children of LILLIAN GARBER and LESTER MYERS are:
>   3-3-4-3-2-1-6-1   LESTER EUGENE[12] MYERS, JR.[135], b. January 14, 1932.
>   3-3-4-3-2-1-6-2   NANCY LOUISE MYERS[135], b. December 28, 1935.
>   3-3-4-3-2-1-6-3   HAROLD WAYNE MYERS[135], b. April 13, 1939.
>   3-3-4-3-2-1-6-4   PEGGY MARIE MYERS[135], b. December 14, 1943.
>   3-3-4-3-2-1-6-5   GARY ELDON MYERS[135], b. August 10, 1946.

[156] REINETTE MAGDALENA[11] GARBER *(SAMUEL LEVI[10], JACOB A.[9], LEVI[8], JACOB W.[7], ABRAHAM[6], JOHANNES "JOHN H."[5], JO HANNES[4] GERBER, NICLAUS[3], CHRISTIAN[2], ULRICH[1])[135]* was born September 23, 1917, and died August 21, 1978. She married GLENN SANGER[135] June 10, 1938.

Children of REINETTE GARBER and GLENN SANGER are:
>   3-3-4-3-2-1-7-1   RICHARD CARL[12] SANGER[135], b. February 02, 1941.
>   3-3-4-3-2-1-7-2   RALPH EDWARD SANGER[135], b. August 09, 1942.
>   3-3-4-3-2-1-7-3   CHARLES LEROY SANGER[135], b. April 05, 1944.
>   3-3-4-3-2-1-7-4   FREDERICK LEE SANGER[135], b. August 19, 1945.
>   3-3-4-3-2-1-7-5   LARRY WILLIAM SANGER[135], b. January 25, 1948.

[157] JACOB MARTIN[11] GARBER *(PETER ISAAC[10], JACOB A.[9], LEVI[8], JACOB W.[7], ABRAHAM[6], JOHANNES "JOHN H."[5], JO HANNES[4] GERBER, NICLAUS[3], CHRISTIAN[2], ULRICH[1])[135]* was born August 29, 1901, and died February 10, 1993, in McLean, VA. He married (1) RUTH PENCE[135] in August 18, 1923. He married (2) ZULA HAMILTON DOVE[135] July 12, 1985.

Child of JACOB GARBER and RUTH PENCE is:
>   3-3-4-3-2-2-1-1   RICHARD MARTIN[12] GARBER[135], b. December 04, 1942.

[158] EDWARD FRANKLIN[11] GARBER *(PETER ISAAC[10], JACOB A.[9], LEVI[8], JACOB W.[7], ABRAHAM[6], JOHANNES "JOHN H."[5], JO HANNES[4] GERBER, NICLAUS[3], CHRISTIAN[2], ULRICH[1])[135]* was born September 21, 1903, and died March 10, 1990. in Elkton, Rockingham Co., VA. He married HAZEL GERTRUDE THOMAS[135] June 10, 1929.

Children of EDWARD GARBER and HAZEL THOMAS are:
>   3-3-4-3-2-2-2-1   HARRY EDWARD[12] GARBER[135], b. July 28, 1931.
>   3-3-4-3-2-2-2-2   SHIRLEY ANN GARBER[135], b. May 29, 1935, d. February 07, 1987.
>   3-3-4-3-2-2-2-3   CHARLES NELSON GARBER[135], b. December 20, 1947.

[159] FANNIE VIRGINIA[11] GARBER *(PETER ISAAC[10], JACOB A.[9], LEVI[8], JACOB W.[7], ABRAHAM[6], JOHANNES "JOHN H."[5], JO HANNES[4] GERBER, NICLAUS[3], CHRISTIAN[2], ULRICH[1])[135]* was born March 19, 1905, and died January 15, 1955. She married LUTHER PAUL ALT March 30, 1933. [135].

Children of FANNIE GARBER and LUTHER ALT are:
>   3-3-4-3-2-2-3-1   MARLIN PAUL[12] ALT[135], b. December 16, 1933.
>   3-3-4-3-2-2-3-2   DARWIN FAY ALT[135], b. September 22, 1935.
>   3-3-4-3-2-2-3-3   DAWN MARCIA ALT[135], b. October 08, 1937.

[160] CLARENCE BENJAMIN[11] GARBER *(PETER ISAAC*[10], *JACOB A.*[9], *LEVI*[8], *JACOB W.*[7], *ABRAHAM*[6], *JOHANNES "JOHN H."*[5], *JO HANNES*[4] *GERBER, NICLAUS*[3], *CHRISTIAN*[2], *ULRICH*[1]*)*[135] was born October 11, 1906. He married (1) GLADYS EAGLE[135] June 01, 1927. He married (2) RUTH KIRACOFE[135] December 29, 1949.

Child of CLARENCE GARBER and GLADYS EAGLE is:
    3-3-4-3-2-2-4-1   JOYCE LILLIE[12] GARBER[135], b. January 18, 1931.

Children of CLARENCE GARBER and RUTH KIRACOFE are:
    3-3-4-3-2-2-4-2   FRANCES ANN[12] GARBER[135], b. November 29, 1951, d. January 23, 1992.
    3-3-4-3-2-2-4-3   CLARENCE BENJAMIN GARBER, JR.[135], b. May 27, 1953.

[161] ERNEST CLINE[11] GARBER *(PETER ISAAC*[10], *JACOB A.*[9], *LEVI*[8], *JACOB W.*[7], *ABRAHAM*[6], *JOHANNES "JOHN H."*[5], *JO HANNES*[4] *GERBER, NICLAUS*[3], *CHRISTIAN*[2], *ULRICH*[1]*)*[135] was born August 27, 1909. He married CHARLOTTE VIRGINIA DEAN[135] May 19, 1931.

Children of ERNEST GARBER and CHARLOTTE DEAN are:
    3-3-4-3-2-2-5-1   HAROLD DAVID[12] GARBER[135], b. March 17, 1941.
    3-3-4-3-2-2-5-2   JOSEPH WILLIAM GARBER[135], b. November 22, 1947.

[162] ELIZABETH SUSAN[11] GARBER *(PETER ISAAC*[10], *JACOB A.*[9], *LEVI*[8], *JACOB W.*[7], *ABRAHAM*[6], *JOHANNES "JOHN H."*[5], *JO HANNES*[4] *GERBER, NICLAUS*[3], *CHRISTIAN*[2], *ULRICH*[1]*)*[135] was born June 02, 1914. She married FORREST SITES[135] June 08, 1933.

Children of ELIZABETH GARBER and FORREST SITES are:
    3-3-4-3-2-2-6-1   ROGER ALAN[12] SITES[135], b. January 18, 1945.
    3-3-4-3-2-2-6-2   ROBERT FORREST SITES[135], b. September 02, 1948.

[163] ISAAC JONATHAN[11] GARBER *(DANIEL BENJAMIN*[10], *JACOB A.*[9], *LEVI*[8], *JACOB W.*[7], *ABRAHAM*[6], *JOHANNES "JOHN H."*[5], *JO HANNES*[4] *GERBER, NICLAUS*[3], *CHRISTIAN*[2], *ULRICH*[1]*)*[135] was born January 05, 1906. He married NEVA MASON KENDRICK[135] August 08, 1929.

Children of ISAAC GARBER and NEVA KENDRICK are:
    3-3-4-3-2-3-2-1   HELEN KENDRICK[12] GARBER[135], b. April 29, 1930.
    3-3-4-3-2-3-2-2   CHARLES DANIEL GARBER[135], b. May 08, 1934.

[164] WILLIAM JACOB[11] GARBER *(DANIEL BENJAMIN*[10], *JACOB A.*[9], *LEVI*[8], *JACOB W.*[7], *ABRAHAM*[6], *JOHANNES "JOHN H."*[5], *JO HANNES*[4] *GERBER, NICLAUS*[3], *CHRISTIAN*[2], *ULRICH*[1]*)*[135] was born January 17, 1909. He married ESTHER VIRGINIA PENCE[135] September 01, 1934.

Child of WILLIAM GARBER and ESTHER PENCE is:
    3-3-4-3-2-3-3-1   MARY KATHERINE[12] GARBER[135], b. January 10, 1937.

[165] JOSEPH DANIEL[11] GARBER *(DANIEL BENJAMIN[10], JACOB A.[9], LEVI[8], JACOB W.[7], ABRAHAM[6], JOHANNES "JOHN H."[5], JO HANNES[4] GERBER, NICLAUS[3], CHRISTIAN[2], ULRICH[1])[135]* was born April 12, 1912, and died January 29, 1995, in Washington, VA. He married GLADYS WIMMER[135] December 26, 1935.

Children of JOSEPH GARBER and GLADYS WIMMER are:
>   3-3-4-3-2-3-4-1   NADA GLADYS[12] GARBER[135], b. November 07, 1936.
>   3-3-4-3-2-3-4-2   GLORIA DAWN GARBER[135], b. May 07, 1940.
>   3-3-4-3-2-3-4-3   DAVID DWIGHT GARBER[135], b. October 08, 1944.

[166] ANNA ELIZABETH[11] GARBER *(DANIEL BENJAMIN[10], JACOB A.[9], LEVI[8], JACOB W.[7], ABRAHAM[6], JOHANNES "JOHN H."[5], JO HANNES[4] GERBER, NICLAUS[3], CHRISTIAN[2], ULRICH[1])[135]* was born February 20, 1918. She married GALEN BENJAMIN CRIST[135] August 10, 1943.

Children of ANNA GARBER and GALEN CRIST are:
>   3-3-4-3-2-3-5-1   RONALD FREDERICK[12] CRIST[135], b. May 16, 1947, m. GLORIA ANN
>   RICHARDSON[135], March 06, 1971.
>   3-3-4-3-2-3-5-2   WAYNE EDWARD CRIST[135], b. February 04, 1952.

[167] MARY VIRGINIA[11] GARBER *(DANIEL BENJAMIN[10], JACOB A.[9], LEVI[8], JACOB W.[7], ABRAHAM[6], JOHANNES "JOHN H."[5], JO HANNES[4] GERBER, NICLAUS[3], CHRISTIAN[2], ULRICH[1])[135]* was born July 15, 1922 in Waynesboro, VA. She married (1) JESSE BROWNING GEISER[135] August 30, 1947. He was born Bet. 1909 - 1916, and died October 24, 1988, in Bridgewater, Rockingham Co., VA. She married (2) HAROLD ASHBY JENNINGS November 28, 1992.

Child of MARY GARBER and JESSE GEISER is:
>   3-3-4-3-2-3-6-1   JUDITH KAREN[12] GEISER[135], b. February 15, 1956, m. (1) HARRY ESTLE
>   DIXON[135], August 09, 1980, b. October 01, 1943, m. (2) LARRY
>   VICIDOMINI[135], December 30, 1995.

[168] CLARENCE A.[11] GARBER *(ANTHONY A.[10], DANIEL SAMUEL[9], LEVI[8], JACOB W.[7], ABRAHAM[6], JOHANNES "JOHN H."[5], JO HANNES[4] GERBER, NICLAUS[3], CHRISTIAN[2], ULRICH[1])[136]* was born September 03, 1908, in Levi Garber house near Mt. Sidney, Augusta Co., VA[136], and died May 01, 1998, in Huntington, MD. He married BEULAH ARMENTROUT[136] October 31, 1928[136]. She was born December 10, 1908[136].

Children of CLARENCE GARBER and BEULAH ARMENTROUT are:
> [186] 3-3-4-3-3-1-3-1   ROBERT EDWARD[12] GARBER, b. September 14, 1929.
>   3-3-4-3-3-1-3-2   FRED HOUSTON GARBER[136], b. December 05, 1930, m. VIRGINIA ANN
>   LAUBINGER[137], May 03, 1952.
>   3-3-4-3-3-1-3-3   LINDA MAE GARBER[138], b. September 03, 1949.

[169] RUTH ELIZABETH[11] GARBER *(ANTHONY A.[10], DANIEL SAMUEL[9], LEVI[8], JACOB W.[7], ABRAHAM[6], JOHANNES "JOHN H."[5], JO HANNES[4] GERBER, NICLAUS[3], CHRISTIAN[2], ULRICH[1])[138]* was born November 17, 1909, in Levi Garber house near Mt. Sidney, Augusta Co., VA*139*. She married CLYDE L. CLINE*140* January 03, 1936.

Child of RUTH GARBER and CLYDE CLINE is:
    3-3-4-3-3-1-4-1   ROSE MARIE[12] CLINE*141*, b. February 27, 1950.

[170] PAULINE A.[11] GARBER *(ANTHONY A.[10], DANIEL SAMUEL[9], LEVI[8], JACOB W.[7], ABRAHAM[6], JOHANNES "JOHN H."[5], JO HANNES[4] GERBER, NICLAUS[3], CHRISTIAN[2], ULRICH[1])[142]* was born January 29, 1911. She married HAMILTON BEECHER MILLER*142* October 27, 1933.

Children of PAULINE GARBER and HAMILTON MILLER are:
    3-3-4-3-3-1-5-1   GAYNELLA REBECCA[12] MILLER*142*, b. July 07, 1941.
    3-3-4-3-3-1-5-2   WAYNE HAMILTON MILLER*142*, b. October 06, 1948.

[171] CLEATIS FRANKLIN[11] GARBER *(HOMER FRANKLIN[10], DANIEL SAMUEL[9], LEVI[8], JACOB W.[7], ABRAHAM[6], JOHANNES "JOHN H."[5], JO HANNES[4] GERBER, NICLAUS[3], CHRISTIAN[2], ULRICH[1])[142]* was born April 19, 1911, in Levi Garber House near Mt. Sidney in Augusta Co., VA*143*. He married (1) DORIS ELIZABETH MILLER*143* June 21, 1942, in First Presbyterian Church, New Orleans*143*, daughter of HARLAND MILLER and CORA TERRY. She was born March 30, 1921*144*. He married (2) NANCY MOORE*145* Abt. 1986.

More about CLEATIS FRANKLIN GARBER:
Occupation: Federal Investigator for General Accounting Office
Residence: Waynesboro, VA

Children of CLEATIS GARBER and DORIS MILLER are:
[187]   3-3-4-3-3-4-1-1   BARBARA ELIZABETH[12] GARBER, b. July 22, 1945.
[188]   3-3-4-3-3-4-1-2   DAVID FRANKLIN GARBER, b. July 12, 1947.

[172] HAROLD LAVERN[11] GARBER *(HOMER FRANKLIN[10], DANIEL SAMUEL[9], LEVI[8], JACOB W.[7], ABRAHAM[6], JOHANNES "JOHN H."[5], JO HANNES[4] GERBER, NICLAUS[3], CHRISTIAN[2], ULRICH[1])[146]* was born March 10, 1912, in Levi Garber House near Mt. Sidney, Augusta Co., VA*147*, and died March 04, 2002, in Summit Square, 501 Oak Ave., Waynesboro, VA. He married NORMA ISABELLE FISHER February 25, 1937, in Washington, DC*148*. She was born March 15, 1918, in Waynesboro, VA, and died November 05, 1998, in Waynesboro, VA.

More about HAROLD LAVERN GARBER:
Burial: March 07, 2002, Tinkling Springs Presbyterian Church in Augusta Co., VA
Education: BS from Bridgewater College and MS from Virginia Polytechnic Institute
Occupation: Research Chemist at DuPont's nylon plant in Waynesboro, VA
Religion: Elder and Deacon of the Tinkling Spring Presbyterian Church

More about NORMA ISABELLE FISHER:
Burial: November 1998, Tinkling Springs Presbyterian Church in Augusta Co.,, VA

Children of HAROLD GARBER and NORMA FISHER are:

[189] 3-3-4-3-3-4-2-1   HAROLD LAVERN[12] GARBER, JR., b. December 20, 1937, Niagara Falls, NY.

[190] 3-3-4-3-3-4-2-2   FREDERIC COWAN GARBER, b. June 29, 1942, Waynesboro Hospital, Waynesboro, VA.

[191] 3-3-4-3-3-4-2-3   DENETTE BELLE GARBER, b. January 23, 1947, Waynesboro Hospital, Waynesboro, VA.

[173] PAUL WILSON[11] GARBER *(HOMER FRANKLIN[10], DANIEL SAMUEL[9], LEVI[8], JACOB W.[7], ABRAHAM[6], JOHANNES "JOHN H."[5], JO HANNES[4] GERBER, NICLAUS[3], CHRISTIAN[2], ULRICH[1])[149]* was born December 31, 1913, in Levi Garber House near Mt. Sidney, Augusta Co., VA[150], and died July 16, 2001, at his residence at 100 Berkeley Drive, Waynesboro, VA, where he lived from 1989 until 2001[151]. He married RUBY ELIZABETH SIPE[151] April 04, 1942, in Tinkling Springs Presbyterian Church, Augusta Co., VA[152], daughter of ROBERT SIPE and BERTHA SHIFFLETT. She was born March 20, 1919, in the H.L. Shifflett farm house on Rt. 340, 4 miles W. of Elkton, VA, in Rockingham Co.[153].

More about PAUL WILSON GARBER:
Burial: July 19, 2001, Middle River Church of the Brethren in Augusta Co., Virginia[154]
Graduation: 1928, New Hope High School in New Hope, VA
Occupation: Bet. 1930 - 1989, Grocery store clerk/owner, farmer and dog warden
Religion: Bet. 1913 - 2001, Member of the Middle River Church of the Brethren from 1913 to about 1956 and then moved membership to the Waynesboro Church of the Brethren.
Residence: 1942, Effective May 15 lived in a new apartment at 312 Florence Ave., Waynesboro, VA, after marriage.
Social Security Number: Issued in District of Columbia

More about RUBY ELIZABETH SIPE:
Occupation: Bet. 1940 - 1983, Nurse-Worked at Waynesboro Hospital (1940-1942), King's Daughters Hospital (1952-1957) and Waynesboro's DuPont Plant (1958-1983)
Residence: September 2002, Moved to the Bridgewater Retirement Community, Apt. 104, 319 First St., Bridgewater, VA 22812

Children of PAUL GARBER and RUBY SIPE are:

[192] 3-3-4-3-3-4-3-1   WAYNE EDWARD[12] GARBER, b. September 11, 1944, Rockingham Memorial Hospital, Harrisonburg, VA.

[193] 3-3-4-3-3-4-3-2   DON PAUL GARBER, b. April 18, 1946, Rockingham Memorial Hospital, Harrisonburg, VA.

[194] 3-3-4-3-3-4-3-3   CAROLYN ANN GARBER, b. May 27, 1952, Kings Daughters Hospital in Staunton, VA.

[174] MARGARET ELIZABETH[11] GARBER *(HOMER FRANKLIN[10], DANIEL SAMUEL[9], LEVI[8], JACOB W.[7], ABRAHAM[6], JOHANNES "JOHN H."[5], JO HANNES[4] GERBER, NICLAUS[3], CHRISTIAN[2], ULRICH[1])[155]* was born November 04, 1915, in Augusta Co., VA[155], and died April 1981, in Myrtle Beach, SC[156]. She married (1) STEWART HALL[157] October 26, 1934, in the Homer F. Garber house at New Hope, VA[157]. She married (2) WALTER WESLEY WOODSIDE, SR. December 26, 1940 in FL[158]. He was born September 15, 1916, in Marion, IL[159,160,161], and died January 13, 1983, in Arlington, VA[161].

More about MARGARET ELIZABETH GARBER:
Burial: Arlington National Cemetery, Arlington, VA
Occupation: Confidential Assistant, Department of Interior

More about WALTER WESLEY WOODSIDE, SR.:
Burial: Arlington National Cemetery, Arlington, VA
Occupation: Attorney at Law
Residence: Arlington, VA

Children of MARGARET GARBER and WALTER WOODSIDE are:
    3-3-4-3-3-4-4-1   SUSANN JEAN[12] WOODSIDE[162], b. September 29, 1942, Jacksonville, FL[162].

More about SUSANN JEAN WOODSIDE:
Occupation: Real Estate Broker

[195]   3-3-4-3-3-4-4-2   DONNA RAY WOODSIDE, b. March 22, 1945, Philadelphia, PA.
[196]   3-3-4-3-3-4-4-3   WALTER WESLEY WOODSIDE, JR., b. September 21, 1949.

[175] ANNA LEE "DOLLY" VIRGINIA[11] GARBER (*HOMER FRANKLIN*[10], *DANIEL SAMUEL*[9], *LEVI*[8], *JACOB W.*[7], *ABRAHAM*[6], *JOHANNES "JOHN H."*[5], *JO HANNES*[4] *GERBER, NICLAUS*[3], *CHRISTIAN*[2], *ULRICH*[1])[162] was born March 24, 1928, in Levi Garber house near Mt. Sidney, Augusta Co., VA[162]. She married OWEN EARLY HARNER June 23, 1948, in Margaret Woodside's House at Greenbelt, MD, son of RAY HARNER and HAZEL EARLY. He was born June 18, 1929, in New Hope, VA[162].

More about ANNA LEE "DOLLY" VIRGINIA GARBER:
Occupation: Homemaker
Residence: Ft. Defiance, VA

More about OWEN EARLY HARNER:
Occupation: Chemical Technician at E. I. DuPont

Children of ANNA GARBER and OWEN HARNER are:
[197]   3-3-4-3-3-4-5-1   SHARON LEIGH[12] HARNER, b. February 25, 1949, Staunton, VA.
[198]   3-3-4-3-3-4-5-2   SUSAN ANN HARNER, b. November 02, 1950, Waynesboro, VA.
[199]   3-3-4-3-3-4-5-3   PEGGY TERESA HARNER, b. June 15, 1952, Staunton, VA.
[200]   3-3-4-3-3-4-5-4   JAMES OWEN HARNER, b. March 15, 1955, Staunton, VA.
[201]   3-3-4-3-3-4-5-5   MICHAEL GARBER HARNER, b. August 05, 1961, Staunton, VA.

[176] CATHERINE LOUISE[11] GARBER (*MINOR WILLIAM*[10], *DANIEL SAMUEL*[9], *LEVI*[8], *JACOB W.*[7], *ABRAHAM*[6], *JOHANNES "JOHN H."*[5], *JO HANNES*[4] *GERBER, NICLAUS*[3], *CHRISTIAN*[2], *ULRICH*[1])[162] was born March 11, 1913, in Augusta Co., VA[162], and died October 23, 2005, in Harrisonburg, Rockingham Co., VA. She married RAYMOND KISER CRIST[162] November 11, 1949[162], son of NOAH CRIST and ETTA KISER. He was born October 15, 1905, and died June 24, 1991 in Harrisonburg, VA.

More about CATHERINE LOUISE GARBER:
Burial: October 25, 2005, Middle River Cemetery

Education: Graduate of Madison College, Class of 1934
Occupation: Seamstress
Residence: Harrisonburg, VA

More about RAYMOND KISER CRIST:
Burial: Middle River Cemetery
Occupation: Linotypes

Child of CATHERINE GARBER and RAYMOND CRIST is:
    3-3-4-3-3-6-1-1   WILLIAM RAY[12] CRIST[162], b. June 25, 1951[162].

[177] NELSON KEITH[11] NORFORD (*EARL RAYMOND*[10], *BARBARA ELIZABETH*[9] *GARBER, LEVI*[8], *JACOB W.*[7], *ABRAHAM*[6], *JOHANNES "JOHN H."*[5], *JO HANNES*[4] *GERBER, NICLAUS*[3], *CHRISTIAN*[2], *ULRICH*[1])[163] was born February 09, 1925. He married LINDA JEAN KIENY[163] October 12, 1947.

Children of NELSON NORFORD and LINDA KIENY are:
    3-3-4-3-7-2-1-1   LESLIE K.[12] NORFORD[163], b. April 02, 1951.
    3-3-4-3-7-2-1-2   LARY C. NORFORD[163], b. December 27, 1953.
    3-3-4-3-7-2-1-3   LESA A. NORFORD[163], b. March 29, 1956.
    3-3-4-3-7-2-1-4   LORI J. NORFORD[163], b. September 21, 1961.

[178] RICHARD FRANCES[11] NORFORD (*EARL RAYMOND*[10], *BARBARA ELIZABETH*[9] *GARBER, LEVI*[8], *JACOB W.*[7], *ABRAHAM*[6], *JOHANNES "JOHN H."*[5], *JO HANNES*[4] *GERBER, NICLAUS*[3], *CHRISTIAN*[2], *ULRICH*[1])[163] was born May 03, 1931. He married ALICE MURACHANIAN[163] June 15, 1957.

Child of RICHARD NORFORD and ALICE MURACHANIAN is:
    3-3-4-3-7-2-3-1   BRADLEY C.[12] NORFORD[163], b. February 04, 1961.

[179] JEAN GARBER[11] NORFORD (*EARL RAYMOND*[10], *BARBARA ELIZABETH*[9] *GARBER, LEVI*[8], *JACOB W.*[7], *ABRAHAM*[6], *JOHANNES "JOHN H."*[5], *JO HANNES*[4] *GERBER, NICLAUS*[3], *CHRISTIAN*[2], *ULRICH*[1])[163] was born July 29, 1933. She married JOHN H. HUBBELL[163] June 11, 1955.

Children of JEAN NORFORD and JOHN HUBBELL are:
    3-3-4-3-7-2-4-1   ANN R.[12] HUBBELL[163], b. January 13, 1958.
    3-3-4-3-7-2-4-2   SHELTON E. HUBBELL[163], b. February 02, 1960.

[180] LOIS[11] SHOEMAKER (*ETHEL V.*[10] *HUFFMAN, FRANCES "FANNIE" V.*[9] *GARBER, LEVI*[8], *JACOB W.*[7], *ABRAHAM*[6], *JOHANNES "JOHN H."*[5], *JO HANNES*[4] *GERBER, NICLAUS*[3], *CHRISTIAN*[2], *ULRICH*[1])[163] was born September 09, 1928. She married C. J. STONECIPHER[163] August 31, 1947.

Child of LOIS SHOEMAKER and C. STONECIPHER is:
    3-3-4-3-8-3-1-1   BONNIE LOU[12] STONECIPHER[163], b. June 24, 1948,
               m. DENNIS HARNED[163], May 02, 1965.

[181] MARTHA[11] GLICK *(CARL[10], JOHN WILLIAM[9], REBECCA[8] WINE, MICHAEL[7], MAGADALENE[6] GARBER, JOHANNES "JOHN H."[5], JO HANNES[4] GERBER, NICLAUS[3], CHRISTIAN[2], ULRICH[1])[164].* She married ROBERT BROWN[164].

Children of MARTHA GLICK and ROBERT BROWN are:
3-10-1-10-6-1-1-1	CAROL[12] BROWN[164].	
3-10-1-10-6-1-1-2	GERALD "JERRY" BROWN[164].	
3-10-1-10-6-1-1-3	TEDDY BROWN[164].	
3-10-1-10-6-1-1-4	RACHEL ANN BROWN[164], b. January 26, 1951[164].	

[182] J. RUTH[11] GLICK *(CARL[10], JOHN WILLIAM[9], REBECCA[8] WINE, MICHAEL[7], MAGADALENE[6] GARBER, JOHANNES "JOHN H."[5], JO HANNES[4] GERBER, NICLAUS[3], CHRISTIAN[2], ULRICH[1])[164].* She married RAY HATHCOCK.

Children of J. GLICK and RAY HATHCOCK are:
3-10-1-10-6-1-3-1	BARBARA[12] HATHCOCK.
3-10-1-10-6-1-3-2	JIMMIE HATHCOCK.
3-10-1-10-6-1-3-3	MERRILIN HATHCOCK.

[183] JEAN[11] MATTEWS *(RUTH[10] SENGER, MARTHA JANE[9] GLICK, REBECCA[8] WINE, MICHAEL[7], MAGADALENE[6] GARBER, JOHANNES "JOHN H."[5], JO HANNES[4] GERBER, NICLAUS[3], CHRISTIAN[2], ULRICH[1])[164]* was born 1923[164]. She married DICK SMITH[164].

Children of JEAN MATTEWS and DICK SMITH are:
3-10-1-10-7-1-1-1	TOMMY[12] SMITH[164], b. 1942[164].	
3-10-1-10-7-1-1-2	PAUL SMITH[164], b. 1943[164].	
3-10-1-10-7-1-1-3	PENNY SMITH[164], b. 1945[164].	
3-10-1-10-7-1-1-4	JIMMY SMITH[164], b. 1946[164].	
3-10-1-10-7-1-1-5	TEDDY SMITH[164], b. 1948[164].	
3-10-1-10-7-1-1-6	JOHNNIE SMITH[164], b. 1950[164].	
3-10-1-10-7-1-1-7	SUSAN SMITH[164], b. 1952[164].	
3-10-1-10-7-1-1-8	RICHARD SMITH[164], b. 1954[164].	
3-10-1-10-7-1-1-9	DAVID SMITH[164], b. 1956.	
3-10-1-10-7-1-1-10	CASEY SMITH[164], b. 1958[164].	
3-10-1-10-7-1-1-11	CHRIS SMITH[164], b. 1960[164].	
3-10-1-10-7-1-1-12	ALLISON SMITH[164], b. 1964[164].	
3-10-1-10-7-1-1-13	MARTHA SMITH[164], b. 1966[164].	

[184] BILL[11] MATTEWS *(RUTH[10] SENGER, MARTHA JANE[9] GLICK, REBECCA[8] WINE, MICHAEL[7], MAGADALENE[6] GARBER, JOHANNES "JOHN H."[5], JO HANNES[4] GERBER, NICLAUS[3], CHRISTIAN[2], ULRICH[1])[164]* was born 1934. He married VIRGINIA SILL 1960.

Children of BILL MATTEWS and VIRGINIA SILL are:
3-10-1-10-7-1-2-1	DONNA[12] MATTEWS, b. 1961.
3-10-1-10-7-1-2-2	BILLY MATTEWS, b. 1963.
3-10-1-10-7-1-2-3	MARY ANNE MATTEWS, b. 1965.

3-10-1-10-7-1-2-4 BOBBY MATTEWS, b. 1971.
3-10-1-10-7-1-2-5 LINDA RUTH MATTEWS, b. 1976.

[185] ROY[11] JOHNSON (*ETHEL*[10] *MILLER, SARAH FRANCES*[9] *GLICK, REBECCA*[8] *WINE, MICHAEL*[7]*, MAGADALENE*[6] *GARBER, JOHANNES "JOHN H."*[5]*, JO HANNES*[4] *GERBER, NICLAUS*[3]*, CHRISTIAN*[2]*, ULRICH*[1]*)*[164] was born 1933[164]. He married MARY[164].

Child of ROY JOHNSON and MARY is:
 3-10-1-10-8-2-3-1 MAX R.[12] JOHNSON[164].

U.S. Generation No. 8

[186] ROBERT EDWARD[12] GARBER (*CLARENCE A.*[11]*, ANTHONY A.*[10]*, DANIEL SAMUEL*[9]*, LEVI*[8]*, JACOB W.*[7]*, ABRAHAM*[6]*, JOHANNES "JOHN H."*[5]*, JO HANNES*[4] *GERBER, NICLAUS*[3]*, CHRISTIAN*[2]*, ULRICH*[1]*)*[165] was born September 14, 1929. He married CHRISTINE MARIE BALDERSON[166] September 03, 1955.

Children of ROBERT GARBER and CHRISTINE BALDERSON are:
 3-3-4-3-3-1-3-1-1 MICHAEL ANDREW[13] GARBER[166], b. December 24, 1952.
 3-3-4-3-3-1-3-1-2 JOHN ROBERT GARBER[166], b. December 1958.

[187] BARBARA ELIZABETH[12] GARBER (*CLEATIS FRANKLIN*[11]*, HOMER FRANKLIN*[10]*, DANIEL SAMUEL*[9]*, LEVI*[8]*, JACOB W.*[7]*, ABRAHAM*[6]*, JOHANNES "JOHN H."*[5]*, JO HANNES*[4] *GERBER, NICLAUS*[3]*, CHRISTIAN*[2]*, ULRICH*[1]*)*[167] was born July 22, 1945[168]. She married GILBERT AUSTIN.

Children of BARBARA GARBER and GILBERT AUSTIN are:
 3-3-4-3-3-4-1-1-1 DANIELLE[13] AUSTIN, m. HENRY CARVAJAL.
 3-3-4-3-3-4-1-1-2 JESSICA AUSTIN.
 3-3-4-3-3-4-1-1-3 NATHANIEL AUSTIN.

[188] DAVID FRANKLIN[12] GARBER (*CLEATIS FRANKLIN*[11]*, HOMER FRANKLIN*[10]*, DANIEL SAMUEL*[9]*, LEVI*[8]*, JACOB W.*[7]*, ABRAHAM*[6]*, JOHANNES "JOHN H."*[5]*, JO HANNES*[4] *GERBER, NICLAUS*[3]*, CHRISTIAN*[2]*, ULRICH*[1]*)*[169] was born July 12, 1947[170]. He married KAREN ESTELLE KIRK[171]. She was born May 17, 1947, in Washington, DC[171].

Children of DAVID GARBER and KAREN KIRK are:
[202] 3-3-4-3-3-4-1-1-1 ELIZABETH ANN[13] GARBER, b. January 27, 1970, Harrisonburg, VA.
 3-3-4-3-3-4-1-1-2 THOMAS FRANKLIN GARBER[171], b. April 04, 1985, Waynesboro, VA[171].
 3-3-4-3-3-4-1-1-3 MICHAEL KIRK GARBER[171], b. December 02, 1987, Waynesboro, VA.

[189] HAROLD LAVERN[12] GARBER, JR. (*HAROLD LAVERN*[11]*, HOMER FRANKLIN*[10]*, DANIEL SAMUEL*[9]*, LEVI*[8]*, JACOB W.*[7]*, ABRAHAM*[6]*, JOHANNES "JOHN H."*[5]*, JO HANNES*[4] *GERBER, NICLAUS*[3]*, CHRISTIAN*[2]*, ULRICH*[1]*)* was born December 20, 1937, in Niagara Falls, NY[172]. He married

(1) ANITA LOUISE LEAVELL August 21, 1960, in Waynesboro United Methodist, Waynesboro, VA. She was born June 15, 1938, in Waynesboro Hospital, Waynesboro, VA. He married (2) KATHI SUSAN MEYERS[173] May 03, 1969[174]. She was born February 08, 1947, in Cincinnati, OH.

More about HAROLD LAVERN GARBER, JR.:
Degree: BS Chemistry
Occupation: Antique furniture refinisher
Residence: Aynor, SC

More about ANITA LOUISE LEAVELL:
Occupation: Artist

More about KATHI SUSAN MEYERS:
Occupation: Social Worker for Horry County, SC

Child of HAROLD GARBER and ANITA LEAVELL is:
[203]   3-3-4-3-3-4-2-1-1   HAROLD LAVERN[13] GARBER III, b. January 17, 1962, Waynesboro
                               Community Hospital, Waynesboro, VA.

Child of HAROLD GARBER and KATHI MEYERS is:
[204]   3-3-4-3-3-4-2-1-2   FREDERICK JOHN[13] GARBER, b. May 25, 1974.

[190] FREDERIC COWAN[12] GARBER *(HAROLD LAVERN[11], HOMER FRANKLIN[10], DANIEL SAMUEL[9], LEVI[8], JACOB W.[7], ABRAHAM[6], JOHANNES "JOHN H."[5], JO HANNES[4] GERBER, NICLAUS[3], CHRISTIAN[2], ULRICH[1])[175]* was born June 29, 1942, in Waynesboro Hospital, Waynesboro, VA[176]. He married DONNA MARIE DEGROFF[177] May 16, 1964, in Leakesville, NC[178], daughter of JOHN DEGROFF and HAZEL VELIE. She was born April 01, 1945, in Poughkeepsie, NY[178].

More About FREDERIC COWAN GARBER:
Residence: Chesapeake City, MD

Children of FREDERIC GARBER and DONNA DEGROFF are:
[205]   3-3-4-3-3-4-2-2-1   KIMBERLY ANN[13] GARBER, b. December 12, 1964, Waynesboro, VA.
[206]   3-3-4-3-3-4-2-2-2   KRISTIN LYNETTE GARBER, b. June 16, 1968, Waynesboro, VA.
[207]   3-3-4-3-3-4-2-2-3   KEVIN DEGROFF GARBER, b. May 06, 1967, Waynesboro Community
                               Hospital, Waynesboro, VA.

[191] DENETTE BELLE[12] GARBER *(HAROLD LAVERN[11], HOMER FRANKLIN[10], DANIEL SAMUEL[9], LEVI[8], JACOB W.[7], ABRAHAM[6], JOHANNES "JOHN H."[5], JO HANNES[4] GERBER, NICLAUS[3], CHRISTIAN[2], ULRICH[1])* was born January 23, 1947, in Waynesboro Hospital, Waynesboro, VA[179]. She married LYNWOOD NEIL STEVERSON August 11, 1973, in Tinkling Springs Presbyterian Church, Augusta Co., VA[180]. He was born October 02, 1948, in Norfolk, VA.

More about DENETTE BELLE GARBER:
Degree: DeNette graduated from William & Mary with degree in Elementary Education.
Residence: Richmond, VA

More about LYNWOOD NEIL STEVERSON:
Occupation: Henrico County Judge

Child of DENETTE GARBER and LYNWOOD STEVERSON is:
     3-3-4-3-3-4-2-3-1   BRYAN CHRISTOPHER[13] STEVERSON[180], b. October 22, 1978, Richmond, VA; m. JENNIFER NOEL EROE, July 26, 2003, Ashburn, VA; b. December 07, 1978, Reno, NV.

More about BRYAN CHRISTOPHER STEVERSON:
Occupation: G.S.A. Environmental Protection Specialist

More about JENNIFER NOEL EROE:
Occupation: Teacher in Loudon County, VA

[192] WAYNE EDWARD[12] GARBER *(PAUL WILSON[11], HOMER FRANKLIN[10], DANIEL SAMUEL[9], LEVI[8], JACOB W.[7], ABRAHAM[6], JOHANNES "JOHN H."[5], JO HANNES[4] GERBER, NICLAUS[3], CHRISTIAN[2], ULRICH[1])[181]* was born September 11, 1944, in Rockingham Memorial Hospital, Harrisonburg, VA[182]. He married GAIL EILEEN TWOMBLY[183] September 17, 1966, in Waynesboro Church of the Brethren, Waynesboro, VA[183], daughter of CARROLL TWOMBLY and MARY COX. She was born June 07, 1946, in Alexandria Hospital, Alexandria, VA[184].

More about WAYNE EDWARD GARBER:
Degree: 1966, B.S. Bus. Admin., VPI & SU, Blacksburg, VA
Occupation: Human Resource Director and Executive Search Consultant

More about GAIL TWOMBLY GARBER:
Degree: 1992, B.A. Management, National-Louis University, McLean, VA

Children of WAYNE GARBER and GAIL TWOMBLY are:
[208] 3-3-4-3-3-4-3-1-1   MARC WAYNE[13] GARBER, b. February 01, 1971, Saint Mary's Hospital, Richmond, VA.

More about MARC WAYNE GARBER:
Degrees:1993, B.B.A., Radford University 1999, J.D. Law, George Mason University

     3-3-4-3-3-4-3-1-2   HOLLY MICHELLE GARBER[185], b. August 29, 1980, Fairfax Memorial Hospital, Falls Church, VA[185].

More about HOLLY MICHELLE GARBER:
Degree: 2002, B.S. Bus. Admin., Longwood University

[193] DON PAUL[12] GARBER *(PAUL WILSON[11], HOMER FRANKLIN[10], DANIEL SAMUEL[9], LEVI[8], JACOB W.[7], ABRAHAM[6], JOHANNES "JOHN H."[5], JO HANNES[4] GERBER, NICLAUS[3], CHRISTIAN[2], ULRICH[1])[185]* was born April 18, 1946, in Rockingham Memorial Hospital, Harrisonburg, VA[185]. He married (1) ROXANNE KAISER[186] July 24, 1971, in Sunnyvale, CA, daughter of FRED KAISER and BARBARA LAHR. She was born about 1948 in Coronado, CA. He married (2) MICHELLE MONTESCLARES[186] January 1976, in San Francisco, CA[186]. She was born December 19, 1950, in San

Francisco, CA[186]. He married (3) JANA FAITH KIENA[187] August 18, 1996, in San Diego, CA[188], daughter of EDWARD KIENA and CAROLYN KIENA. She was born December 21, 1960, in Staten Island, NY[188,189].

More about DON PAUL GARBER:
Graduation: 1968, B.S. Industrial Engineering, VPI & SU
           1972, J.D. Law, Hastings College of Law
Occupation: Director for Sentra Gas and Electric in San Diego, CA

More about ROXANNE KAISER:
Graduation: B.S. Printing Techniques & Management, California Polytechnic Institute

More about MICHELLE MONTESCLARES:
Occupation: Housewife, dance instructor, English teacher

More about JANA FAITH KIENA:
Occupation: Certified Professional Accountant (CPA)

Children of DON GARBER and MICHELLE MONTESCLARES are:
3-3-4-3-3-4-3-2-1   ALISA MICHELLE[13] GARBER[190], b. July 01, 1979, Falls Church, VA[190].

More about ALISA MICHELLE GARBER:
Occupation: Irish dance instructor

3-3-4-3-3-4-3-2-2   CHASE ALAIN GARBER[190], b. March 08, 1983, Falls Church, VA[190].

[194] CAROLYN ANN[12] GARBER (PAUL WILSON[11], HOMER FRANKLIN[10], DANIEL SAMUEL[9], LEVI[8], JACOB W.[7], ABRAHAM[6], JOHANNES "JOHN H."[5], JO HANNES[4] GERBER, NICLAUS[3], CHRISTIAN[2], ULRICH[1])[191] was born May 27, 1952, in Kings Daughters Hospital in Staunton, Va. She married DAVID HOMER PETTIT[192] August 18, 1973, in Waynesboro Church of the Brethren, Waynesboro, VA[193]. He was born March 02, 1952, in Waynesboro Community Hospital, Augusta Co., VA[194].

More about CAROLYN ANN GARBER:
Occupation: Social Worker for adoption services

More about DAVID HOMER PETTIT:
Occupation: Aft. 1977 He is an attorney in private practice in Charlottesville, VA.

Children of CAROLYN GARBER and DAVID PETTIT are:
3-3-4-3-3-4-3-3-1   ALLAN DAVID[13] PETTIT[194], b. April 20, 1978, Roanoke Memorial Hospital, Roanoke, VA[194].

More about ALLAN DAVID PETTIT:
Occupation: Construction management

3-3-4-3-3-4-3-3-2   ANDREW G. PETTIT[194], b. February 08, 1980, Martha Jefferson Hospital, Charlottesville, VA[194].

More about ANDREW G. PETTIT:
Occupation: Concrete sales and quality control

3-3-4-3-3-4-3-3-3   BROOKE ELIZABETH PETTIT[194], b. September 05, 1986, Martha Jefferson Hospital, Charlottesville, VA[194].

More about BROOKE ELIZABETH PETTIT:
Occupation: Student

[195] DONNA RAY[12] WOODSIDE (*MARGARET ELIZABETH*[11] *GARBER, HOMER FRANKLIN*[10], *DANIEL SAMUEL*[9], *LEVI*[8], *JACOB W.*[7], *ABRAHAM*[6], *JOHANNES "JOHN H."*[5], *JO HANNES*[4] *GERBER, NICLAUS*[3], *CHRISTIAN*[2], *ULRICH*[1])[195] was born March 22, 1945, in Philadelphia, PA[195]. She married WALTER A. SERGEEFF September 01, 1966, in San Francisco, CA. He was born April 10, 1940, on Russia/China border.

More about DONNA RAY WOODSIDE:
Occupation: Investor

More about WALTER A. SERGEEFF:
Occupation: Investor

Children of DONNA WOODSIDE and WALTER SERGEEFF are:
    3-3-4-3-3-4-4-2-1   KEVIN A.[13] SERGEEFF, b. October 27, 1971, Encino, CA.
    3-3-4-3-3-4-4-2-2   JENNIFER S. SERGEEFF, b. December 06, 1972, Encino, CA.
    3-3-4-3-3-4-4-2-3   PAMELA A. SERGEEFF, b. December 06, 1972, Encino, CA.

[196] WALTER WESLEY[12] WOODSIDE, JR. (*MARGARET ELIZABETH*[11] *GARBER, HOMER FRANKLIN*[10], *DANIEL SAMUEL*[9], *LEVI*[8], *JACOB W.*[7], *ABRAHAM*[6], *JOHANNES "JOHN H."*[5], *JO HANNES*[4] *GERBER, NICLAUS*[3], *CHRISTIAN*[2], *ULRICH*[1])[195] was born September 21, 1949[195]. He married MARSHELLA ANNE THOMAS June 03, 1972, in Arlington, VA, daughter of FREDRICK THOMAS and NANCY TAYLOR. She was born October 26, 1948, in Washington, DC.

More about WALTER WESLEY WOODSIDE, JR.:
Occupation: U.S. Park Ranger

Children of WALTER WOODSIDE and MARSHELLA THOMAS are:
    3-3-4-3-3-4-4-3-1   WALTER WESLEY[13] WOODSIDE III, b. September 06, 1974, Alexandria, VA.
    3-3-4-3-3-4-4-3-2   AMBER MICHELLE WOODSIDE, b. November 09, 1976, Asheville, NC.
    3-3-4-3-3-4-4-3-3   HEATHER NICOLE WOODSIDE, b. September 21, 1978, Homestead, FL.

[197] SHARON LEIGH[12] HARNER (*ANNA LEE "DOLLY" VIRGINIA*[11] *GARBER, HOMER FRANKLIN*[10], *DANIEL SAMUEL*[9], *LEVI*[8], *JACOB W.*[7], *ABRAHAM*[6], *JOHANNES "JOHN H."*[5], *JO HANNES*[4] *GERBER, NICLAUS*[3], *CHRISTIAN*[2], *ULRICH*[1])[195] was born February 25, 1949, in Staunton, VA[195]. She married (1) JEFFERSON A. DYER. He was born September 28, 1953, in Cookeville, TN.

She married (2) WILLIAM SOUTHARD TUTTLE[196] November 08, 1968, in New Hope, VA[196]. He was born in Staunton, VA.

More about SHARON LEIGH HARNER:
Occupation: Bank manager and financial advisor

Child of SHARON HARNER and JEFFERSON DYER is:
  3-3-4-3-3-4-5-1-1   THOMAS K.[13] DYER, b. July 01, 1987, Bristol, TN.

Children of SHARON HARNER and WILLIAM TUTTLE are:
  3-3-4-3-3-4-5-1-2   WILLIAM CHRISTOPHER[13] TUTTLE[196], b. August 26, 1969, m. HEIDI
                       BINKO, June 15, 2002, Staunton, VA, b. October 03, 1974, Fredonia, NY.
  3-3-4-3-3-4-5-1-3   NICOLE LEIGH TUTTLE[196], b. March 21, 1972, Staunton, VA, m.
                       EDWARD C. CRIDLEBAUGH III, July 13, 2003, Jamaica,
                       b. August 18, 1970, High Point, NC.

More about EDWARD C. CRIDLEBAUGH III:
Occupation: Social Worker

[198] SUSAN ANN[12] HARNER *(ANNA LEE "DOLLY" VIRGINIA[11] GARBER, HOMER FRANKLIN[10], DANIEL SAMUEL[9], LEVI[8], JACOB W.[7], ABRAHAM[6], JOHANNES "JOHN H."[5], JO HANNES[4] GERBER, NICLAUS[3], CHRISTIAN[2], ULRICH[1])[197]* was born November 02, 1950, in Waynesboro, VA[197]. She married JERRY ROBINSON COFFMAN[198] July 15, 1972, in New Hope, VA[198]. He was born May 07, 1950, in OH.

More about SUSAN ANN HARNER:
Occupation: Nursing

More about JERRY ROBINSON COFFMAN:
Occupation: Insurance Broker

Children of SUSAN HARNER and JERRY COFFMAN are:
[209] 3-3-4-3-3-4-5-2-1   ANNE MARIE[13] COFFMAN, b. December 20, 1972, Limestone, ME.
       3-3-4-3-3-4-5-2-2   ALISON SUSANNE COFFMAN[199], b. October 07, 1977, Richmond, VA,
                            m. BRANT NICHOLAS MARKOW[199], October 12, 2001, New Hope,
                            VA[199], b. October 30, 1972, Richmond, VA.

More about ALISON SUSANNE COFFMAN:
Occupation: Education Coordinator

More about BRANT NICHOLAS MARKOW:
Occupation: Teacher

       3-3-4-3-3-4-5-2-3   MATTHEW ROBINSON COFFMAN[199], b. October 06, 1980, Winchester,
                            VA[199].

More about MATTHEW ROBINSON COFFMAN:
Education: Communications graduate from EMU

[199] PEGGY TERESA[12] HARNER *(ANNA LEE "DOLLY" VIRGINIA[11] GARBER, HOMER FRANKLIN[10], DANIEL SAMUEL[9], LEVI[8], JACOB W.[7], ABRAHAM[6], JOHANNES "JOHN H."[5], JO HANNES[4] GERBER, NICLAUS[3], CHRISTIAN[2], ULRICH[1])*[200] was born June 15, 1952, in Staunton, VA[200]. She married JOHNNIE MILTON BARR, JR.[201] October 26, 1974, in New Hope, VA[201]. He was born July 29, 1952, in Staunton, VA.

More about PEGGY TERESA HARNER:
Occupation: Homemaker

More about JOHNNIE MILTON BARR, JR.:
Occupation: Consulting Engineer

Children of PEGGY HARNER and JOHNNIE BARR are:
| 3-3-4-3-3-4-5-3-1 | SARAH LINDSEY[13] BARR[201], b. October 26, 1981, Richmond, VA. |
| 3-3-4-3-3-4-5-3-2 | AMANDA KATHLEEN BARR[201], b. March 17, 1988, Richmond, VA. |

[200] JAMES OWEN[12] HARNER *(ANNA LEE "DOLLY" VIRGINIA[11] GARBER, HOMER FRANKLIN[10], DANIEL SAMUEL[9], LEVI[8], JACOB W.[7], ABRAHAM[6], JOHANNES "JOHN H."[5], JO HANNES[4] GERBER, NICLAUS[3], CHRISTIAN[2], ULRICH[1])*[202] was born March 15, 1955, in Staunton, VA[202]. He married CONNIE ELIZABETH DILLON[203] July 09, 1977, in Staunton, VA[203]. She was born July 22, 1955.

More about CONNIE ELIZABETH DILLON:
Occupation: School Teacher

Children of JAMES HARNER and CONNIE DILLON are:
3-3-4-3-3-4-5-4-1	TASHA ELIZABETH[13] HARNER[203], b. August 16, 1983, Waynesboro, VA.
3-3-4-3-3-4-5-4-2	ARIANA LAUREL HARNER[203], b. April 14, 1987, Waynesboro, VA.
3-3-4-3-3-4-5-4-3	JAMES DILLON HARNER[203], b. September 18, 1993, Waynesboro, VA.

[201] MICHAEL GARBER[12] HARNER *(ANNA LEE "DOLLY" VIRGINIA[11] GARBER, HOMER FRANKLIN[10], DANIEL SAMUEL[9], LEVI[8], JACOB W.[7], ABRAHAM[6], JOHANNES "JOHN H."[5], JO HANNES[4] GERBER, NICLAUS[3], CHRISTIAN[2], ULRICH[1])*[204] was born August 05, 1961, in Staunton, VA. He married LAVONNE KAY BOWMAN[205] October 27, 1990, in Manassas, VA[205]. She was born April 14, 1966.

More about MICHAEL GARBER HARNER:
Occupation: Supervisor Dominion Power

More about LAVONNE KAY BOWMAN:
Occupation: School Teacher and Homemaker

Children of MICHAEL HARNER and LAVONNE BOWMAN are:
3-3-4-3-3-4-5-5-1	KRISTINE LAUREN[13] HARNER[205], b. May 03, 1994, Manassas, VA.
3-3-4-3-3-4-5-5-2	ANGELA LYNN HARNER[205], b. February 02, 1997, Manassas, VA.
3-3-4-3-3-4-5-5-3	MICHAEL BRADLEY HARNER[205], b. January 07, 2000, Manassas, VA.

[202] ELIZABETH ANN[13] GARBER *(DAVID FRANKLIN[12], CLEATIS FRANKLIN[11], HOMER FRANKLIN[10], DANIEL SAMUEL[9], LEVI[8], JACOB W.[7], ABRAHAM[6], JOHANNES "JOHN H."[5], JO HANNES[4] GERBER, NICLAUS[3], CHRISTIAN[2], ULRICH[1])*[206] was born January 27, 1970, in Harrisonburg, VA[206]. She married STEPHEN WADE WETTERLING[206] December 20, 1996[206]. He was born March 13, 1971, in England[206].

More about ELIZABETH ANN GARBER:
Occupation: Housewife

Children of ELIZABETH GARBER and STEPHEN WETTERLING are:

3-3-4-3-3-4-1-1-1-1	LOGAN KIRK[14] WETTERLING[206], b. October 06, 2000, VA.
3-3-4-3-3-4-1-1-1-2	HOPE VIRGINIA WETTERLING[206], b. July 24, 2002, FL.
3-3-4-3-3-4-1-1-1-3	ERIK MAGNUS WETTERLING, b. June 4, 2005, Naples, FL.

[203] HAROLD LAVERN[13] GARBER III *(HAROLD LAVERN[12], HAROLD LAVERN[11], HOMER FRANKLIN[10], DANIEL SAMUEL[9], LEVI[8], JACOB W.[7], ABRAHAM[6], JOHANNES "JOHN H."[5], JO HANNES[4] GERBER, NICLAUS[3], CHRISTIAN[2], ULRICH[1])*[207] was born January 17, 1962, in Waynesboro Community Hospital, Waynesboro, VA. He married CYNTHIA ANN BERRY[207] June 18, 1983, in Waynesboro, Virginia[207]. She was born September 01, 1965, in Waynesboro, VA.

More about HAROLD LAVERN GARBER III:
Occupation: Electrician

Children of HAROLD GARBER and CYNTHIA BERRY are:

3-3-4-3-3-4-2-1-1-1	KRYSTAL LYNNE[14] GARBER, b. May 14, 1991, Charleston, SC.
3-3-4-3-3-4-2-1-1-2	JOHN MATTHEW GARBER, b. June 09, 1995, Charlottesville, VA.

[204] FREDERICK JOHN[13] GARBER *(HAROLD LAVERN[12], HAROLD LAVERN[11], HOMER FRANKLIN[10], DANIEL SAMUEL[9], LEVI[8], JACOB W.[7], ABRAHAM[6], JOHANNES "JOHN H."[5], JO HANNES[4] GERBER, NICLAUS[3], CHRISTIAN[2], ULRICH[1])*[207] was born May 25, 1974[207]. He married CHRISTINA GAIL GORE[207] December 09, 1998. She was born November 05, 1978, in Conway, SC.

More about CHRISTINA GAIL GORE:
Occupation: Housewife

Children of FREDERICK GARBER and CHRISTINA GORE are:

3-3-4-3-3-4-2-1-2-1	BRITTANY NICOLE[14] GARBER[207], b. July 08, 1998, Myrtle Beach, SC[207].
3-3-4-3-3-4-2-1-2-2	CAMERON BAILEY GARBER[207], b. April 18, 2000, Myrtle Beach, SC[207].

[205] KIMBERLY ANN[13] GARBER *(FREDERIC COWAN[12], HAROLD LAVERN[11], HOMER FRANKLIN[10], DANIEL SAMUEL[9], LEVI[8], JACOB W.[7], ABRAHAM[6], JOHANNES "JOHN H."[5], JO HANNES[4] GERBER, NICLAUS[3], CHRISTIAN[2], ULRICH[1])*[208] was born December 12, 1964, in Waynesboro, VA[208]. She married STEVEN ANDREW WOMER[208] June 04, 1988, in Cecil Co., MD[208]. He was born March 16, 1962, in Wilmington, DE[208].

More about STEVEN ANDREW WOMER:
Occupation: Certified Public Account (CPA)

Children of KIMBERLY GARBER and STEVEN WOMER are:

3-3-4-3-3-4-2-2-1-1	JOHN EVERETT-DEGROFF[14] WOMER[208], b. June 11, 1990, Newark, DE[208].
3-3-4-3-3-4-2-2-1-2	VICTORIA LYNETTE WOMER[208], b. February 28, 1994, Wilmington, DE[208].

[206] KRISTIN LYNETTE[13] GARBER *(FREDERIC COWAN[12], HAROLD LAVERN[11], HOMER FRANKLIN[10], DANIEL SAMUEL[9], LEVI[8], JACOB W.[7], ABRAHAM[6], JOHANNES "JOHN H."[5], JO HANNES[4] GERBER, NICLAUS[3], CHRISTIAN[2], ULRICH[1])*[208] was born June 16, 1968, in Waynesboro, VA[208]. She married JEFFREY NICHOLAS KEATING, SR.[208] January 02, 1993, in St. Anthony's of Padua, Wilmington, DE[208], son of JAMES KEATING and MARIE. He was born August 12, 1965, in Wilmington, DE[208].

More about KRISTIN LYNETTE GARBER:
Occupation: VP of Data Base Marketing with Bank One

More about JEFFREY NICHOLAS KEATING, SR.:
Occupation: Proprietor of Micro Ovens of Delaware

Children of KRISTIN GARBER and JEFFREY KEATING are:

3-3-4-3-3-4-2-2-2-1	JEFFREY NICHOLAS[14] KEATING, JR.[208], b. October 30, 1995, Wilmington, DE.
3-3-4-3-3-4-2-2-2-2	SEAN FREDERIC KEATING[208], b. September 13, 1998, Wilmington, DE.

[207] KEVIN DEGROFF[13] GARBER *(FREDERIC COWAN[12], HAROLD LAVERN[11], HOMER FRANKLIN[10], DANIEL SAMUEL[9], LEVI[8], JACOB W.[7], ABRAHAM[6], JOHANNES "JOHN H."[5], JO HANNES[4] GERBER, NICLAUS[3], CHRISTIAN[2], ULRICH[1])*[208] was born May 06, 1967, in Waynesboro Community Hospital, Waynesboro, VA. He married KAREN MARIE BALOURICKI May 18, 1991, in Church of the Holy Family, Newark, DE. She was born November 13, 1968, in Wilmington, DE.

Notes for KAREN MARIE BALOURICKI:
Divorced 1999

Children of KEVIN GARBER and KAREN BALOURICKI are:

3-3-4-3-3-4-2-2-3-1	ASHLEY NICOLE[14] GARBER, b. June 27, 1992, Wilmington, DE.
3-3-4-3-3-4-2-2-3-2	KATIE MARIE GARBER, b. October 05, 1995, Newark, DE.
3-3-4-3-3-4-2-2-3-3	KEVIN DEGROFF GARBER, b. July 14, 1997, Newark, DE.

[208] MARC WAYNE[13] GARBER *(WAYNE EDWARD[12], PAUL WILSON[11], HOMER FRANKLIN[10], DANIEL SAMUEL[9], LEVI[8], JACOB W.[7], ABRAHAM[6], JOHANNES "JOHN H."[5], JO HANNES[4] GERBER, NICLAUS[3], CHRISTIAN[2], ULRICH[1])[209]* was born February 01, 1971, in Saint Mary's Hospital, Richmond, VA[209]. He married CATHLEEN MARIE ROCKWELL[210] November 11, 2000, in Walnut Hills Baptist Church, Williamsburg, VA[211], daughter of EDWARD ROCKWELL and BEVERLY. She was born August 17, 1968, in San Diego County, CA[212].

More about MARC WAYNE GARBER:
Education: 1993, Graduated with a B.B.A., Marketing, Radford University, Radford VA
        1999, J.D. Law, George Mason University, Fairfax, VA

Children of MARC GARBER and CATHLEEN ROCKWELL are:
3-3-4-3-3-4-3-1-1-1	MADELINE MARIE[14] GARBER[213], b. May 24, 2002, Rockingham Memorial Hospital, Harrisonburg, VA.
3-3-4-3-3-4-3-1-1-2	MELANIE MICHELLE GARBER, b. February 20, 2004, Johnston Willis Hospital, Richmond, VA.
3-3-4-3-3-4-3-1-1-3	MASON MARC GARBER, b. March 22, 2007, St. Francis Medical Center, Richmond, VA.

[209] ANNE MARIE[13] COFFMAN *(SUSAN ANN[12] HARNER, ANNA LEE "DOLLY" VIRGINIA[11] GARBER, HOMER FRANKLIN[10], DANIEL SAMUEL[9], LEVI[8], JACOB W.[7], ABRAHAM[6], JOHANNES "JOHN H."[5], JO HANNES[4] GERBER, NICLAUS[3], CHRISTIAN[2], ULRICH[1])[214]* was born December 20, 1972, in Limestone, ME. She married LEWIS TIMOTHY BERGMAN[214] August 03, 1996, in New Hope, VA[214]. He was born February 26, 1969, in Kingsport, TN.

More about ANNE MARIE COFFMAN:
Occupation: Finance Manager

Children of ANNE COFFMAN and LEWIS BERGMAN are:
3-3-4-3-3-4-5-2-1-1	NICHOLAS TIMOTHY[14] BERGMAN[214], b. March 22, 1999, Richmond, VA.
3-3-4-3-3-4-5-2-1-2	WILLIAM ETHAN BERGMAN[214], b. January 14, 2003, Richmond, VA[214].

Endnotes

1. Mason, Floyd, *John H. Garber and Barbara Miller of PA, MD & VA*, 1998.
2. Levi Garber Family Bible Register in Possession of Frederic C. Garber.
3. Mason, Floyd, *John H. Garber and Barbara Miller of PA, MD & VA*, 1998.
4. Levi Garber Family Bible Register in Possession of Frederic C. Garber.
5. Mason, Floyd, *John H. Garber and Barbara Miller of PA, MD & VA*, 1998.
6. "The Clifton B. Garber Family Record," 1989.
7. Mason, Floyd, *John H. Garber and Barbara Miller of PA, MD & VA*, 1998.
8. Levi Garber Family Bible Register in Possession of Frederic C. Garber.
9. Mason, Floyd, *John H. Garber and Barbara Miller of PA, MD & VA*, 1998.
10. "The Clifton B. Garber Family Record," 1989.
11. Mason, Floyd, *John H. Garber and Barbara Miller of PA, MD & VA*, 1998.
12. Hamilton, Merle R., *Jacob Garber Family Record*, 1965.
13. Levi Garber Family Bible Register in Possession of Frederic C. Garber.
14. Hamilton, Merle R., *Jacob Garber Family Record*, 1965.
15. Levi Garber Family Bible Register in Possession of Frederic C. Garber.
16. Personal Knowledge of Wayne Garber.
17. Hamilton, Merle R., *Jacob Garber Family Record*, 1965.
18. Levi Garber Family Bible Register in Possession of Wayne Garber.
19. "The Clifton B. Garber Family Record," 1989.
20. Levi Garber Family Bible Register in Possession of Wayne Garber.
21. "The Clifton B. Garber Family Record," 1989.
22. Mason, Floyd, *John H. Garber and Barbara Miller of PA, MD & VA*, 1998.
23. "The Clifton B. Garber Family Record," 1989.
24. Levi Garber Family Bible Register in Possession of Wayne Garber.
25. Mason, Floyd, *John H. Garber and Barbara Miller of PA, MD & VA*, 1998.
26. "The Clifton B. Garber Family Record," 1989.
27. Mason, Floyd, *John H. Garber and Barbara Miller of PA, MD & VA*, 1998.
28. "The Clifton B. Garber Family Record," 1989.
29. Levi Garber Family Bible Register in Possession of Frederic C. Garber.
30. Mason, Floyd, *John H. Garber and Barbara Miller of PA, MD & VA*, 1998.
31. "The Clifton B. Garber Family Record," 1989.
32. Levi Garber Family Bible Register in Possession of Frederic C. Garber.
33. Mason, Floyd, "John H. Garber and Barbara Miller of PA, MD & VA," 1998.
34. "The Clifton B. Garber Family Record," 1989.
35. Levi Garber Family Bible Register in Possession of Frederic C. Garber.
36. Mason, Floyd, *John H. Garber and Barbara Miller of PA, MD & VA*, 1998.
37. "The Clifton B. Garber Family Record," 1989.
38. Levi Garber Family Bible Register in Possession of Frederic C. Garber.
39. Mason, Floyd, *John H. Garber and Barbara Miller of PA, MD & VA*, 1998.
40. "The Clifton B. Garber Family Record," 1989.
41. Levi Garber Family Bible Register in Possession of Frederic C. Garber.
42. Mason, Floyd, *John H. Garber and Barbara Miller of PA, MD & VA*, 1998.
43. "The Clifton B. Garber Family Record," 1989.
44. Mason, Floyd, *John H. Garber and Barbara Miller of PA, MD & VA*, 1998.
45. Hamilton, Merle R., *Jacob Garber Family Record*, 1965.
46. Levi Garber Family Bible Register in Possession of Frederic C. Garber.

47. "The Clifton B. Garber Family Record," 1989.
48. Hamilton, Merle R., *Jacob Garber Family Record*, 1965.
49. Levi Garber Family Bible Register in Possession of Frederic C. Garber.
50. Hamilton, Merle R., *Jacob Garber Family Record*, 1965.
51. Levi Garber Family Bible Register in Possession of Frederic C. Garber.
52. "The Clifton B. Garber Family Record," 1989.
53. Mason, Floyd, *John H. Garber and Barbara Miller of PA, MD & VA*, 1998.
54. Hamilton, Merle R., *Jacob Garber Family Record*, 1965.
55. Levi Garber Family Bible Register in Possession of Frederic C. Garber.
56. "The Clifton B. Garber Family Record," 1989.
57. Hamilton, Merle R., *Jacob Garber Family Record*, 1965.
58. Levi Garber Family Bible Register in Possession of Frederic C. Garber.
59. "The Clifton B. Garber Family Record," 1989.
60. Levi Garber Family Bible Register in Possession of Frederic C. Garber.
61. "The Clifton B. Garber Family Record," 1989.
62. Levi Garber Family Bible Register in Possession of Frederic C. Garber.
63. "The Clifton B. Garber Family Record," 1989.
64. Hamilton, Merle R., *Jacob Garber Family Record*, 1965.
65. Levi Garber Family Bible Register in Possession of Frederic C. Garber.
66. Hamilton, Merle R., *Jacob Garber Family Record*, 1965.
67. Levi Garber Family Bible Register in Possession of Frederic C. Garber.
68. "The Clifton B. Garber Family Record," 1989.
69. Hamilton, Merle R., *Jacob Garber Family Record*, 1965.
70. Levi Garber Family Bible Register in Possession of Frederic C. Garber.
71. Hamilton, Merle R., *Jacob Garber Family Record*, 1965.
72. Levi Garber Family Bible Register in Possession of Frederic C. Garber.
73. Ryman, Blaine R., *Descendants of Jacob Garber*, July 2, 1998.
74. Levi Garber Family Bible Register in Possession of Frederic C. Garber.
75. Ryman, Blaine R., *Descendants of Jacob Garber*, July 2, 1998.
76. Levi Garber Family Bible Register in Possession of Frederic C. Garber.
77. Ryman, Blaine R., *Descendants of Jacob Garber*, July 2, 1998.
78. Levi Garber Family Bible Register in Possession of Frederic C. Garber.
79. Ryman, Blaine R., *Descendants of Jacob Garber*, July 2, 1998.
80. Glick Family Bible in Possession of Wayne Garber.
81. "The Clifton B. Garber Family Record," 1989.
82. Levi Garber Family Bible Register in Possession of Frederic C. Garber.
83. Ryman, Blaine R., *Descendants of Jacob Garber*, July 2, 1998.
84. Levi Garber Family Bible Register in Possession of Frederic C. Garber.
85. Ryman, Blaine R., *Descendants of Jacob Garber*, July 2, 1998.
86. Levi Garber Family Bible Register in Possession of Frederic C. Garber.
87. Personal knowledge of Carolyn Ann Garber.
88. Levi Garber Family Bible Register in Possession of Frederic C. Garber.
89. Glick Family Bible in Possession of Wayne Garber.
90. Personal Knowledge of Wayne Garber.
91. Levi Garber Family Bible Register in Possession of Frederic C. Garber.
92. Personal Knowledge of Wayne Garber.
93. Levi Garber Family Bible Register in Possession of Frederic C. Garber.
94. Ryman, Blaine R., *Descendants of Jacob Garber*, July 2, 1998.

95. Levi Garber Family Bible Register in Possession of Frederic C. Garber.
96. Ryman, Blaine R., *Descendants of Jacob Garber*, July 2, 1998.
97. Levi Garber Family Bible Register in Possession of Frederic C. Garber.
98. Ryman, Blaine R., *Descendants of Jacob Garber*, July 2, 1998.
99. Levi Garber Family Bible Register in Possession of Frederic C. Garber.
100. Ryman, Blaine R., *Descendants of Jacob Garber*, July 2, 1998.
101. Levi Garber Family Bible Register in Possession of Wayne Garber.
102. Ryman, Blaine R., *Descendants of Jacob Garber*, July 2, 1998.
103. Levi Garber Family Bible Register in Possession of Wayne Garber.
104. Ryman, Blaine R., *Descendants of Jacob Garber*, July 2, 1998.
105. Levi Garber Family Bible Register in Possession of Wayne Garber.
106. Ryman, Blaine R., *Descendants of Jacob Garber*, July 2, 1998.
107. Levi Garber Family Bible Register in Possession of Wayne Garber.
108. Ryman, Blaine R., *Descendants of Jacob Garber*, July 2, 1998.
109. Levi Garber Family Bible Register in Possession of Frederic C. Garber.
110. Personal knowledge of Carolyn Ann Garber.
111. Personal Knowledge of Wayne Garber.
112. Glick Family Bible in Possession of Wayne Garber.
113. Notes of Cora Garber given to Wayne E. Garber.
114. Click Family Bible in the Possession of Wayne Garber.
115. Notes of Cora Garber given to Wayne E. Garber.
116. Click Family Bible in the Possession of Wayne Garber.
117. Notes of Cora Garber given to Wayne E. Garber.
118. "The Clifton B. Garber Family Record," 1989.
119. Ryman, Blaine R., *Descendants of Jacob Garber*, July 2, 1998.
120. Levi Garber Family Bible Register in Possession of Wayne Garber.
121. Ryman, Blaine R., *Descendants of Jacob Garber*, July 2, 1998.
122. Levi Garber Family Bible Register in Possession of Wayne Garber.
123. Ryman, Blaine R., *Descendants of Jacob Garber*, July 2, 1998.
124. Levi Garber Family Bible Register in Possession of Frederic C. Garber.
125. Personal Knowledge of Wayne Garber.
126. Levi Garber Family Bible Register in Possession of Frederic C. Garber.
127. Tombstone, Middle River Church of the Brethren, Augusta Co., VA.
128. Levi Garber Family Bible Register in Possession of Frederic C. Garber.
129. Tombstone, Middle River Church of the Brethren, Augusta Co., VA.
130. Personal Knowledge of Wayne Garber.
131. Levi Garber Family Bible Register in Possession of Frederic C. Garber.
132. Ryman, Blaine R., *Descendants of Jacob Garber*, July 2, 1998.
133. Notes of Cora Garber given to Wayne E. Garber.
134. Levi Garber Family Bible Register in Possession of Frederic C. Garber.
135. Ryman, Blaine R., *Descendants of Jacob Garber*, July 2, 1998.
136. Levi Garber Family Bible Register in Possession of Frederic C. Garber.
137. Ryman, Blaine R., *Descendants of Jacob Garber*, July 2, 1998.
138. Levi Garber Family Bible Register in Possession of Frederic C. Garber.
139. Interview with Cleatis Garber Conducted by Wayne Garber, Nov. 18, 2003.
140. Levi Garber Family Bible Register in Possession of Frederic C. Garber.
141. Ryman, Blaine R., *Descendants of Jacob Garber*, July 2, 1998.
142. Levi Garber Family Bible Register in Possession of Frederic C. Garber.

143. Interview with Cleatis Garber Conducted by Wayne Garber, Nov. 18, 2003.
144. Levi Garber Family Bible Register in Possession of Frederic C. Garber.
145. Personal Knowledge of Wayne Garber.
146. Levi Garber Family Bible Register in Possession of Frederic C. Garber.
147. Personal knowledge of Donna DeGroff Garber.
148. Interview with Cleatis Garber Conducted by Wayne Garber, Nov. 18, 2003.
149. Personal Knowledge of Wayne Garber.
150. Interview with Cleatis Garber Conducted by Wayne Garber, Nov. 18, 2003.
151. Personal Knowledge of Wayne Garber.
152. Commonwealth of Virginia Certificate of Marriage in the Possession of Wayne Garber.
153. Statement of Ruby S. Garber to Wayne Garber, Son, During Interview on Nov. 19, 2003.
154. Funeral Service Bulletin of Waynesboro Church of the Brethren.
155. Levi Garber Family Bible Register in Possession of Frederic C. Garber.
156. Personal Knowledge of Susanne Jean Woodside.
157. Interview with Dolly Harner Conducted by Wayne Garber, Nov. 19, 2003.
158. Levi Garber Family Bible Register in Possession of Frederic C. Garber.
159. Interview with Cleatis Garber Conducted by Wayne Garber, Nov. 18, 2003.
160. Funeral Service Announcement of Lizzie Lou Sipe.
161. Personal Knowledge of Susanne Jean Woodside.
162. Levi Garber Family Bible Register in Possession of Frederic C. Garber.
163. Ryman, Blaine R., *Descendants of Jacob Garber*, July 2, 1998.
164. Notes of Cora Garber Given to Wayne E. Garber.
165. Levi Garber Family Bible Register in Possession of Frederic C. Garber.
166. Ryman, Blaine R., *Descendants of Jacob Garber*, July 2, 1998.
167. Personal Knowledge of Wayne Garber.
168. Levi Garber Family Bible Register in Possession of Frederic C. Garber.
169. Personal Knowledge of Wayne Garber.
170. Levi Garber Family Bible Register in Possession of Frederic C. Garber.
171. Personal Knowledge of Karen Kirk Garber.
172. Personal Knowledge of Cynthia Ann Berry Garber.
173. Personal Knowledge of Donna DeGroff Garber.
174. Personal Knowledge of Cynthia Ann Berry Garber.
175. Personal Knowledge of Wayne Garber.
176. Birth Certificate.
177. Personal Knowledge of Wayne Garber.
178. Personal Knowledge of Donna DeGroff Garber.
179. Levi Garber Family Bible Register in Possession of Frederic C. Garber.
180. Personal Knowledge of Donna DeGroff Garber.
181. Personal Knowledge of Wayne Garber.
182. Birth Certificate.
183. Personal Knowledge of Wayne Garber.
184. Birth Certificate.
185. Personal Knowledge of Wayne Garber.
186. Personal Recollections of Don Garber.
187. Personal Knowledge of Jana Garber.
188. Personal Recollections of Don Garber.
189. Personal Recollections of Jana Garber.
190. Personal Recollections of Don Garber.

191. Personal Knowledge of Wayne Garber.
192. Personal Knowledge of Carolyn Garber Pettit.
193. Personal Knowledge of Carolyn Ann Garber.
194. Personal Knowledge of Carolyn Garber Pettit.
195. Levi Garber Family Bible Register in Possession of Frederic C. Garber.
196. Personal Knowledge of Anna Lee "Dolly" Harner.
197. Levi Garber Family Bible Register in Possession of Frederic C. Garber.
198. Personal Knowledge of Anna Lee "Dolly" Harner.
199. Personal Knowledge of Susan Harner Coffman.
200. Levi Garber Family Bible Register in Possession of Frederic C. Garber.
201. Personal knowledge of Anna Lee "Dolly" Harner.
202. Levi Garber Family Bible Register in Possession of Frederic C. Garber.
203. Personal Knowledge of Anna Lee "Dolly" Harner.
204. Levi Garber Family Bible Register in Possession of Frederic C. Garber.
205. Personal Knowledge of Anna Lee "Dolly" Harner.
206. Personal Knowledge of Karen Kirk Garber.
207. Personal Knowledge of Cynthia Ann Berry Garber.
208. Personal Knowledge of Donna DeGroff Garber.
209. Personal Knowledge of Wayne Garber.
210. Statement by Cathy Rockwell Garber.
211. Personal Knowledge of Wayne Garber.
212. Statement by Cathy Rockwell Garber.
213. Personal Knowledge of Wayne Garber.
214. Personal Knowledge of Susan Harner Coffman.

Hans Zimmerman 12
Harland Miller 257
Harold Ashby Jennings 256
Harold David Garber 255
Harold Garber 73, 98, 117, 136, 144,
    161, 169, 175, 258, 263, 269
Harold Lavern Garber 245, 257, 258,
    262, 263, 269
Harold Mckinney 247
Harold Wayne Myers 254
Harpines 34
Harriet Bickers 248
Harrison Ross 80, 220
Harry Bickers 248
Harry Edward Garber 254
Harry Estle Dixon 256
Harry Stover 238, 247
Hazel Early 259
Hazel Gertrude Thomas 254
Hazel Jeanette Heddings 252
Hazel Margery Garber 228
Hazel Thomas 254
Hazel Velie 263
Heather Nicole Woodside 266
Hedrick C. Gordon 240
Hedrick Gordon 240
Heidi Binko 147
Helen Clemmer 250
Helen Katherine Clemmer 250
Helen Kendrick Garber 255
Helen Rebecca Garber 243
Henry Flory 210
Henry Garber 194
Henry Jacob Garber 224
Henry Miller 206, 208
Henry Sanger 206
Henry Showalter 232
Herbert Roach 228
Hettie Ellen Showalter 232
Hettie Showalter 205, 232
Hilda Stobbe 225
Holly Michelle Garber 191, 264
Homer F. Garber 78, 104, 113, 127, 158,
    183, 189, 227, 239, 258
Homer Franklin Garber 4, 101, 102, 104,
    113, 183, 234, 245
Homer Garber 6, 68, 99, 105, 106, 115,
    116, 119, 120, 150, 183, 239, 245
Hope Virginia Wetterling 269
Howard Miller Garber 230
Hubert Michael Garber 232

I

Ida Barbara Cline 230
Ida Elizabeth Flory 235
Ida Frances Long 230
Ida Nancy Jane Garber 224
Ida Stover 234, 237
Ida Wagner 230
Infant Norford 235
Infant Reed 236
Infant Son Garber 220, 243
Ira Levi Garber 224
Irene Edith Garber 243, 252
Irene Garber 252
Isa D. Miller 244
Isa Miller 244
Isaac Alexander Reed 236
Isaac Burner 216
Isaac Garber 233, 255

Isaac Jonathan Garber 243, 255
Isaac Landis 214
Isaac Miller 205
Isaac Reed 236
Isaac Wine 217
Israel Denlinger 215
Israel Jones 209
Issac Click 210
Issac Flory 210
Issac Long 205
Issac Miller 208
Iva Leslie 237

J

J. Early 244
J. Foley 239
J. G. Miller 238
J. Glick 237, 261
J. Harman Stover 238
J. Miller 206, 238, 246
J. Ruth Glick 248, 261
J. Samuel Foley 239
J. Stover 238
J. M. "Boss" White 240
Jack Donald Herrington 241
Jacob A. Garber 65, 223, 233
Jacob Baughman 203
Jacob Beiler 12
Jacob C. Bowman 204
Jacob Cline 250
Jacob Custer 199
Jacob Flory 198, 210, 211, 225, 235
Jacob G. Garber 193, 197
Jacob Gerber 15, 167
Jacob H. Flory 63, 235
Jacob Hoover 203, 205
Jacob Huff 219, 235
Jacob Huffman 235
Jacob Humbert 40, 80, 195, 197
Jacob L. Huffman 63, 235
Jacob Landis 214
Jacob Long 209
Jacob Martin Garber 243, 254
Jacob Michael Garber 223
Jacob Miller 19, 34, 46, 196, 197, 205,
    206
Jacob Minnich 200, 219
Jacob Rife 194, 196
Jacob Rudolph Cline 250
Jacob Sanger 206, 212
Jacob Shickel 206
Jacob Stoner 29, 32, 194, 196, 214, 225
Jacob Stoner Flory 214, 225
Jacob Thomas 208
Jacob Trout 203
Jacob W. Garber 3, 4, 5, 15, 17, 46, 50-
    57, 62, 65, 102, 105, 161, 167, 168,
    189, 195-197, 201, 203, 209, 224,
    233, 244, 254, 273- 276
Jacob Wine 199, 202, 216
Jacob Yount 210
Jake Stover 206
James Arnold Manuel 232
James Boots 225
James Dillon Harner 268
James Dinkle Garber 244
James Edward Cline 250
James Edward Shifflett 253
James F. Garber 240. 241
James Franklin Garber 228, 229

James Franklin Pugh 240
James Garber 229, 240, 244
James Garber White 240
James H. Landis 228
James Harner 268
James Henry Borden 221
James Keating 270
James M. Herrington 241
James Manuel 232
James Norford 235
James Owen Harner 259, 268
James Robert Manuel 232
James Warren Huffman 251
James William Garber 226, 227
Jana Faith Kiena 265
Janet Tanner 39
Jean Boon Batchelor 237
Jean Carol Conner 252
Jean Garber Norford 247
Jean Mattews 248, 261
Jean Norford 260
Jefferson A. Dyer 266
Jefferson Dyer 267
Jeffrey Keating 270
Jeffrey Nicholas Keating 270
Jennifer Noel Eroe 264
Jennifer S. Sergeeff 266
Jeremiah8 Kessler 215
Jerry Coffman 147, 267
Jerry Robinson Coffman 267
Jesse Auten Heddings 251
Jesse Browning Geiser 256
Jesse Geiser 256
Jesse Heddings 251
Jesse W. Garber 215
Jessica Austin 262
Jim Mckinney 247
Jimmie Hathcock 261
Jimmy Smith 261
Jo Hannes Gerber 2, 17, 24, 25-28, 193-
    271
Jo Hannes Gerber/garver 25, 27
Joel Flory 211
Joel Frantz 200
Joel Glick 206
Johannes "John H." Garber   2, 17, 22,
    24-26, 34, 35, 193-271
Johannes Garber 15, 25, 28, 30, 31, 33,
    193
Johanns Garber 8, 36
John A. Miller 209
John Adam Garber 160, 225, 237
John Arion 201
John Arion 44
John B. Miller 206
John B. Minnich 219
John Brower 47, 201
John Burkholder 230
John C. Miller 211
John Calvin Moomaw 231
John Click 210
John Cline Garber 233, 242
John Custer 199
John D. Miller 205
John Daniel Garber 221
John David Garber 233, 244
John David Western 242
John Degroff 144, 263
John E. Sanger 213
John Emery Grover 215

Patricia Glick 247
Paul Custer 199
Paul Leslie Garber 237
Paul Miller 248
Paul Smith 261
Paul Wilson Garber 5, 6, 64, 112, 123-126, 131-135, 139, 145, 150, 183, 245, 258, 265
Pauline A. Garber 245, 257
Pauline Garber 257
Pauline May Byrd 236
Pearl Glick 248
Peggy Harner 268
Peggy Marie Myers 254
Peggy Teresa Harner 259, 268
Pences 34
Penny Smith 261
Penolope Owen 249
Peter Becker 25
Peter Franklin Wampler 242
Peter Garber 65, 83, 97, 158, 223, 232, 233, 243
Peter Isaac Garber 233, 243
Peter M. Minnich 219
Peter Miller 44, 46, 47, 49, 51, 65, 200, 206, 222, 223
Peter Minnich 200
Peter Wine 218
Peter Wright 219
Philip Kessler 215
Phillip W. Garber 215
Phoeba Miller 207
Phoebe Minnich 219
Polly Firebaugh 205
Polly Flory 211
Polly Garber 210
Priscilla Elizabeth Garber 223, 231
Priscilla Garber 231

R

R. H. Yarbrough 228
R. W. Slonaker 234
Rachel Ann Brown 261
Rachel Kessler 215
Ralph Edward Sanger 254
Ralph W. Garber 244
Ray Harner 259
Ray Hathcock 261
Ray Miller 238, 249
Ray Renalds 232
Raymond Crist 260
Raymond Kiser Crist 259, 260
Raymond S. Garber 244
Rebecca Bowman 203, 204
Rebecca Campbell 208
Rebecca E. Garber 244
Rebecca Elizabeth Manuel 232
Rebecca Flory 213
Rebecca Frances Shifflett 253
Rebecca Friend 214
Rebecca Garber 171, 196, 204, 209-224, 230, 232, 243, 244
Rebecca Glick 237
Rebecca Leedy 206
Rebecca Long 211
Rebecca Miller 205, 211
Rebecca Myers 230
Rebecca Rhodes 44, 202
Rebecca Sanger 213
Rebecca Stoner 29, 196

Rebecca Wine 76, 202, 216, 225, 233, 237, 238, 247-249, 261, 262
Rebekah Garber 201, 222, 230, 242, 249

Regena Sherfey 206
Regina Garber 234
Regina Miller 206
Regina Ziegler 206, 207
Reinette Garber 254
Reinette Magdalena Garber 243, 254
Rena Barbara Western 77, 242, 245, 246, 249, 250
Rena Western 92, 115, 116, 246
Reuben Arnold Garber 201, 224
Reuben Garber 224
Richard Bruce Weider 253
Richard Carl Sanger 254
Richard Frances Norford 247, 260
Richard Martin Garber 254
Richard Miller 248
Richard Norford 260
Richard Smith 261
Richard Thomas Wampler 250
Riggle 206, 207
Robert Brown 15, 261
Robert E. Garber 240, 241
Robert Edward Garber 256, 262
Robert Estes Garber 229, 240
Robert Forrest Sites 255
Robert Franklin Garber 244
Robert Garber 236, 241, 262
Robert Ham 51, 224
Robert Holt 212
Robert Issac Garber 224, 236
Robert Johnson 249
Robert Keith White 240
Robert Lee Hartman 253
Robert Parsons 236
Robert Sipe 124, 258
Roger Alan Sites 255
Roger Allen Huffman 251
Rolla E. Shoemaker 247
Rolla Shoemaker 247
Ronald Frederick Crist 256
Rose Marie Cline 257
Roxanne Kaiser 124
Roxanne Kaiser 264, 265
Roy Johnson 249, 262
Roy Quinter Garber 236
Roy W. Slonaker 77, 234
Royce Errol Thompson 253
Ruby Elizabeth Sipe 6, 102, 123, 124, 127, 131, 135, 145, 170, 183, 258
Ruby Garber 123, 124, 129, 131, 134, 135, 137, 139-141, 153, 229, 241 see also Ruby Elizabeth Sipe
Ruby Leah Margaret Garber 236
Ruth Elizabeth Garber 245, 256
Ruth Emma Wampler 242
Ruth Emman Shaver 230
Ruth Garber 239, 257
Ruth Johnson 249
Ruth Kiracofe 255
Ruth Mae Garber 244
Ruth Pence 254
Ruth Senger 238, 248, 261

S

S. R. Garver 27, 28

Sada Estella Houff 242
Sada Houff 242
Sadie Ivy Garber 228
Sallie Belle Reed 77, 101, 102, 184, 245
Sallie Miller 205
Sallie Moyers 205
Sallie Reed 4, 92, 104, 106, 115, 131, 245
Sallie Sanger 213
Sallie Wright 221
Sally Garber 106, 209
Saloma Miller 207
Saloma Rebecca Cline 230
Salome Frantz 200, 207
Salome Hoover 203
Samuel Abraham Garber 223, 232
Samuel Arnold 44, 52, 201
Samuel Bechtel 28
Samuel Bechtly 27
Samuel Bechtol 28
Samuel Bell Garber 221
Samuel Bowman 203, 204
Samuel Carroll Shifflett 253
Samuel E. Long 205
Samuel F. Miller 207, 211
Samuel F. Sanger 213
Samuel Flory 198, 210, 212
Samuel Francis Funkhouser 252
Samuel Frank 206
Samuel Frantz 200
Samuel Frederick Huffman 250
Samuel G. Glick 206
Samuel Garber 19, 24, 25, 44, 46, 68, 75, 80, 193-196, 202, 203, 209, 220, 223, 232, 234, 237, 243
Samuel Garver 19, 20
Samuel Glick 172, 174, 183, 225, 233
Samuel Landis 214
Samuel Leedy 198
Samuel Levi Garber 233, 243
Samuel M. Garber 219
Samuel Miller 44, 56, 196, 200, 201, 205, 206, 208, 219, 226-228, 239-241
Samuel Miller Garber 201, 219
Samuel Myers 233
Samuel N. Flory 212
Samuel N. Wine 216
Samuel Neher 207
Samuel Preston Garber 221
Samuel Sanger 205, 212, 213
Samuel Stoner 209
Samuel T. Glick 76, 174, 183, 225
Samuel Wine 72, 217
Samuel Zigler 205
Sandra Mae Weeks 252
Sara Alyce Garber 253
Sara Beth Alexander 241
Sara Garber 211
Sarah "Sallie" Garber 195
Sarah "Sally" C. Garber 220
Sarah A. Garber 202
Sarah Arrington 214
Sarah Bowman 204
Sarah C. Garber 220
Sarah Catherine Flory 212
Sarah Catherine Garber 224
Sarah Catherine Miller 204
Sarah Catherine Wright 206
Sarah Claudia Yarbrough 228, 229
Sarah E. Flory 214

Pictures

Places

Ancestors of Paul Wilson Garber

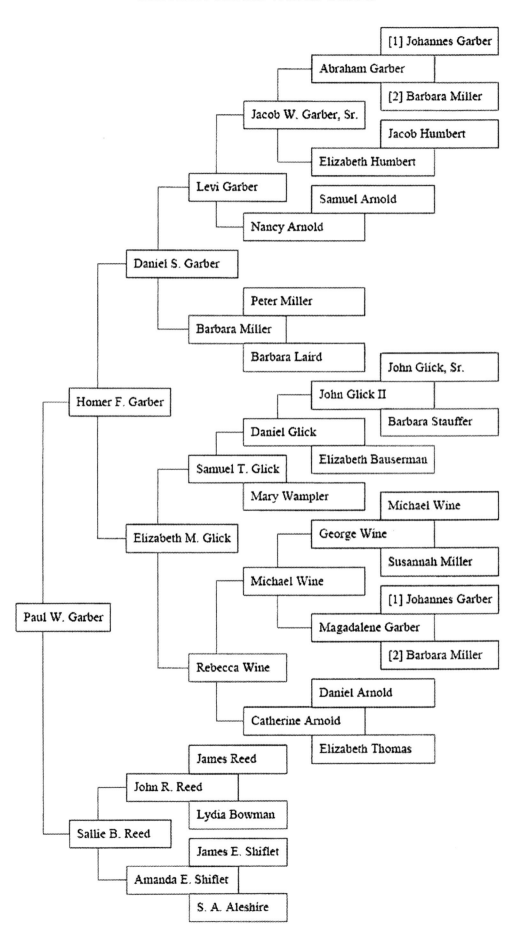

Printed in the United States
95204LV00002B/95-514/A